D1224800

BLACK CHURCH STUDIES

AN INTRODUCTION

More Praise for *Black Church Studies: An Introduction*

"*Black Church Studies* is an exciting and exacting introduction for a discipline whose day has finally and at long last come. This cooperative work presents complex data in a manner readily accessible to critical and confessional communions. The authors have radiantly illumined the promise and peril facing the black faithful everywhere and for this we give thanks."
—Alton B. Pollard III, Dean, Howard University of Divinity

"*Black Church Studies* is an ideal textbook. The authors concisely present an overview of a range of subjects in Black Christian church studies—historical, theological, ethical, sociological. By doing so, they connect historical and contemporary aspects of Black American churches to provide coherence of subject matter for students. They introduce students to important people, places, and ideas of Black Church life throughout the text with study questions, new terms in boldface, chapter summaries, and listings of additional readings. In this first-of-a-kind text, the authors brilliantly lay out the bare bones of Black Church studies.

"As a teacher, I know . . . this text is an invaluable resource, providing a place for me to begin work with students in a study that can seem overwhelming without this guidebook. *Black Church Studies* is essential to anyone who teaches about Black Christian religious life in the United States. And it's about time!"
—Stephanie Y. Mitchem, Associate Professor, Religious Studies and Women's Studies, University of South Carolina

"Exhilarating scholarship, a comprehensive work that brilliantly chronicles the history of Black Church sacred beliefs, theological understandings, and ecclesial practices. The Black Church and the theological academy will find this scholarship on the cutting edge of what it means to be Black and Christian in America."
—Forrest E. Harris, Director, Vanderbilt Divinity School's Kelly Miller Smith Institute on Black Church Studies; President, American Baptist College, Nashville

"I enthusiastically commend this text which remarkably introduces the academic field of Black Church Studies without losing sight of the need to 'make it plain' for those in the pews. This is an indispensable resource for teachers, preachers, and activists committed to the ongoing goal of liberation and human fulfillment."
—Jeffrey L. Tribble, Sr., Assistant Professor of Ministry, Columbia Theological Seminary, Decatur, Georgia

"*Black Church Studies* breaks through the past and into the twenty-first century, revealing the beauty, mystery, and power of the Black Church. These emerging scholars tell us from whence we have come, where we now are, and where we need to go. The breadth, scope, and penetrating insights of this work make this readily accessible text the best current source to assist all who hunger to understand our church—and to serve it."
—Darryl M. Trimiew, President of the Society of Christian Ethics (2008), Professor and Chair of Philosophy and Religion, Medgar Evers College, Brooklyn

"This comprehensive and timely book provides much needed attention to the nature and make-up of Black Church Studies. Drawing on an interdisciplinary approach, this volume offers an intriguing framework for understanding the impact of the Black Church on the study of African American religion. It is a must read. I recommend it highly."
—Anthony B. Pinn, Agnes Cullen Arnold Professor of Humanities, Rice University

BLACK CHURCH STUDIES
AN INTRODUCTION

STACEY FLOYD-THOMAS JUAN FLOYD-THOMAS
CAROL B. DUNCAN STEPHEN G. RAY JR. NANCY LYNNE WESTFIELD

ABINGDON PRESS
Nashville

BLACK CHURCH STUDIES: AN INTRODUCTION

Copyright © 2007 by Abingdon Press

All rights reserved.

This book is printed on acid-free paper.

Library of Congress Cataloging-in-Publication Data

Black church studies: an introduction / Stacey Floyd-Thomas . . . [et al.].
   p. cm.
   Includes biblographical references and index.
   ISBN 978-0-687-33265-6 (pbk.: alk. paper)
   1. African American churches.   2. African Americans—Religion. I. Floyd-Thomas, Stacey.

BR563.N4B56585   2007
277.3'008996073—dc22   2007015621

All Scripture quotations unless noted otherwise are taken from the New Revised Standard Version of the Bible, copyright 1989 Division of Christian Education of the National Council of the Churches of Christ in the United States of America. Used by permission. All rights reserved.

Scripture quotations marked (KJV) are from the King James or Authorized Version of the Bible.

The stained glass windows that grace the opening of each chapter are by artist Maurice Jenkins. Copyright © 2001 by Covenant Baptist Church, Washington, D.C. Used by permission. The titles of the pieces are "Generations" (chap. 1), "Heritage" (chap. 2), "Compassion" (chap. 3), "Creation" (chap. 4), "Liberation" (chap. 5), "Inclusiveness" (chap. 6), "Service (chap. 7), and a segment of "Victory" (chap. 8).

07 08 09 10 11 12 13 14 15 16 —10 9 8 7 6 5 4 3 2 1

MANUFACTURED IN THE UNITED STATES OF AMERICA

To the founders of Black Church Studies:

Major Jones

C. Eric Lincoln

Henry L. Mitchell

Shelby Rooks

Kelly Miller Smith

Gayraud S. Wilmore

"AN INTRACOMMUNAL, INTERDISCIPLINARY COLLABORATION COMMITTED TO SOCIAL JUSTICE THROUGH FAITH, THOUGHT, AND ACTION."

The Black Religious Scholars Group (BRSG) promotes meaningful dialogue and partnership between Black religious scholars, Black churches, and community organizations in order to promote the goals of Black religion of liberation and human flourishing. The BRSG aims to advance the tradition of the Black church-based community of supporting the souls of Black folk through spiritual empowerment, human fulfillment, and socioeconomic uplift, as well as to make the academic work of Black religious scholars more relevant, accessible, and pertinent to the larger needs of the Black Church community.

The BRSG advances the field of Black Church Studies, establishing it as a model for critical interdisciplinary inquiry that is also inspirational in nature. It serves as an information clearinghouse and communication network for scholars and students of Black Church Studies and African American Religious Studies, as well as an international consortium for scholars, religious leaders, and community activists. The BRSG publishes scholarly materials relevant to the needs of the Church and the Black community, convenes scholarly consultations, organizes workgroups, panels, and regional conferences, and supports research projects pertaining both to African American Religious Studies generally and Black Church Studies specifically. It is especially committed to developing mentoring, advocacy, and support mechanisms for seminary and graduate students of African descent in order to shape positively their academic experiences and better prepare them for their professional careers and vocational callings.

Thus, the BRSG is devoted to developing creative endeavors, sharing expertise, cultivating resources, and facilitating collaborative conversations that will forward its mission, hope, and prayer of linking divine justice to social justice.

CONTENTS

Contents

Contents

FOREWORD

During the height of the Black Power/Black Consciousness period in the late 1960s, Union Theological Seminary in New York City had three Black professors, the largest number of Black faculty on the teaching staff of any divinity school in the country: Professor C. Eric Lincoln in Church and Community, Professor Lawrence N. Jones in administration and Religion in Higher Education, and Assistant Professor James Cone in Theology. While all three went on to achieve great distinction in their respective fields, a student at Union at that time, as I was, could take only three courses related to African Americans. Since then, remarkable progress has been made, largely due to the perseverance and pressure exerted on academia by scholars and students. As a result, the field of Black Church Studies has come into being. All of us are indebted to the labor of love of the co-authors, Stacey and Juan Floyd-Thomas, Carol B. Duncan, Stephen G. Ray Jr., and Nancy Lynne Westfield, in producing the first comprehensive and coherent introduction to Black Church Studies. Each chapter gives an overview of the sub-field, summarizes the concepts and content of current studies, includes questions for discussion, and biographies of major authors.

I am particularly pleased that the co-authors have chosen to use the title "Black Church" (or "Negro Church") reflecting a tradition that extends from the classical Black scholars like W.E.B. Du Bois, Carter G. Woodson, Benjamin Mays and Joseph Nicholson, E. Franklin Frazier, and C. Eric Lincoln to the present day. While there has always been recognition of the diversity and multiplicity among Black churches, these scholars have also valued the cultural unity that cuts across denominational and sectarian lines.

As an institution, the Black Church is unrivaled in its historical influence in Black culture and among Black people. As the only coherent institutional area to emerge from slavery, it still carries burdens and performs functions far beyond its spiritual ones—in education, economics, politics, art, music, counseling and therapy, and community outreach, etc. It is the only institution where Black people feel ownership when they speak of "my pastor, my church." They do not say "my Democratic Party" or even "my NAACP." There is a loyalty and commitment to the Black Church that has enabled it to survive the decline in membership experienced by mainline white denominations over the past forty years.

Finally, it is a great pleasure to see the success achieved by one of my former Vassar students, Professor Stacey Floyd-Thomas. She is one of the emerging voices and scholars in Christian Social Womanist Ethics and Black Church Studies. Besides Stacey, I want to thank all of the co-authors for producing a highly readable, well-organized, comprehensive, and eminently usable book for courses in Black Church Studies.

Lawrence H. Mamiya
Paschall-Davis Professor of Religion and Africana Studies, Vassar College
Co-author, *The Black Church in the African American Experience*

ACKNOWLEDGMENTS

This book, the first of its kind, would not have come to life without the collaborative efforts of the contributors, Black churches, the academy, and a visionary publisher. As Black religious scholars, we believe that too much of scholarship is done in isolation and without collaboration. The writing of this book, grown out of a collaboration that finds its institutional roots in the organization known as the Black Religious Scholars Group (BRSG), has been a labor of love, and perhaps more importantly, is meant to be a symbol of the necessity for collaboration by Black scholars of religion for ongoing concerns of teaching and scholarship. The guiding vision of the BRSG was to "make it plain" as the Black Church adage goes, by making palpable for the Black Church the valuable resources found within Black theological education and religious studies. This vision was initially expressed by three Black graduate students (then, Stacey Floyd, Juan Thomas Jr., and Duane Belgrave Sr.) during a Black Theology Group session of the 1996 American Academy of Religion/Society of Biblical Literature Annual Meeting in New Orleans, Louisiana. Those attending that session realized that because the discussion and work of Black religious scholars tends to be firmly situated within academic circles, we have lost sight of the goal of Black religion in general and Black Christianity in particular: liberation and human fulfillment in all areas of life.

We recognized that faithfulness to our call as religious scholars, preachers, and community activists required relevant theological activity, accessible to the larger African Diasporan Church and society. Our commitment to exploring ways in which more meaningful dialogue and partnership might occur between Black religious scholars and the larger Black community and its churches led us to organize public forums at Black churches prior to our annual scholarly meetings. This volume is a testament to those consultations and the vision they embody: to continue the tradition of church/community organizing for the spiritual empowerment, human flourishing, and socio-economic uplift of Black folk. We are also committed to an educated leadership, both laity and clergy. We honor and celebrate those pastors and churches where the consultations have been held:

1997	Glide Memorial United Methodist Church, San Francisco, CA	Rev. Cecil Williams
1998	New Covenant Baptist Church, Orlando, FL	Rev. Dr. Randolph Bracy Jr.
1999	Union Baptist Church, Cambridge, MA	Rev. Jeffrey L. Brown
2000	New Visions Baptist Church, Nashville, TN	Rev. Dr. Sherman Tribble
2002	Grant AME Church, Toronto ON, Canada	Rev. Virgil Woods
2003	First Iconium Baptist Church, Atlanta, GA	Rev. Timothy McDonald III
2004	Macedonia Missionary Baptist Church, San Antonio, TX	Rev. Jerry Wm. Dailey
2005	Hickman Temple AME Church, Philadelphia, PA	Rev. Dr. Vernal Simms
2006	Covenant Baptist Church, Washington, DC	Rev. Dr. Dennis and Rev. Dr. Christine Wiley
2007	St. Stephen's Cathedral COGIC San Diego, CA	Bishop George D. McKinney, Ph.D.

It is our intention that the BRSG will continue to facilitate these dialogues with the hope that they will contribute to the well-being and advancement of our people and communities. We take seriously the voices, experiences, and stories of the people in the pews of Black churches.

As contributors and co-authors of this book, we are deeply indebted to many, many people for their support, generosity, and backing. We want to thank our colleagues Dale Andrews, Cheryl Kirk-Duggan, Anthony Pinn, Rodney Sadler, Darryl Trimiew, and Anne Streaty Wimberly who have worked as our consultants and collaborators. We are thankful to those institutions that have nourished this work. We are particularly grateful to Brite Divinity School for serving as the BRSG institutional headquarters, for providing fiscal resources and in-kind support for our work. When we needed space in which to write during a critical phase of this book project, Lutheran Theological Seminary at Philadelphia provided us with housing and full use of its library and classrooms, and we are grateful for such a glowing act of generosity. We also want to express our gratitude to Concord Baptist Church in Brooklyn, New York (and pastor Rev. Dr. Gary Simpson), for serving as a BRSG institutional affiliate and offering us financial and collegial support. Additionally, we would like to show special appreciation for the Louisville Institute for rewarding BRSG with a general grant to fund several of the BRSG consultations (2002–2005) that provided the ongoing impetus for this work.

We wish to thank Brite Divinity School seminarians and Black Church Studies research assistants Chris Driscoll, Jacob Robinson, and Rodney Thomas, as well as Boston University School of Theology doctoral candidate, Nicole L. Johnson, for their efforts in helping us with the task of completing this text. We also want to express our wholehearted appreciation to Rev. Dr. Christine Wiley and Rev. Dr. Dennis Wiley, co-pastors of Covenant Baptist Church in Washington, D. C., for allowing us to use their church's gorgeous stained glass windows as the cover and interior art for this book and subsequent volumes of the "Making It Plain" series. Aside from being visually stunning, artist Maurice Jenkins' graphic images of God and God's people reflect the enduring power of merging faith and art in ways that can educate, excite, and ultimately empower people in previously unimaginable ways.

Our deepest and most heartfelt thanks are extended to Abingdon Press, our primary institutional sponsor and affiliate: for their ability to see the merit of this project, for supporting it and the supplemental series, and for using the model as a prototype. So many perspectives that have been pushed to the margins will now be brought to the center with the help of their pioneering publishing trajectory. Toward this end, we thank Robert A. Ratcliff and John F. Kutsko for their unprecedented support for the vision of this book and the companion volume series of supplemental texts that will follow; Neil Alexander and Harriet Olsen for lending institutional leadership and financial support for the expansion of the BRSG; and Barbara Dick for being the midwife in the production process. It is our hope that this book will be a testament to the value of collaboration between the academy, the Church, and academic presses.

INTRODUCTION

WHAT IS BLACK CHURCH STUDIES?

The proliferation of scholarly research on various aspects of Black Christian faith since the 1960s serves as the *raison d'être* for this comprehensive book. Even as we express our abundant joy at the completion of this project, as the authors of this volume we must admit that the idea of bringing this work to fruition has been a twofold concern. On the one hand, this has been a daunting task because of the vast array of scholarship on Black Christianity. On the other hand, we faced the inherent difficulty of interpreting and articulating the substantive nature of an entire people's sacred beliefs and practices in a single volume. Added to these issues was the exhilarating challenge of multiple authors with various perspectives, areas of expertise, and backgrounds yet united by a common goal—maintaining the highest standards of Black Church Studies as an area of academic inquiry—collaborating toward a shared and singular vision in this book. Having faced and overcome these issues to a certain degree of satisfaction, we hope that this text will serve its intended purpose as an introduction to the academic study of the Black Church in North America. Therefore, we must begin with a functional definition of what we mean in this volume by the phrase "Black Church Studies."

Black Church Studies as a discrete academic enterprise began in the 1970s with teaching, scholarship, and ministerial praxis focused on developing the worship life, ecclesial practices, and theological understandings of African American churches. These writings in Black Church Studies arose largely as a response to earlier commentators: W.E.B. Du Bois in *The Negro Church* (1903), Carter G. Woodson in *The History of the Negro Church* (1921), E. Franklin Frazier in *The Negro Church in America* (1963), and Benjamin E. Mays and Joseph Nicholson in *The Negro's Church* (1969) among others. These writers largely defined and examined the African American Church using assimilation to the white mainline Church as well as oppression by white mainstream society as the yardstick to measure the existence and evolution of the Black Church. Within the last four decades, pioneering texts, including: Henry Mitchell's *Black Preaching* (1970), C. Eric Lincoln's *The Black Experience in Religion* (1974), Gayraud Wilmore's *Black Religion and Black Radicalism* (1989), and C. Eric Lincoln and Lawrence Mamiya's *The Black Church in the African-American Experience* (1990), provided unprecedented interpretations of African American Christianity with levels of rigor, depth, and sophistication that informed a subsequent generation of ministers, religious scholars, and theologians such as ourselves. Although these seminal works gave new perspectives on the significance of the Black Church in the history of modern Christendom, the authors of this work believe that there needed to be a more contemporary, comprehensive, and cohesive approach to teaching and learning about Black Christianity in North America.

Under the vision of Rev. Dr. Henry H. Mitchell, along with the considerable assistance of the Lilly and the Irwin-Sweeney-Miller foundations, the Black Church Studies program at Colgate Rochester Crozer Divinity School was established in 1969. From this auspicious beginning, Colgate Rochester's Black Church Studies program became the first and oldest program of its kind in the nation. Before the creation of the Black Church Studies program, Colgate Rochester Divinity School's African American alumni included some of the most visible national leaders of African American theological and ecclesiastical life: Howard Thurman, Mordecai Wyatt Johnson, Joseph H. Jackson, Samuel Dewitt Proctor, and Martin Luther King, Jr., to name only a few. In the aftermath of the tumultuous upheavals of the 1960s, the passionate dreams and courageous efforts of students challenged the faculty, administration, and staff members of the Colgate Rochester Crozer Divinity School to inaugurate a Black Church Studies program that was consistent with the divinity school's historic tradition of progressive views and prophetic ministry.

In 1966, Colgate Rochester hired Rev. Dr. Henry H. Mitchell as the first Martin Luther King, Jr., Professor of Black Church Studies. He became the founding director of the Black Church Studies (BCS) program at Colgate Rochester. In that capacity, Mitchell developed a curriculum that featured courses with critical methodological approaches, deep theological reflection, and profound social witness. In addition to its academic agenda, the Black Church Studies program also provided opportunities for the intellectual, professional, and inspirational development of transformational leadership within the African American community offered through classes, lectureships, symposia, worship services, voluntary community services, as well as social gatherings and celebrations. In keeping with the long tradition of the school to provide ministers for the Black Church in the context of the universal Christian mission, the BCS program sought integration in all dimensions of the curriculum. It prepared women and men of all races and backgrounds for professional ministry and scholarly training that appreciated African Americans' contributions to the entirety of Christian faith, life, and witness in North America. In the nearly four decades since the inauguration of Colgate Rochester Crozer Divinity School's BCS program, similar full-fledged efforts have been initiated at Vanderbilt University Divinity School, Duke Divinity School, Candler School of Theology, Lutheran Theological Seminary at Philadelphia, Garrett-Evangelical Theological Seminary, Fuller Theological Seminary, and Brite Divinity School, among other theological institutions.

At its core, Black Church Studies was originally envisioned as a pragmatic academic enterprise that was experimental in its pedagogy and experiential in its praxis. In other words, pioneering BCS programs and curricula worked ceaselessly to devise innovative teaching-learning methods within seminary and university classrooms as well as imaginative vision of ministerial leadership in service of the Black Christian tradition. In its earliest manifestation, the BCS curricula developed by Rev. Dr. Mitchell consisted of the following sub-disciplines: Black Biblical Studies, Black Theology, Black Church History, Black Philosophy[1], Black Ministry Studies[2], and Black Preaching. During the heady days at the start of Black Church Studies, the nascent BCS courses consistently drew seminarians of all backgrounds—whites, Latinos, Asians, and Native Americans, as well as Blacks—who took these courses not only as a sign of solidarity with the vision and experience of Black Christianity but also as a means of expanding their own personal faith expression and ministerial potential. Moreover, many of the courses taught by Black as well as white faculty were not related to Black Church Studies as such. Overall, these courses were used to enrich the curriculum of the seminary as a whole. But the lack of textbooks and BCS faculty for the study of ministerial practice in the Black churches and community led Rev. Dr. Mitchell to propose the "Martin Luther King, Jr. Program in Developing a Bibliography in Black Church Studies" to the Irwin Sweeney Miller Fund in an attempt to expand the resources useful for the scholarly examination of Black Christianity. The new funding provided for faculty and students to engage in six weeks of intensive study of the African roots of African American religion by visiting West Africa, then a two-week intensive study in the Caribbean, and finally a six-week summer study at the Interdenominational Theological Center in Atlanta, Georgia, and the Colgate Rochester Crozer Divinity School in Rochester, New York. In 1975, nineteen Doctor of Ministry (D.Min.) degrees were awarded, marking the first generation of ministers and scholars whose academic preparation reflected the impact of BCS on theological education.

Consequently, Black Church Studies in the contemporary context is a *multidisciplinary* and *interdisciplinary* enterprise that is a vital component of the intellectual richness of the academy. It is a field of study that describes and analyzes the legacy, traditions, and social witness of the Black Church in North America. Black Church Studies is *multidisciplinary* because it encompasses several fields of study that are brought into conversation to illumine the object of study, in this case the Black Church. The term *interdisciplinary* relates more to a conscious effort to integrate the "knowledge and perspectives of multiple disciplines of expertise to holistically solve problems through research and education."[3] For example, since its inception, it is common for Black Church Studies to combine Homiletics, Biblical Hermeneutics, Church History, Theology, Ethics, Sociology of Black Religion (herein referred to as Black Church and Society), Christian Education, Practical Theology / Pastoral Care, and Sacred Worship in order to prepare ordained and lay ministerial leadership for the Black Church. One example of this multidisciplinary work is bringing biblical interpretation, theological reflection, ethical considerations, sociological analysis, and pastoral care to bear on health crises in the Black community (e.g., HIV/AIDS infection, sickle-cell anemia, teen pregnancy, malnutrition, rising cancer rates, and post-traumatic stress disorder).

Given the hybrid nature of Black Church Studies as a multidisciplinary field of study with an emphasis on interdisciplinary theoretical and methodological approaches, Black Church Studies joins the study of the Black Church with reflection upon those aspects of the prophetic witness and ministry that have characterized this tradition from its historic beginnings. It does this by connecting the study of being the Black Church with the project of *doing* Black Church. The foundation of this understanding of Black Church Studies is the often-noted resistance within the Black Church to the separation of theory and practice, most often encapsulated in the dictum "will it preach?" The approach this book takes is, therefore, one that merges the practices and theologies that animate the Black Church in ways that will hopefully resonate not only in the classroom but also in the church and the community. Seeing that the Black Church is an institution that serves to solve the complicated problems that arise in a racist, sexist, and classist society, the study of the Black Church must demonstrate the ability to investigate and interrogate the intricacies of this complex structure through multidisciplinary and interdisciplinary work. Black Church Studies, in addressing complicated problems of diverse audiences, is a discipline concerned not only with the study and description of the Black Church as a religious phenomenon but also with using what is gleaned from the research to strengthen the Church as it meets contemporary challenges in and beyond the Black community. Before going on to a description of how this book is situated within the field, a brief explanation of what we mean by the "Black Church" is necessary.

THE HISTORIC BLACK CHURCH TRADITION

The Black Church emerges from the religious, cultural, and social experience of Black people. With its roots on the continent of Africa and the Middle Passage, the Black Church provided structure and meaning for African people and their descendants in the Americas who struggled to survive the ravages and brutality of slavery and racial oppression. Sociologist C. Eric Lincoln described that, for Black people, the church "was their school, their forum, their political arena, their social club, their art gallery, their conservatory of music. It was lyceum and gymnasium as well as sanctum sanctorum."[4] In that spirit, the Black Church functioned as the center of Black life, culture, and heritage for much of the history of the African American experience in North America.

For many decades, the form of the Black Church has been described primarily as those churches whose worship life and cultural sensibilities have reflected, historically and traditionally, a connection to the larger African American community. This ecclesial formation had three primary expressions: (a) independent Black, Methodist, and Holiness-Pentecostal denominations; (b) Black congregations and fellowship in predominantly white denominations such as Roman Catholics, Presbyterians, and Episcopalians; and (c) more recently, non-denominational Christian churches that have multicultural, multiracial, and multiethnic membership but the ministerial leadership and cultural identity is African American in nature. While this book uses this definition as a starting point, we also understand the term *Black Church* as a designation for the multiple communities of African descent and Christian faith present in many North American contexts. For the purposes of this book, the term *Black Church*, then, moves beyond historic, denominational affiliations and toward a more expansive understanding of the Black Church as an African Diasporan reality.

EXPLANATION OF THE BLACK CHURCH AS TRADITION

Next, it is necessary to explain what we mean in using the term *Black Church*. Over the course of the last century, the concept of the Black Church—and *Negro Church* before that—was a scholarly construct that achieved popular resonance throughout American culture and society. For the sake of simplicity and efficacy, the term *Black Church* became a euphemistic generalization for the collective identity of African American Christians in both academic and societal contexts.

Given the conceptual ambiguity and methodological problems involved in examining the Black Church as an *institution*, per se, we find it more useful to study the Black Church as a *tradition*. Obviously, this shift poses some equally formidable theoretical challenges. However, the semantic change allows us to discuss the dynamism and evolutionary character of African American Christianity. As one scholar notes, a living or organic tradition can be defined as a "historically extended, socially embodied argument, and an argument precisely in part about the goods which constitute that tradition."[5] For our purposes, we consider the Black Church tradition not as a fixed historical product but rather as a fluid historic process in which Black Christians engage one another, invent, embrace, and inherit this tradition that they argue over and care deeply about, whether overtly or not. Dating back to its days as the "invisible institution," the creation and development of the historic Black Church tradition never has been completely clear. Nevertheless, the Black Church tradition possesses distinctive characteristics and constitutive elements, including key questions, symbols, rituals, ideas, and beliefs that are always subject to adaptation, improvisation, reinterpretation, and even abandonment.

POLITICS OF THE BOOK

A central theme, early in the field of Black Church Studies, was freedom as an organizing principle in the individual lives and collective experience of Black Christians. This book aligns itself with this indispensable perspective and views liberation as the driving force of this conversation. Liberation serves as a central consideration for the authors for several reasons. First, a liberation motif is consistent with the flow of Black Church Studies exemplified in the conversations of Black theology and Womanist approaches in religion. Second, our focus on liberation reintroduces and reasserts a much needed conversation for an era—in the wake of September 11, 2001, terror attacks—filled with the most dreaded aspects of globalization such as endemic poverty, religious extremism, ethnic wars, and terrorism. Third, liberation calls any particular tradition, like the Black Church tradition, out of itself and toward a more holistic understanding. Fourth, the emphasis on liberation within Black Christianity allows a discussion that moves beyond social description and toward the necessity of dialogue concerning ethics, practical theology, education, pastoral care, and so forth. In other words, we hope to provoke conversations that greatly inform the mission and ministry of the Black Church tradition. Liberation necessitates the interplay of theory and practice within the Christian context. Liberation serves as the focal point for a much broader discussion about Black Church Studies, one that extends the impact of such knowledge and wisdom of Black Christianity in meaningful ways that unite rather than divide the academy, the church, and the community.

As a note on usage, there are several terms and concepts that we utilize throughout this text in the hopes of transforming the language and thoughts of all readers. First, readers will note that the terms *Black, African American, Negro,* and *Afro-American* are used interchangeably in this book. We use *Black* as our preferred descriptive label of racial identification because, contrary to any negative connotations about the pigmentation of human skin or pejorative assessments of personal traits and behavior, we reclaim the term as a unifying description of peoples, communities, and cultures of African descent that span the limits of historic time and geographic space. However, anyone reading this book who remembers the dramatic tensions and ideological debates that accompanied the transition from *Negro* to *Black* within American popular culture and jargon circa the late 1960s will doubtless retain a level of skepticism towards the establishment of a single, normative usage. Moreover, contemporary devotees of post-modernism and political correctness might equally contend that using the term *Black* is a means of expressing a mode of racial identification that is essentialist, overly generalized, and assumes levels of racial authenticity. Our emphasis of the term *Black* counters those claims by asserting racial notions of Blackness that are richly layered, complex, and diverse. Nevertheless, we do alternate among *Black, African American*, and *Afro-American* largely in order to maintain contextual and emphatic options for using these multiple terms. Conversely, we have tried to minimize the use of outdated terms like *Negro* and *colored* in reference to Black Americans except in the case of direct quotations or the titles of articles, books, sermons, and so forth. Most important, we have chosen to capitalize *Black* as a means of moving beyond skin color towards a notion of shared history, cultural heritage, and group identity as well as a challenge to the pervasiveness of white supremacist thought. The general consensus of the authors of this book is that there is no equally logical or compelling basis for capitalizing the term *white*.

Another key element that the student will notice is that there is minimal emphasis on the white church in the chapters of this book. We have presumed that it is wholly appropriate in a book about Black Church Studies to rely on sources, analyses, and criticism that not only emerge from the scholarship of Black intellectuals and church people but also interpret the life and practices of the Black Church when it is at its best. Rather than using the norms and practices of the white church as a benchmark or standard of comparison, our descriptions and analyses of the Black Church tradition are based upon its own assessment of the problems and issues it seeks to address, on its own terms, in order to best meet the needs of its adherents and practitioners.

Unlike previous works that address the genesis of the Black Church tradition in the North American context, this book focuses on Black people as central to their own story of faith. Toward this end, discussion of the Black Church tradition is told from the standpoint of the thoughts, beliefs, and practices of Black Christians rather than viewed through the lens of America's white mainline churches. By this token, we approach Black Church Studies as a systematic investigation of how people of African descent in North America have made and remade their Christian witness themselves over time and space with their experiences placed center stage. In pursuing this objective, we assert the self-evident truth that Black Church Studies has more than enough excellent cultural resources, research methods, and theoretical approaches of its own. It does not depend on the comparison, validation, and assessment of whites. In other words, though external factors, influences, and actors that have had impact on the development of African American Christianity receive appropriate attention where and when necessary, this book does not view the mission and ministry of the Black Church as either outside or subordinate to its own religious saga.

By making these editorial and pedagogical decisions, we are also challenging the presumption that white faith communities and religious institutions must necessarily be the normative expression of human *being* and human *doing*. A conversation about Black people without mention of white people is possible and necessary as Black people are in-and-of ourselves a distinct and distinguished people with our own rites, rituals, customs, values, and traditions. We do not exist as a reaction to white people, as a distorted reflection of white culture, or as an exotic, sepia-toned version of white people.

Keeping that in mind, this book is about the religious experiences of Black people, the lives they forged separately and together, the sacred institutions they created, and how they realized and claimed themselves to be children of God in spite of the virulent persistence of white supremacy. We can no longer write, study, preach, pray, or live the spirituality of Black folk—or that of any other people on the planet—according to the evaluative criteria of others since the substance and significance of Black lives are not replicas of those others.

Another dimension of this approach to this subject will be noticed in our use of language to describe historical Black persons and communities. The most significant instance is in our use of the term *enslaved Africans*, as opposed to the more commonly used word *slave*. It is our goal to remind the reader that the condition of inhuman bondage in which these persons found themselves neither exclusively defined nor exhausted the depth of their humanity. In the work of this book, this has an added poignancy because of the witness of so many Black Christians in a state of enslavement and subjugation, who still realized a spiritual, mental, and eventually even physical state of freedom.

ORGANIZATION OF THE BOOK AND PEDAGOGICAL AIMS

As Black Church Studies scholars informed by and in dialogue with the Church, we have chosen to organize the book in the organizational patterns true to the way in which the larger intellectual community organizes the transmission of knowledge. So, while we are taking a multidisciplinary/interdisciplinary approach to the topic, this book's discussion is organized by the disciplinary categories of the academy: Black Church History, Black Biblical Studies, Black Theology, Sociology of Black Religion, African American Christian Social Ethics, African American Christian Education, Black Church Worship and Nurture, and Black Preaching. While Black Church Studies is neither solely defined by nor solely aimed at the academy, much of the research, writing, and reflection happens in the academy by scholars in various fields; thus, our organizing choice.

Most teachers of Black Church Studies are faced with pulling together the wide variety of sources needed for the complex study of the Black Church tradition. Teachers, in an effort to design courses with comprehensive themes, have often gathered resources written as scholarly works for constitutive elements of Black Church studies. Texts often used are Gayraud Wilmore's *African-American Religious Studies*, Timothy Fulop and Albert Raboteau's *African-American Religion*, and C. Eric Lincoln and Lawrence Mamiya's *The Black Church in the African-American Experience*. While these texts are invaluable resources, they do not render a comprehensive overview for students and teachers who are unfamiliar with the scope and tradition of the Black Church. This book is written for students and teachers who want a comprehensive resource. As such, it is meant to serve as a foundational text that the other established books may augment. A key feature of this book is the inclusion of teaching aids. A detailed Table of Contents provides a helpful guide through the material. Charts and graphs throughout the text provide ease in accessing vital concepts, facts, and data. Biographies of significant persons, study questions, and a brief list of essential texts in the chapter's subject area can be found at the end of each chapter. Further resources to strengthen the conversation are provided in the back of the book:

- Notes: citations and notes, grouped by chapter
- Glossary: definitions of key terms, set in boldface at first appearance in the text

- Bibliography: all cited sources, plus additional study resources
- Authors' Biographies: biographical information about the book's authors
- Index: key terms, significant individuals, and important topics

This book is addressed to students in introductory courses about Black Church Studies and related fields. It is also aimed at a wider spectrum of students—those who are a part of the Black Church tradition and those who may be part of other religious traditions and communities. The authors invite students of any background to explore the unique Christian tradition, aptly described by C. Eric Lincoln as something more than "a black patina on a white happening." It is a unique response to a historical occurrence that can never be replicated for any other people in America.[6] While our intent is to offer this book as a thorough study of the history, tradition, and expressions of the Black Christian tradition, we understand it to be a tool offered as an inspiration for further study.

The order of the chapters that follow is our attempt to provide a comprehensive structural approach to Black Church Studies. Our approach begins with the conviction that students of Black Church Studies must have a sound understanding of the historical development of the Black Church in the United States. The first chapter on history is the prerequisite for interpreting the Black Church's contemporary reality. The systematic examination of that reality is then the lens through which we make sense of the Church as a tradition. As with all traditions, the Black Church is engaged with the formation of future generations and does this through the work of its teaching and identity formation. Throughout most of its history, the Black Church has situated the Bible at the center of the Church's self-understanding. The Bible has provided the framing and content for the mission and ministry of the Black Church tradition. Engagement with key existential questions and with the religious experiences of the Black community has been the crux of the theological reflection within the Church and an emphasis of the sociological impact of the Black Church in North American culture and society. Consequently, the moral traditions and social ethics of the Church guide Black Christians in how they can best live out their faith in order to positively impact society on an individual and collective basis. Finally, our approach asserts that education, worship and nurture, and preaching are the *telos* of the Church as it expresses itself in the world throughout time. So, by ordering the chapters in this way, we are suggesting a way that is fundamentally significant as we encourage students to read and think in this disciplinary trajectory.

Chapter 1, "Black Church History," tells the story of the evolution of Black Christian faith from the enslavement of Africans to the emergence of African American church denominations and beyond. This account reflects that Black Christian faith has historically affirmed humanity in a world that sought to deny the equality of all God's children. Chapter 2, "Black Biblical Studies," explores the complex relationship that African Americans have had with the Bible in shaping both Black Christian spirituality and sense of social justice. The chapter illustrates how African Americans overcame the misuses and misinterpretations of the biblical text by whites and incorporated Scripture within Black life and culture both as a critique against social injustice and as affirmation of God's engagement in human affairs. Chapter 3, "Black Theologies," outlines the various sources and norms of the Black Church's theological tradition. Particular attention is paid to the place of Black Christians' experience and worldview within theological reflection. The chapter also identifies the two dominant streams of theological reflection in the Black Church and describes their role in constructing piety and motivating social action within the Black Church. Chapter 4, "The Black Church, Culture, and Society," explores gender, sexuality, race, and class as interlocking social relations of power in the Black Church. The chapter situates the Black Church as the most autonomous institution in Black community development in the continental United States while also discussing the implications of understanding the Black Church in diasporan and transnational contexts. Chapter 5, "African American Christian Social Ethics," explores the moral tradition of the Black Church as it confronts the social ills and special concerns unique to the Black community. Herein, the study of the virtues and approaches to liberation unique to the Black Church moral tradition illustrates the ways Black Christians preserve and promote their community by putting a liberating faith in action. Chapter 6, "Christian Education in the Black Church Tradition," suggests that the Black Church is a problem-solving institution in a racist, sexist, classist, oppressive, and hegemonic context. As such, church life is deemed a "classroom" for teaching and learning theological practices of survival, liberation, faith, and hope. Christian education in the Black Church fosters the cultural and religious identity of its people while equipping the people to survive the ravages of oppression. Chapter 7, "Black Christian Worship as Nurture," presents worship as the distinctive and vital celebration of God's presence and activity in the lives of Black people by providing an overview of the nature, necessity, and functions of nurture in Black worship. It explores in fuller detail the content and approaches to nurture found in key activities, liturgical events, and the roles of the pastor and congregation in nurture. Chapter 8, "Black Preaching Praxis," identifies and addresses developments in the narrative preaching practices, biblical interpretations, and complex rhetorical strategies of Black preaching praxis and the apprenticeship tradition of the Black Church. Central to this exploration is the dialectic between pastoral and prophetic preaching that has been critical to the formation and mission of the Black Church in proclaiming a Word of revelation, empowerment, and justice.

As you read this book, be aware that Black Church Studies is an under-analyzed dimension in the study of North American church life as well as a much needed model for continued study of previously relegated and marginalized expressions of the church in North American life and culture. We hope this book will whet your appetite for additional reflection, learning, research, and activism.

When the history books are written in future generations, the historians will have to pause and say, "There lived a great people—a black people—who injected new meaning into the veins of civilization." This is our challenge and our overwhelming responsibility.
—Rev. Dr. Martin Luther King, Jr.

CHAPTER ONE

BLACK CHURCH HISTORY

INTRODUCTION

This chapter is not a typical history, full of names, dates, places, and statistics ready for memorization and repetition. It certainly has those elements, but it is more than that. Rather than strictly being a chronological account of the emergence of particular African American church denominations, our goal is to tell the story of the evolution of Black Christian faith. Having been denied presence and rendered invisible in the broad scope of Church history due to enslavement, segregation, and the persistence of **racism**, Black Christians have been believers much longer than they have had access to institutional modes of religion and worship. African Americans came to Christianity not simply through the church but through a faith in the God of love and liberation. From slavery to freedom, Black Christians have historically upheld the cross of Jesus because it affirmed their humanity in a world that sought to deny the equality of all God's children. This history reflects that Black Christians' faith in God's love and liberating power led to the establishment of the institution and tradition known as the Black Church.

Historian Gayraud Wilmore asserts that the radical nature of the historic Black Church tradition is defined by three factors: the quest for independence from white control; the revalorization of the image of Africa [and African peoples]; and the acceptance of protest and agitation as theological prerequisites for Black liberation and the liberation of all oppressed peoples.[1] From its origins in traditional African societies to its contemporary manifestations, religion has permeated every dimension of African American history and culture—from art, music, and literature, to the formation of social institutions, economic collectives, and political philosophies. Prior to the incursion of Europeans into sub-Saharan Africa, most Africans participated in religious practices that were not only indigenous to the continent but were also specific to their family or kinship group, and society. Even before the United States came into existence as a recognizable nation, the conundrum of what it meant to be *Black* and *Christian* was intensely connected in both law and social practice. From the moment Africans were imported to British North America and enslaved in 1619 until the end of American chattel slavery as a result of the Civil War, they and their descendants sought to create communal and kinship networks within the context of slave traders and slaveholders deliberately separating families and exacerbating intraracial differences among enslaved populations. Viewed in this sense, the Black Church has been the Black community's foremost means to overcome the cumulative dehumanization of slavery, segregation, and social injustice.

FROM SLAVE RELIGION TO LIBERATING FAITH: THE MAKING OF BLACK CHRISTIANS

To understand the history of the Black Church in America, it is important to return to its origins. The Black Church arose from the deepest, darkest depths of the slave ship. As millions of **enslaved Africans** were forced to travel the Atlantic Ocean during the **Middle Passage**, aboard vessels ironically named *King of Dahomey*, *Brotherhood*, *The Virgin Mary*, and *John the Baptist*, their fervent prayers and pleas to the Almighty Creator marked the start of a radically different religious enterprise in the New World. As historian Charles Long asserts,

> The Middle Passage . . . was never forgotten by the Africans, neither during slavery nor in freedom. The watery passage of the Atlantic, that fearsome journey, that cataclysm of modernity, has served as a mnemonic structure, evoking a memory that forms the disjunctive and involuntary presence of these Africans in the Atlantic world.[2]

From the bowels of those dreaded wooden ships, untold millions of African women, men, and children began to shed many of the social, ethnic, and psychological distinctions that had kept them divided in their native lands on the continent.[3] In the hull of any given slave ship, en route to the most dehumanizing and devastating form of enslavement known to humankind, millions of Africa's children

4

turned their souls to an unknown, unnamed God that might hold the answer to their present fate.

Early African American religion was an effort by enslaved Africans to safeguard themselves against the disruption of their religious worldview. Enslaved Africans gradually merged their composite African religiosity with western notions of Christianity through complex cultural processes of **enculturation**, adaptation, and assimilation.[4] Whether enslaved or free, African American converts to Christianity of the colonial era subordinated European sacred rhetoric to their own hermeneutical interpretation of personal salvation, conviction of sin, charismatic praise and worship, the equality of all peoples, and the divine promise of heaven.

When slavery was introduced to the English colony of Jamestown in 1619, there was no official distinction of *slave* in English law. By the end of the seventeenth century, however, this changed with a series of influential legal measures approved by the Virginia House of Burgesses known as the **Slave Codes**. These laws profoundly defined race relations in North America more than a century before the ratification of the U.S. Constitution. By 1650, the Virginia legislators established the premise that Africans were considered enslaved for life as a *de facto* (by custom) issue. A noteworthy 1662 law emphasized that the child of an enslaved or indentured mother inherited the legal status of the mother; this was the first such law and clearly violated English common law and custom. Another 1662 law stated that "if any christian shall [commit] Fornication with a negro man or woman, hee or shee soe [sic] offending" would be doubly fined as opposed to those found guilty of a similar offense between two "Christians." By 1667, the House of Burgesses passed a law that Christian baptism no longer allowed for the liberation of enslaved peoples. In 1670, the Virginia legislature ratified a law that any non-Christian servants brought by ship "shall be slaves for their lives"; this indicated that slavery was *durante vita* (for life) and *de jure* (by law) by its legal definition. By 1705, legislation was passed stating that enslaved labor was to be considered chattel (private property).[5]

Since enslaved Blacks were denied fellowship within institutional Christianity, they created what historian Albert Raboteau called "slave religion" through a process known as **syncretism**.[6] Slave religion is important to the origins of the Black Christian experience in America for two distinct reasons. On one hand, the retention of **African traditional religions** in the western hemisphere had been evident in the persistence of such religious practices as spirit possession, river baptisms (total immersion), the ring shout, call-and-response, conjuring practices, and cross-cultural identification of African divine spirits with Roman Catholic saints in African-derived religious traditions such as *Santería* from Cuba and *Vodoun* from Haiti.[7] On the other hand, it laid a religious foundation for the historic Black Church whereby the spiritual and cultural sensibilities of enslaved Africans found common ground with various icons, rituals, and traditions within Western Christianity, which otherwise might not have been recognized. In this fashion, slave religion soon became the means to galvanize people of African descent into a more cohesive community based on their religiosity as well as their race.

Race, Slavery, and the Great Awakenings

The major turning point in African American Christianity and the creation of the historic Black Church tradition came in conjunction with the pietism and religious revivalism known as the first Great Awakening. This extensive social movement of the mid- to late-eighteenth century stemmed from growing dissatisfaction among white Americans with a deterministic and increasingly formal style of Protestantism that seemed to deny most people a chance for salvation. During the early 1730s, famed Congregationalist preacher Jonathan Edwards began an emotional, participatory ministry aimed at bringing more people into the church. By the 1740s, George Whitefield had carried an equally evangelical style of Christianity to the British colonies in North America. In their "fire and brimstone" sermons, Edwards and Whitefield—while they did not advocate emancipation—preached to Black people as well as white people.[8]

Some people of African descent had converted to Christianity before Whitefield's arrival in North America. But two factors prevented widespread Black conversion. First, most slave masters feared that enslaved Blacks who embraced Christianity would interpret their new religious status as a step toward freedom, justice, and equality. Second, many enslaved Blacks continued to derive spiritual satisfaction from their ancestral religions and were not attracted to Christianity of the European settlers.

With the first Great Awakening, however, a remarkable conversion began along cultural and spiritual lines. Enslaved Africans and eventually their African American counterparts not only became Christians but also, in turn, influenced white religiosity. This was because this religious movement unwittingly emphasized key points of convergence between

Western Christianity and African traditional religions. For instance, the prevalent belief in a Supreme Being, ancestral veneration, and animism within African traditional religions resembled the Trinitarian belief in the *Father, Son,* and *Holy Ghost* central to the mainstream Christian doctrine. Moreover, the pietistic style of preaching adopted by Whitefield and other evangelicals had some overt similarities to the forms of "spirit possession" that were commonplace in West African societies. Like their African and African American counterparts—both enslaved and free— the white evangelists and revivalists of the first Great Awakening emphasized singing, emotionalism, physical movement, and personal rebirth. The practice of total body immersion during baptism in lakes, rivers, and ponds that gave the Baptist church tradition its name paralleled West African water rituals.

Because it drew African Americans into an evangelical movement that helped shape American society, the first Great Awakening increased the infusion of Western Christianity into Black religious experience. Revivalists appealed to the poor of all races and emphasized spiritual equality. Evangelical Anglicans, Baptists, Methodists, Congregationalists, and Presbyterians opened their fledgling churches to Black people during the colonial era. Members of these early interracial churches addressed each other as *brother* and *sister* regardless of race; Black members received communion with white members, served as church officers, and were subject to the same church discipline.

By the late 1700s, Black men such as Jupiter Hammon, David George, George Liele, and Andrew Bryan were being ordained as deacons, priests, and ministers—even though they were enslaved—and preached to white congregations. They thereby influenced white people's perception of how services should be conducted. Black worshipers also influenced white preachers. Regardless of race, the Baptists exhibited a worship style that was revival-minded and enthusiastic; this, however, had a particular impact on African Americans who resonated with a form of Christianity that was reminiscent of African traditional religions.

During the first Great Awakening, enslaved preacher George Liele, the first Black Baptist preacher and missionary in Georgia, often preached at the Silver Bluff Baptist Church in Silver Bluff, South Carolina, the first Black Baptist church organized in North America. This church was equally notable because the congregation included free and enslaved Blacks. Andrew Bryan, one of Liele's original followers, was ordained to the ministry, and his church certified, in 1788. Bryan enjoyed the support of several prominent white men of Savannah who cited the positive effect of religion on slave discipline. When his own master died, Andrew Bryan was able to purchase his freedom. In 1794, Bryan raised enough money to erect a church in Savannah, calling it the Bryan Street African Baptist Church—the first Baptist church for African Americans in Georgia, as well as the first Baptist church, either Black or white, in Savannah. By 1800, the church had grown to about seven hundred; they reorganized as the First African Baptist Church of Savannah, and two hundred fifty members were dismissed in order to establish a branch outside of Savannah.[9] The pioneering ministerial work of such leaders as George Liele, David George, and Andrew Bryan, whether enslaved or free, boldly established the historic Afro-Protestant tradition within the African American religious experience.[10]

Enslaved Blacks found significant reasons to embrace the Baptist tradition in the antebellum South. Most separate Black Baptist congregations such as the Silver Bluff community (1770s) were typically Southern and rural with notable exceptions like New York City's Abyssinian Baptist Church (1808). Even though there was a definite concept of the *call to ministry* for educated clergy and trained leadership within Baptist church doctrine, there was limited concern for educational qualifications regarding catechism and formal training. This was particularly advantageous for Black men and women who were forbidden access to any level of education by state law. Furthermore, the Baptists espoused belief in the equality of all believers and placed great emphasis on moral self-determination—what historian Nathan Hatch has called the "individualization of conscience"[11]—as well as independence and democratic order. Due to the congregational polity of Baptist churches, the decentralized autonomy of local communities of the faithful was vitally important for a fellowship of Black Christians who were forced, because of the virulent web of racial and religious persecution, to remain *invisible*. This seeming invisibility was further enhanced by the minimal supervision/monitoring of their worship services by white authorities. The general Baptist belief in human potential to fulfill God's will spoke very intensely to an enslaved people who were continuously condemned as being subhuman by whites.

Another key development in the historic Black Church tradition was the emerging influence of Methodism among enslaved and free Blacks in North America. In a similar fashion, as a denomination based on connectional churches, the centralization of Methodist societies via regional meetings and conferences inherently led to a greater sense of church fellowship as well as a considerable pooling of resources. The accepted role of traveling or itinerant ministers proved less hierarchal than other denominations, and allowed Black men and women the opportunity to preach in various churches. Notable Methodist leaders such as John Wesley and Francis Asbury believed the gospel was meant for all people regardless of color; they argued that true Methodist societies must deny Christian fellowship to slaveholders. This level of anti-slavery advocacy was rare by any standard, and it had a definite allure for African Americans seeking a faith free of religious hypocrisy and moral contradiction.

By the end of the eighteenth century, along with the dawning of the American Republic in the wake of the Revolutionary War, independent Black churches quickly became the core of African American communities in their quest for freedom from domination from white ecclesiastical bodies and other expressions of white supremacy. The roots of the independent Black Church movement are traced most often to the establishment of the **Free African Society**, organized in Philadelphia in 1787, by Richard Allen, Absalom Jones, and other African American members of St. George's Methodist Episcopal Church. The incident that led to the formation of the Free African Society was the forced removal of Absalom Jones from St. George's by the white trustees while he and other Black members were kneeling at the altar in prayer. Because of differences in religious views, Allen left the Free African Society in 1789 and Jones became its leader. Under Jones's leadership, the Free African Society began holding worship services on New Year's Day, 1791, and the society soon gave way to the formation of a church. Over the next few years, Absalom Jones and the church's charter members petitioned the Episcopal Church to become an Episcopal parish, yet fervently insisted upon remaining free of white control. As a result, Jones and the members founded St. Thomas African Episcopal Church in Philadelphia, thus making it the first independent Black Church in Philadelphia. By 1805, Jones was ordained as the first African American Episcopalian priest in the nation.

Like Rev. Jones and Black Episcopalians, Richard Allen was vitally important to the formation of the independent Black Church movement. When his predominantly white congregation supported the racist actions of the trustees, Allen eventually organized his fellow Black Methodists in order to form the Bethel Church in 1793. Richard Allen was subsequently ordained by Methodist bishop Francis Asbury in 1799 and became the first Black Methodist minister. Realizing the great desire to build their own house of worship for African Americans, Allen bought land and built the sanctuary for the Bethel Church in Philadelphia. It remains, even now, as the property in this country with the longest continual ownership by an African American group. Richard Allen was elected the church's first bishop in 1816. Other African-identified churches in the area, having also been discriminated against by white Christians, aligned themselves with Bishop Allen, thus establishing the African Methodist Episcopal (AME) Church as the first Black Church denomination in the United States, with "Mother Bethel" AME Church its flagship institution.[12] In 1848, Frederick Douglass maintained that the Mother Bethel AME Church in Philadelphia, with roughly three thousand worshipers every Sunday, was the "largest church in this Union." [13]

The founding of the African Methodist Episcopal Zion Church (AME Zion) was another key example of the independent Black Church movement in America. The church's roots can be traced back to the John Street Methodist Church of New York City. Following acts of overt racial discrimination such as forcing Blacks to leave worship, many Black Methodists left to form their own churches. The first church founded by the AME Zionists was built in 1800 and was henceforth named "Mother Zion." Initially these early churches were part of the Methodist denomination regarding theological instruction, ordination of ministers, and other ecclesiastical concerns, although the congregations remained separate in terms of their racial identification. James Varick was elected in 1821 and ordained as the first bishop of the AME Zion church a year later.[14]

After 1816, the great enthusiasm among free Blacks surrounding the independent Black Church movement led to a burgeoning number of AME and AME Zion churches within cities in the Northern and Southern Unites States, thus establishing the AME and AMEZ as two new and distinctive Wesleyan denominations. Furthermore, the establishment of predominantly African United Baptist churches in Canada during the early half of the nineteenth century offered signs of Black Christians' excitement over the creation of their own churches and denominations across national borders. Overall, the independent Black Church movement was vital to the fabric of free Black communities in the North. The churches that were organized, supported, and led by Black Christians during the nineteenth century illustrated a sense of freedom in performing religious functions and guarding moral discipline and communal values, in addition to providing and promoting education, social insurance, fraternal associations, and recreation.[15]

During much of the second Great Awakening of the early nineteenth century, independent Black churches in the North were community centers in the truest sense. They housed schools and were meeting places for a variety of organizations as well as various voluntary associations. Antislavery societies often met in churches, and the churches harbored fugitive slaves. This went hand-in-hand with the community leadership that Black ministers provided to anxious church members worried about the tenuous state of their quasi-freedom, and with those ministers' work in keeping Black Northerners confident of God's grace and protection. The independent Black churches spoke against slavery in the plantation South as well as racial oppression in the North. These churches also grappled with what they considered weaknesses among African Americans. However, it must be noted that Black ministers seldom, if ever, spoke with a unanimous voice.

By the 1830s and 1840s, some Black leaders began to criticize the existence of separate Black churches. During this era, the AME Church had at least 296 congregations in the United States and Canada with more than seventeen thousand members. Frederick Douglass called them "Negro pews, on a higher and larger scale."[16] Such churches, Douglass and others maintained, were part and parcel of a segregationist spirit that divided America by skin color. Foreshadowing criticisms that would persist throughout the nineteenth and twentieth centuries, Douglass also denounced what he considered the illiteracy and anti-intellectualism of most Black ministers. Yet growing numbers of African Americans during the 1800s regarded such churches as crucial sources of cultural pride, spiritual renewal, and social dignity, and saw them as a legitimate alternative to the racial prejudice and mistreatment perpetrated by their white Christian counterparts. As an example, Douglass eventually affiliated himself with the AME Zion Church because of its more progressive social outlook.

The Black Church as the *Invisible Institution* in the Old South

By the nineteenth century, most African Americans in the antebellum South practiced a form of Protestantism that was loosely related to that of their white counterparts. Ironically, interracial Methodist and Baptist church fellowships persisted in the South much longer than they did in Northern cities. The Southern congregations usually had racially segregated seating, but Blacks and whites joined in communion and church discipline, and they even shared cemeteries in some locales. Another aspect of this interracial Christianity was evident in that many plantation owners as well as white missionary organizations established churches on Southern estates for the express purpose of indoctrinating enslaved men, women, and children during the antebellum era. In these plantation churches, white ministers typically preached to their Black congregants that the Holy Bible taught that Black people deserved to be subjugated because of the "Curse of Ham" and that "good slaves" must obey their earthly masters as they did God.[17] As it might be imagined, this was not what enslaved African Americans wanted to hear. There is evidence that at times enslaved Blacks walked out on ministers who preached this way. In his ex-slave narratives, Cornelius Garner recalled, "dat ole white preacher jest was telling us slaves to be good to our marsters. We ain't keer'd a bit 'bout dat stuff he was telling us 'cause we wanted to sing, pray, and serve God in our own way [sic]."[18]

Instead of attending and adhering to church services sponsored by slave masters, enslaved Blacks were able to create the **invisible institution**, a secretive Black Church tradition. They consecrated themselves to the purpose of resisting, escaping when possible, and ultimately surviving enslavement in the plantation South, giving rise to the **hush harbors** (alternately referred to as "brush arbors"). In the aftermath of legendary slave rebellions and plots of insurrection—organized by enslaved Black preachers such as Gabriel Prosser, Denmark Vesey, and Nat Turner—the spread of religion among the enslaved Black population was deemed illegal by nearly all the state legislatures throughout the American South.[19] In light of this, these loose-knit congregations met in secret and were led by enslaved Black men and women, who were often "self-called" and illiterate.[20] The biblical references and teachings of these hush harbors, as well as the slave rebellions plotted by Prosser, Vesey, Turner, and countless others, were largely centered on the Old Testament narrative of Exodus with its emphasis on God's deliverance of Moses and the Israelites from inhumane slavery.

Finding immediate parallels between the Israelites' plight in Pharaoh's Egypt and the struggle of African Americans against American slavery, enslaved Black Christians preferred the lessons garnered from the Exodus story to the theology professed by white supremacists—Christian meekness, docile slaves, and divinely cursed Black people.[21] Moreover, gathering together in wooded areas far from the prying eyes and relentless whips of those who enslaved them, Black Christians held worship services characterized by a sense of engaged ecstasy with singing, dancing, praying, moaning, clapping, and shouting. In such stolen moments, enslaved Black women, men, and children gradually wrested their humanity from the grip of inhumane bondage through their worship of the sacred.

The Black Church as the *Visible Institution* in the Antebellum North

The ability for Africans and African Americans to openly identify and voluntarily assemble as Christian communities of faith in the antebellum North gave rise to Black churches as visible institutions in the United States. Without question, this was a momentous advance for the Black Church tradition. While the invisible institution was the central means available to enslaved Blacks in the plantation South to express their Christian faith and their aspirations for freedom, the majority of free Blacks of the time had specific reasons to identify themselves with the Methodist tradition. Most Black Methodist congregations were typically Northern and urban. The Methodist denominations had great appeal to a growing number of Northern Blacks because of their practices of personal sanctification, and what historian Evelyn Brooks Higginbotham refers to as a politics of respectability reflected in their worship styles, highly ordered liturgies, closely supervised ministry, and generally prosperous memberships.[22] Simply put, the "method of the Methodists" brought a viable institutional order to Black worship without losing the authenticity of Black spirit-filled worship.

The second Great Awakening significantly transformed American society and culture during the first half of the nineteenth century, a change to which the contributions of African Americans was central. Regardless of race, American evangelicals were motivated to carry Christian morality into politics by inspiring a new era of revivalism in America by emphasizing a sense of "practical Christianity." In keeping with their beliefs, they felt that those who were truly saved would not be content with their own salvation. Rather, they would help to save others. In particular, Black evangelicals of this period called for "a *liberating* faith" that would advance both material and spiritual well-being.

13

The Black Church and the Antislavery Struggle

The most powerful and politically important development of the second Great Awakening was connected to confronting the enslavement of African Americans in the United States. Abolitionists were typically people who committed themselves to ending slavery on both state and national levels. Two separate expressions of the abolitionist movement arose and continued up to the climax of the American Civil War. The first of these abolitionist movements existed in the antebellum South among the enslaved, with the help of the small number of free Black and sympathetic white people. Enslaved African Americans, individually and in groups, sought their liberation through both violent and nonviolent means. The second abolitionist movement was comprised of white and Black antislavery advocates in the North, with strategic outposts in the upper South. Although far more white people were involved in the Northern aspect of the abolitionist struggle than its Southern counterpart, the presence and involvement of African Americans in the Northern branch was central to its work in several ways. For instance, even as liberal white reformers like William Lloyd Garrison, the Grimké sisters (Sarah and Angelina), and Theodore Weld began to dominate the larger, more renowned abolitionist organizations, free Blacks like David Walker, Maria Stewart, Henry Highland Garnet, and others became involved in direct arguments and political action against slavery in the South and its influences in the North. While African Americans could not participate in antislavery organizations in the upper South, many still cooperated covertly and informally with white abolitionists there. Whether looking at the series of failed slave revolts or the **Underground Railroad**, these forms of resistance to American slavery in the antebellum South made it possible for a modest number of enslaved people to free themselves, even though they proved unable to bring the entire institution of slavery to an end.[23]

The independent Black churches of the antebellum North were especially significant in the abolitionist movement. With a few noteworthy exceptions, the leading Black abolitionists were ministers. Among them were Henry Highland Garnet, Theodore S. Wright, Samuel E. Cornish, Jehiel C. Berman, Charles B. Ray, James C.W. Pennington, Nathaniel Paul, Alexander Crummell, Samuel Ringgold Ward, and Daniel A. Payne. Some of these African American men were leaders of the African Baptist Church or the AME Church, while others preached to Black

14

congregations affiliated with predominantly white churches.[24] A few Black ministers, such as Amos N. Freeman of Brooklyn, New York, served white abolitionist congregations. These clergy used their pulpits to attack slavery, racial discrimination, proslavery white churches, and the American Colonization Society (ACS).[25]

The Black Church and the Civil War

It is important to remember that the first half of the nineteenth century witnessed a massive expansion and consolidation of chattel slavery in the United States. During this period, along with family and socialization, religion offered enslaved Black men, women, and children the most help in surviving the "peculiar institution."[26] Some slave masters denied enslaved Blacks access to Protestant Christianity because of the prospect that it would prompt African Americans to seek manumission and racial equality as a result of prolonged exposure to the gospel. Meanwhile, some portions of the enslaved Black populace actively ignored Christianity because they could not embrace the professed religion of white Americans.

By the 1850s, the growing concern of Southerners with the presence of free Blacks in their midst led to the threat of extinction for the free Black community. Pressures increased to either deport free Blacks or enslave them. As a result, some Black leaders, like prototypical Black nationalists Martin R. Delany and Henry Highland Garnet, began to look more favorably on migration to and colonization of Africa by African Americans. That quest was interrupted by the outbreak of the Civil War.[27]

What must be understood is that African Americans—whether free or enslaved—did not side with the Union because of abstract notions of federal authority versus states' rights or industrial capitalism versus agricultural economy. The significance of the Civil War within the African American experience was defined by the insurmountable struggle to liberate all people of African descent and make certain that freedom, justice, and equality would be the rightful inheritance for them and their progeny.[28] As the foremost recruiter for the all-Black 54th Massachusetts Colored Infantry, Frederick Douglass once encouraged the growing throngs of Black folks to "Remember that in a contest with oppression the Almighty has no attribute which can take sides with oppressors."[29]

Another interesting development that became a prevalent aspect of the Civil War's impact on the historic Black Church tradition was the watch night service on New Year's Eve. According to Methodist practice, a watch night was a church meeting that had singing, prayer, and preaching that began late in the evening and continued until shortly after midnight. What was otherwise a generic worship activity took on ultimate significance for every member of the African American community in the United States on December 31, 1862. In heavy anticipation of President Lincoln's signing of the decree (later known as the **Emancipation Proclamation**) ending the government-sanctioned enslavement of African Americans in slave holding states (it excluded neutral states), watch night services were coordinated in order to be held particularly for Black women, men, and children in all churches in the North as well as the South. Since that first so-called "Emancipation Day," watch night services on New Year's Eve have become a staple within countless Black churches, regardless of denominational affiliation, as a commemoration of the event that marked the beginning of slavery's end.

By the time President Abraham Lincoln signed the Emancipation Proclamation on January 1, 1863, Union forces were facing incredible numbers of casualties, with a desperate need for more troops. This situation may eventually have inspired the growing pressure on the white political and military leadership of the North to put African Americans in the blue soldier's garb of the Union Army. When this opportunity arose, hundreds of thousands of Black men and women in the North and even the South leapt at the chance to strike a fatal blow against chattel slavery.

Although the Civil War was not the first American conflict in which Black soldiers fought, it was the first war that allowed African Americans to serve as chaplains. In this tumultuous struggle to end slavery in the United States, the chaplains had a very demanding task in seeing to the physical and spiritual maintenance of the Black troops gathering to the Union cause. Each chaplain was assigned to a regiment of one thousand soldiers, so that one hundred eighty chaplains attended to the religious needs of nearly one hundred eighty thousand Black troops enlisted by the Union forces from 1863 to 1865. Only fourteen of the chaplains designated for Black Union troops were African Americans. These chaplains had to do more than simply serve as worship leader for the troops.[30] In addition to such pastoral duties as visiting the sick and wounded, holding prayer meetings, and burying the dead, chaplains often had to ensure that wounded Black troops received medical care, and that soldiers' pay was sent to their next of kin. Moreover, since they were usually the only Black commissioned officers in their regiments, African American chaplains often had to become advocates and intermediaries for Black troops in many dealings with their white commanding officers.

Historian William Edward Burghardt (W.E.B.) Du Bois indicated that, when word of their emancipation spread among the enslaved Black populace of the American South following January 1, 1863, the majority of them "were in religious and hysterical fervor. This was the coming of the Lord. This was the fulfillment of prophecy and legend. It was the Golden Dawn . . . It was everything miraculous and perfect and promising."[31] This was the substance of Black liberation in the aftermath of the Emancipation Proclamation and later the Thirteenth Amendment, ratified on January 31, 1865, legislation that abolished slavery in the United States finally and forever. Du Bois further states that, amid the dizzying and devastating events of the Civil War,

> To these Black folk it was the Apocalypse. The magnificent trumpet tones of Hebrew Scripture, transmuted and oddly changed, became a strange new gospel. All that was Beauty, all that was Love, all that was Truth, stood on the top of these mad mornings, and sang with the stars. A great human sob shrieked in the wind, and tossed its tears upon the sea—free, free, free.[32]

MAKING THE *INVISIBLE INSTITUTION* VISIBLE: THE EVOLUTION OF THE MODERN BLACK CHURCH TRADITION

The evolution of the historic Black Church tradition in America since emancipation can be discussed in two ways. Most generally and popularly, the Black Church is any Christian congregation predominantly populated by Blacks, including those that are parts of denominational traditions that began among whites (that is, Southern Baptists, American Baptists, Presbyterians, Episcopalians, Lutherans, Roman Catholics, Seventh Day Adventists, Assemblies of God, and so on). Alternately, the Black Church tradition can be defined as the specific Protestant denominations that were created, founded, governed, and populated by Blacks, reflecting an organized religiosity that merges Protestant doctrines of faith with an unapologetic cultural and political awareness in order to be intentionally relevant to the social and spiritual plight of African Americans. Taken together, the first seven denominations accounted for more than 80 percent of all Black Christians during the first half of the twentieth century (see list below). The Black Church in the South was hailed as the invisible institution that helped millions of African Americans survive slavery in this country. In the same way, the modern Black Church in the North must be considered the **visible institution** that helped hundreds of thousands of Black migrants adjust to urban life while affirming an enduring set of core values consisting of freedom, justice, and equality, as well as an abiding pride in a common racial identity for the entire Black community.

When people talk about and/or study the historic Black Church tradition, they are typically referring to the following denominations:[33]

BLACK CHURCH DENOMINATIONS

Year Founded	Denomination
1787 / 1816	African Methodist Episcopal (AME) Church
1796 / 1820	African Methodist Episcopal Zion (AMEZ) Church
1870	Christian Methodist Episcopal (CME) Church
1895	National Baptist Convention
1915	National Baptist Convention of America
1988	National Missionary Baptist Convention of America
1961	Progressive National Baptist Convention (PNBC)
1897 / 1906	Church of God in Christ (COGIC)
1992	Full Gospel Baptist Church Fellowship

In the years after slavery was abolished, the historic Black Church became the most important institution among African Americans, other than the family. Not only did churches fill deep spiritual and inspirational needs, they also offered enriching music, provided charity and compassion to the needy, developed community and political leaders—and did all of this free of white supervision. Before slavery's demise, free and enslaved Black people often attended white churches. Although these Black Christians were encouraged to participate in church services conducted by white ministers, racist white churchgoers treated them shabbily.

The Creation of the "Negro Church" after Emancipation

Once liberated from bondage, the *freedpeople* eventually organized their own churches with their own ministers. Most freed Blacks considered white ministers incapable of preaching a meaningful message befitting the reality of Black worshipers. In the wake of her emancipation, formerly enslaved Nancy Williams commented, "Ole white preachers used to talk wid dey tongues widdout sayin' nothin', but Jesus told us slaves to talk wid our hearts [*sic*]. "[34] In the meantime, even though many had been denied access to formal education, Black preachers nevertheless communicated powerfully and passionately with their parishioners, doing so in a manner that sometimes appalled Northern white missionaries. Despite such denouncements, white missionaries and other observers could not deny the visible impact of Black preachers on their congregations. For instance, a visiting white clergyman was genuinely impressed and humbled upon hearing the stellar sermons of one of these unlettered Black preachers whose devout faith more than compensated for any lack of formal education. This onlooker later recalled, "'He talked about Christ and his salvation as one who understood what he said . . . Here was an unlearned man, one who could not read, telling of the love of Christ, of Christian faith and duty in a way which I have not learned.'"[35]

Other Black and white religious leaders anguished over what they considered moral laxity and displaced values among the freedpeople. The ministers preached about temperance, thrift, honesty, integrity, and the eradication of sexual promiscuity, moral attitudes which were very much in keeping with the ethos of Victorian-era America. They demanded an end to anti-social behavior such as alcoholism, debauchery, prostitution, petty larceny, or any other criminal activity that would inhibit the advancement of African Americans as a race.

In addition to the federal government's efforts through the Freemen's Bureau, concerned private citizens, both Blacks and whites, volunteered to go into the American South to provide material assistance and educational opportunities to newly freed African Americans. Founded by the Congregational Church, the American Missionary Association (AMA) had a major impact in helping the freedpeople to make a smoother transition from slavery to emancipation.[36] Black churches became integral to the struggle to help Black women, men, and children adapt to their new future. For Black and white Northern teachers, such as Gideon's Band,

19

who migrated to the South after the Civil War, education was considered to have a deeply moral component. As essential as it was to teach Black Southerners how to read, write, and *figure* (the ability to know and do arithmetic), these same educators also believed these schools could extol moral virtues and social values such as honesty, punctuality, discipline, thrift, and temperance.[37] All of this was meant to hasten students on their path to American citizenship. In spite of nagging poverty, culture shock, and the escalation of violent backlash by Southern whites, the missionary zeal of teachers as well as the enthusiasm of the freedpeople was able to develop Black freedmen's schools as symbols of freedom and empowerment.

Second only to the immediate need for food, clothes, and shelter, education was the most sought after commodity among emancipated African Americans. When Booker T. Washington recounts the unbridled zeal of the freedpeople for education in his autobiography, he notes,

> Few were too young, and none too old, to make the attempt to learn. As fast as any kind of teachers could be secured, not only were day schools filled, but night schools as well. The great ambition of the older people was to try to learn to read the Bible before they died.[38]

In addition to understanding that acquiring proficiency in reading, writing, and arithmetic granted Black folks a greater sense of their freedom; they also believed that education would ensure that their greatest desire—the ability to read the Bible for themselves—would be fulfilled.

Apart from the obvious task of providing higher education and moral instruction, the historically Black colleges and universities (HBCUs) were laying the foundation for the creation of an educated Black middle-class. From humble roots, many of these freedmen's schools evolved gradually into the basis for these HBCUs. Many of these schools were founded and supported by white and Black churches. Among their number was:

- Shaw University (1865), Morehouse College (1867), and Bishop College (1881) by the Baptists;
- Morgan State University—formerly known as Morgan College (1867)—and Bennett College (1873) by the Methodists;
- Fisk University (1866), Talladega College (1867), and Hampton University (1868) by the AMA;
- Knoxville College (1875) by the Presbyterians;

- Wilberforce University (1863) and Morris Brown College (1885) by the AME Church; and
- Livingstone College (1879) by the AMEZ Church.

By the end of the nineteenth century, these institutions had become the foremost sources of African American professionals, especially in terms of ministers (overwhelmingly Black men) and teachers (mostly Black women).

Organized in 1897 in Washington, D.C., the Lott Carey Baptist Foreign Mission Convention became the first independent foreign mission society founded by African Americans. Focused specifically on advancing the goals of Christian ministry, education, and health in Africa, the Lott Carey Baptist Foreign Mission Convention was named in memory of Rev. Lott Carey, a freed Black preacher and pioneering missionary. In the late 1800s, Black churches lacked the resources and were ill equipped to sponsor large-scale Christianizing missions to Africa. Nonetheless, such efforts by African American Christians were important because they symbolized a spiritual redemption of the ancestral homeland. Eventually, the Lott Carey Baptist Foreign Mission Convention became the premier African American missionary organization focusing on issues of healthcare, education, poverty, and spirituality in Africa, Asia, the Caribbean, Europe, and Latin America, boasting the participation of three thousand churches and at least one hundred full-time workers overseas.[39]

Black Denominationalism and the Consolidation of the Black Church in Modern America

In the post–Civil War American South—a region that had banned Black religious practice by law as well as by force—most of the newly freed men, women, and children founded and attended Baptist and Methodist churches. These denominations tended to be more autonomous and less subject to outside control. Moreover, their doctrine was usually simple and direct without a complex, articulated theology. Of the Methodist denominations, the AME church made giant strides in the South after the Civil War. For instance, the AME church in Charleston, South Carolina, reemerged after an absence of more than forty years. In 1822, during the tumult over the foiled Denmark Vesey slave revolt, the lone AME church in that city had been forced to disband and its leader to flee. But by the 1870s, there were three AME congregations thriving in Charleston. In another example, the sixteen hundred members of the Front Street Methodist Church in Wilmington, North Carolina, were African Americans who decided to join the AME church soon after the Civil War ended. To further emphasize their desire to fully link their racial and religious identity as a church, the members found a Black minister to replace the long-term white pastor. Faced with the growing attraction of the AME and AME Zion denominations in the post–Civil War South, white Methodists initially encouraged cooperation with Black Methodists and helped establish the Colored Methodist Episcopal (CME) Church, now known as the Christian Methodist Episcopal Church. But the white Methodists lost some of their fervor for this endeavor after they failed to persuade the Black Methodists to dwell solely on spiritual matters and keep political issues out of the CME church.

The Presbyterian, Congregational, and Episcopal churches generally appealed to the more prosperous members of the African American community. Their services tended to be more formal and solemn. Black people who had been free before the Civil War were usually affiliated with these congregations and remained so long after the conflict ended. "Well-to-do" freedpeople organized St. Mark's Protestant Episcopal Church in Charleston, South Carolina, when they separated from the white Episcopal church, but they retained Joseph Seabrook, a white minister, as their rector. Poorer Black people generally found churches such as St. Mark's unwelcoming because of a growing division over what constituted Black Christianity in its most genuine sense.

Black churches, their parishioners, and clergymen would play a vital role in Reconstruction politics. More than one hundred Black ministers were elected to political office after the Civil War. By the end of the 1800s, in a world in which white supremacy and racial segregation dominated the lives and limited the possibilities of African Americans, the historic Black Church was the most important institution, alongside the family, that African Americans possessed and controlled for themselves. Numbering well over 1.3 million congregants in 1890, the South had more Black Baptists than all other denominations combined (AME Zion had 366,000, AME had 310,000, CME and other Methodists had 125,000, and Presbyterians had 114,000).[40] This huge disparity was probably attributable to the fact that the Baptist churches were congregational in nature, thus making them more independent and less bound by formal supervision and church hierarchy than other denominations. By comparison, bishops in both the AME and AME Zion denominations exercised considerable authority over congregations as did white Methodist and Presbyterian leaders. Interestingly, many Southerners, both Black and white, preferred the greater autonomy found in Baptist churches. Whereas the vast majority of Black Southerners belonged to Baptist, Methodist, and Presbyterian congregations in the late nineteenth century, it should be noted that there were probably 15,000 Episcopalians and possibly 200,000 Roman Catholics among the Southern Black population.

Denominational affiliation notwithstanding, the church was integral to the lives of most Black people in the United States. Obviously, it can be assumed that the church satisfied the spiritual needs of the African American community through what historian W.E.B. Du Bois declared to be the key strengths of the historic Black Church, namely "the Preacher, the Music, and the Frenzy."[41] But more than that, Black churches gave African American men, women, and children the opportunity, free from white surveillance, interference, and governance, to discuss, plan, organize, and lead within their own community. Though church members usually had little money to spare, they tithed and contributed heartily to benevolent causes such as helping the sick, the bereaved, and the victims of natural disasters. Black congregations helped thousands of young people to attend school and college, through scholarship fund drives and care packages for needful students. Quite aptly, historian James M. Washington noted that the Black Church tradition could be defined as a "church with the soul of a nation."[42]

As we look at the evolution of the Black Church as a mainstay of the Black community, it is important to note that numerous Black congregations were plagued by **sexism** with detrimental effects on Black women. African American women's contributions in making the Black Church the most dynamic and influential institution within the African American experience have been immeasurable.[43] Female parishioners in Black churches immersed themselves deeply into church activities and eventually became vital to the very existence of the Black Church tradition. There has been, however, the impending challenge posed by the prospect of empowering Black women to assume ministerial roles in churches. When Jarena Lee felt she was called to preach in the earliest days of the AME Church, and she approached Richard Allen, she was given a lukewarm and somewhat disturbing response. Despite his recognition of her abilities to preach, the AME bishop argued that there was no precedent in the *Book of Discipline* for the ordination of women as preachers, thus leaving her unable to fulfill her potential for a life of ministry. As Lee once argued,

> If the man may preach, because the Saviour died for him, why not the woman? seeing he died for her also. Is he not a whole Saviour instead of half one? as those who hold it wrong for a woman to preach, would seem to make it appear.[44]

Sometimes, though infrequently, Black women led congregations in the late nineteenth and early twentieth centuries. For instance, the marked success of the AME Zion Church in attracting members was likely related to its acceptance of women in ordained ministry, as demonstrated by the ordination of Rev. Julia Foote as a minister in 1894 and Mary Jane Small as an elder a few years later. In fact, it must be noted that the AME Zion denomination embraced women's leadership long before the much older AME denomination. In spite of the pioneering efforts of female preachers like Rev. Lee, it was not until 1948 that a woman was ordained in the AME denomination.[45]

Much like the Methodist denominations, the Baptist denominations had a similar dilemma regarding the recognition of women's religious authority and spiritual gifts. As a means of advancing the cause of greater gender inclusion (if not full-blown equality) among Black Baptists, Nannie Helen Burroughs utilized the power of the Black clubwomen's movement in order to establish Women's Day in Baptist churches, in which women delivered sermons and guided the parishioners. But even Burroughs grew disgruntled and complained that Women's Day quickly became little more than an opportunity for the male pastors, deacons, and trustees of Black churches to raise large sums of money, instead of empowering female leadership.[46]

Jim and Jane Crow, the Great Migration, and the Quest for the Promised Land

For many Black Christians, emotional involvement and enthusiastic participation in church services was an escape from their dreary and oppressive daily lives. During his childhood in Greenwood County, South Carolina, Benjamin E. Mays admitted that James F. Marshall, a

Baptist preacher in his hometown, barely had a fifth-grade education yet he "emphasized the joys of heaven and the damnation of hell" and that the "trials and tribulations of the world would all be over when one got to heaven." Although Mays eventually would advocate a more activist vision of ministerial leadership within the Black Church tradition, he often stated that he understood the great need for sermons that tried to mitigate the ravages of white supremacy for Black men, women, and children. As Mays contended, "Beaten down at every turn by the white man, as they were, Negroes could perhaps not have survived without this kind of religion."[47]

In spite of the ability of such sermons to assuage Black people's pain, ministers like Rev. Marshall never developed a language to challenge white supremacy in any direct fashion. With a deeper understanding of what the writer Richard Wright called "the ethics of Jim Crow," every Black preacher readily understood that each, and every, comment about racism and prejudice might invite some form of retaliation or even lynching.[48] In one instance, when a visiting minister came to Marshall's church and began to criticize white people from the pulpit, Marshall stopped the guest speaker at once. This period, according to African American religious historian Gayraud Wilmore, saw the "deradicalization" of the Black Church. Nonetheless, to many whites Black religious gatherings held the threatening potential to inspire Black Christians to protest against the mounting indignities and injustices of Southern life during the era of **Jim and Jane Crow** segregation.[49] The sustained reluctance of many Black ministers of the early twentieth century to advocate for serious progress in race relations remained largely invisible to the collective white imagination that still resonated with racist paranoia. As a result, Black ministers were assaulted and killed, and Black churches were burned with tragic regularity during the late 1800s and early 1900s in the segregated South. Like their white counterparts, Black ministers often stressed middle-class values to their congregations, while suggesting that many Black people found themselves in "shameful situations because of their sinful ways." Rather than offering substantial condemnation of racial prejudice in American society, many pastors preferred to urge their congregants to improve their personal conduct and hygiene as a means of avoiding further rebukes from whites.

But not all religious leaders in the African American community were afraid to tackle the volatile issue of white supremacy. In fact, some church leaders defiantly insisted that African Americans demand their rights. A prime example of this radical thread within the Black Church is AME Bishop Henry McNeal Turner, who consistently spoke out on racial matters in the United States. Without question, Turner must be recognized as one of the most visionary and militant Black religious leaders of the late nineteenth and early twentieth centuries.[50] Having grown up in South Carolina as a free Black in the midst of slavery, Turner eventually became a U.S. Army chaplain during the Civil War, and later became a member of the Georgia House of Representatives during Reconstruction. In 1883, after the U.S. Supreme Court declared the Civil Rights Act of 1875 unconstitutional, "Turner called the Constitution 'a dirty rag, a cheat, a libel and ought to be spit upon by every Negro in the land.'"[51]

As fiery as his attack on American politics was at the time, Turner made an even more intense and significant impact on the African American religious experience. Once he joined the AME Church in the 1850s, Turner became very influential in the recruitment of new converts to Methodism, the proliferation of AME churches, and the mentoring of new church clergy throughout the South after the Civil War. He eventually became a bishop in the AME Church in 1880. Contrary to the dominant opinion in the AME Church largely outlined by the erudite Bishop Daniel Payne, his mentor, Turner became an outspoken supporter of controversial issues such as women's suffrage, opposition to U.S. imperialism, the ordination of women ministers, and the Back-to-Africa movement. More importantly, he demonstrated little patience for anyone who considered Christianity a white man's religion. He boldly yet simply asserted, "God is a Negro" and assaulted those who "believe that God is white-skinned, blue-eyed, straight-haired, projecting-nosed, compressed-lipped, and finely-robed white gentleman" as being completely foolhardy.[52] Turner's provocative "God is a Negro" thesis has given generations of preachers, as well as scholars of the Black Christian tradition, the foundation for a new theological vision that began to delve more meaningfully into the religious experience of African Americans.

It can be argued that the historic Black Church helped hundreds of thousands of African Americans during the **Great Migration** make the transition from being Southern peasants to becoming part of an industrial Black workforce in the urban North and Midwest.[53] Yet the relationship between the Black religious tradition and the everyday lives of African Americans was always in flux. For instance, the growing popularity of the blues and jazz that was being performed in nightclubs during the 1920s was gradually being integrated into urban gospel music.[54] Many nightclub

musicians and singers received their training and first public performances in their home churches. During the Great Depression, the Black
Church helped many African Americans survive economic hardship and
social malaise by enabling them to pool their resources as well as providing spiritual solace and hopeful inspiration.

Black Pentecostalism in Early Twentieth-century America

Undeniably, the most significant area of growth in the Black Church
tradition during the twentieth century was the Holiness and Pentecostal
Movement. The Holiness movement and the advent of the Pentecostal
church movement greatly affected Baptist and Methodist congregations.
Partly in reaction to the elite domination and stiff authority of white
Methodism, the Holiness movement gained a foothold among white people and then spilled over among Black Southerners. Holiness churches
ordained women such as Neely Terry to lead them. Holiness clergy
preached the Wesleyan notion of **sanctification**; an ideal that allowed a
Christian to receive a "second blessing" and to feel the "perfect love of
Christ" through the anointing of the Holy Spirit.[55] Believers thus
achieved an emotional reaffirmation and a new state of grace.

The roots of the Black Holiness movement can be traced to a series of
successful revivals in Mississippi, as well as Memphis, Tennessee, and Los
Angeles, California. William J. Seymour played a key role in the development of the new movement. After hearing Black people in Houston
speak in tongues (exhibit the gift of **glossolalia**, thought by some to be
evidence of baptism in the Holy Ghost), Seymour became part of the
Azusa Street Revivals in Los Angeles in 1906. During these historic
gatherings, Seymour and others also began to speak in tongues. At 312
Azusa Street, Seymour founded the highly evangelistic movement that
shortly became the Pentecostal Church. Claiming the name of the movement from the story of Pentecost in Acts 2, the movement attracted enor-
mous interest from churchgoers of all races and grew rapidly.

Bishop Charles Harrison Mason and Charles P. Jones—two Black former Baptists—joined the early Pentecostal movement and co-founded
the Church of God in Christ (commonly known as COGIC). It eventually became the leading Pentecostal denomination. The name COGIC
had actually developed as early as 1897, while Mason was seeking a
spiritual name that would distinguish the formative church from others

bearing similar titles. By his account, he was persuaded that the name, Church of God in Christ, was a sign of divine revelation based on his reading of 1 Thessalonians 2:14 (KJV): "For ye, brethren, became follow- ers of the *churches of God* which in Judea are *in Christ Jesus*: for ye also have suffered like things of your own countrymen, even as they have of the Jews" [emphasis added]. Returning from a 1907 visit to the Azusa Street Revival, Mason reported that, while there "a flame touched my tongue," and "my language changed."[56] In other words, Mason announced that he had received the spiritual gift of *glossolalia*. When Charles P. Jones rejected Mason's biblical teaching on the baptism of the Holy Spirit, the two leaders parted ways. Jones continued to lead his adherents as a Holiness church, eventually changing the name to the "Church of Christ Holiness" in 1915.

C. H. Mason, however, called a conference in Memphis, Tennessee, and subsequently reorganized the Church of God in Christ as a Holiness Pentecostal body. He remained presiding COGIC bishop until his death in 1961. Bishop Mason organized the Pentecostal General Assembly of the Church of God in Christ, and assigned several Black men to serve as bishops in Mississippi, Arkansas, Texas, Missouri, and California. Of par- ticular note in the history of the COGIC is the influential role of women in leadership and organization. In 1911, Mason appointed Lizzee Woods Roberson to lead the International Women's Department as the first "General Mother/Supervisor" of the church, a post she held until 1945. She transformed that department into a financial powerhouse for the COGIC. Her successor, Lilliona Brooks Coffey, was the organizer of the first International Women's Convention in 1951. From 1945 to 1964, Coffey helped organize many of the departments of the COGIC that still exist today. Moreover, foreign missions and schools were established through the leadership of women in the COGIC. Rev. James O. Patterson Sr., made a COGIC bishop by C. H. Mason in 1953, later became pre- siding bishop in 1968. During his twenty-one-year tenure, Bishop Patterson vastly expanded the scope of the COGIC denomination by building the church's first seminary, Charles Harrison Mason Theological Seminary, as a part of the Interdenominational Theological Center in Atlanta, Georgia, as well as a publishing house and numerous other busi- nesses. Another symbol of the COGIC's legacy is Mason Temple in Memphis, Tennessee, which serves as the denominational headquarters.

The permanence of the Holiness Pentecostal tradition was soon estab- lished as the COGIC movement spread across the South among Black and white people. Though there were racial tensions between Black and white believers, especially in the South, the Pentecostal Church was the only movement of any significance within the historic Black Church tradition that crossed the proverbial color line in American society. The burgeoning COGIC movement was especially unique because it had moved from its roots in Afro-Protestantism to gain members and influence as a multiracial, multicultural, and multiethnic church movement. More notable than the rapid growth of the Holiness movement within the African American religious experience is the fact that the COGIC rejected any prospect for a theology or church ministry that was socially engaged. In spite of the various internal divisions that began to emerge within the historic Black Church traditions (including the COGIC) such as elitism, denominationalism, and secularism, the COGIC and the larger Pentecostal movement had an inexorable impact on the development of Black Christianity in the contemporary United States. They did so partly by promoting a theological doctrine that emphasized a strict interpretation of the gospel, energetic worship experience, sanctification, and the divine gift of speaking in tongues.[57]

The Black Church and the Civil Rights Movement

Unquestionably, the modern **civil rights movement** was the most important social protest event of the twentieth century. The civil rights movement would have been impossible without the historic Black Church tradition. The term *civil rights movement* typically refers to a set of noted protest events and reform movements in the United States from 1954 to 1968 aimed at abolishing public and private acts of racial discrimination against African Americans. The movement focused particularly on the plight of African Americans in the Deep South. The civil rights movement intended to provide racial dignity, economic and political self-sufficiency, and freedom from white supremacy. Central to the movement were certain African American theological and ethical perspectives. These perspectives, derived from the Black Church, were vital in helping Black people—who had been locked out of the formal political process due to racial barriers—mount numerous campaigns over three decades to eradicate racial injustice and, in the process, transform the nation. The greatest accomplishment of the civil rights movement was its success in eliminating the American apartheid system of Jim and Jane Crow.[58]

Without a doubt, *Brown v. Board of Education of Topeka* was a landmark decision of the United States Supreme Court that explicitly outlawed racial segregation of public schools, ruling so on the grounds that the doctrine of "separate but equal" public education could never truly provide Black Americans with facilities of the same standards available to white Americans. For much of the ninety years prior 1954, race relations in the United States had been dominated by Jim and Jane Crow segregation particularly, but not exclusively, in the American South. Under the visionary legal strategy of Thurgood Marshall and the National Association for the Advancement of Colored People (NAACP) legal defense team, the plaintiffs in *Brown v. Board of Education* asserted that this system of racial separation, while masquerading as providing separate but equal treatment of both white and Black Americans, instead perpetuated inferior accommodations, services, and treatment for Black Americans.[59] On May 17, 1954, the Supreme Court, headed by Chief Justice Earl Warren, handed down a unanimous decision that stated, in no uncertain terms, "separate educational facilities are inherently unequal." Despite this momentous ruling, not everyone accepted the *Brown* decision, a point made obvious by the "Massive Resistance" organized throughout the Deep South in opposition to the desegregation ruling from the U.S. Supreme Court.[60]

Stepping into an unexpected leadership role in this struggle for civil rights was Rev. Dr. Martin Luther King, Jr. When Dr. King assumed the pastorate of Dexter Avenue Baptist Church in the early 1950s, neither the church nor its young pastor were obvious candidates for the prominence they would assume in the civil rights movement. King's predecessor at Dexter Avenue, Rev. Vernon Johns, was a renowned and stirring preacher whose unwavering stance on civil rights and human dignity often proved too provocative for one of the most elite African American congregations in Montgomery, Alabama. Having grown tired of Rev. Johns's sharp social commentary, the members of Dexter Avenue had asked him to resign. They hoped the more scholarly King would prove less controversial.[61]

Yet, when Rosa Parks refused to comply with the local segregationist ordinance that required her to give up her seat on a public bus to a white man on December 1, 1955, King was instrumental in defining the leadership of the Montgomery Improvement Association. This group, comprised largely of Black Church members, worked with the NAACP to support Mrs. Parks in her fight against the city ordinance. The result was the Montgomery Bus Boycott, a political and social protest campaign that began on December 5, 1955, in Montgomery, Alabama, intended to oppose the city's policy of racial segregation on its public transit system. The ensuing struggle lasted until December 21, 1956 (roughly 386 days), and resulted not only in a U.S. Supreme Court decision that declared the local and state laws, requiring segregated buses, unconstitutional but also inspired the emergence of the modern civil rights movement under the leadership of Dr. King.[62]

Following the overall success of the Montgomery bus boycott, Dr. King was instrumental in founding the Southern Christian Leadership Conference (SCLC) in 1957, a group created to harness the moral authority and organizing power of Black churches to conduct nonviolent protests in the service of civil rights reform. Dr. King continued to dominate the organization until his death in 1968.[63] The SCLC derived its membership principally from Black communities associated with Baptist churches. Dr. King was an adherent of the philosophies of nonviolent civil disobedience used by Mahatma Gandhi in India's decolonization struggle against the British. In turn, Dr. King applied the Gandhian philosophy of *satyagraha* to the protests organized by the SCLC.[64] The organization's nonviolent principles were criticized by some Blacks and later challenged by the Student Nonviolent Coordinating Committee (SNCC).[65]

Dr. King and the SCLC, applying the principles of nonviolent direct action, experienced a series of victories by strategically choosing the timing, location, and methods in which the protests were conducted, often instigating dramatic stand-offs with segregationist local authorities.[66] Sometimes, these staged confrontations between the marchers and the local authorities turned violent when pro-segregation supporters mobilized resistance, as in Albany, Georgia; Birmingham, Alabama; St. Augustine, Florida; and Selma, Alabama. During the early 1960s, the group was considered more radical than the older NAACP and more conservative than the younger Student Nonviolent Coordinating Committee (SNCC). Notably, SCLC had a mentoring relationship with SNCC in its earlier years. However, by 1966 SNCC had abandoned its nonviolent strategy in favor of greater militancy. Much thought went into the naming of the Southern Christian Leadership Conference. The leadership of the civil rights organization wanted to attract attention from both African American and white people, without the mention of race distancing them from other races. More than that, the group's founders felt that the term *Christian* could be related to all Christians across the nation and reduce their critics' suspicions about their morality or politics.

As the head of SCLC, Dr. King was among the leaders of the six most influential civil rights organizations of the twentieth century: A. Philip Randolph of the Brotherhood of Sleeping Car Porters; Roy Wilkins of the NAACP; Whitney Young Jr. of the National Urban League; James Farmer of the Congress of Racial Equality (CORE); and John Lewis of the SNCC. These groups were instrumental in the organization of the March on Washington for Jobs and Freedom in 1963. Originally conceived as a public event to dramatize the desperate condition of Blacks in the South, the organizers of the march intended to criticize and then challenge the federal government for its utter failure to uphold the constitutional rights of Blacks as well as protect the lives of civil rights workers across the South. However, the group yielded to pressure and influence from President John F. Kennedy and the majority of speakers at the gathering ultimately took on a far less harsh tone than originally imagined. The march did, however, put forward very specific demands: an end to racial segregation in public education; meaningful civil rights legislation, including a law prohibiting racial discrimination in employment; protection of civil rights workers from police brutality; an increased minimum wage for all workers; and self-government for the District of Columbia, then governed by congressional committee.[67]

Another key tension about the 1963 March on Washington arose concerning Dr. King's connection to Bayard Rustin. Rustin was an African American civil rights activist who counseled Dr. King in 1956 to devote himself wholeheartedly to the principles of nonviolence. However, Rustin's open homosexuality and his membership in the Communist Party USA caused many white and African American leaders to demand that Dr. King distance himself from Rustin for the sake of the movement, advice which he followed on several occasions. One occasion in which Dr. King did not surrender to such fears was when he welcomed Rustin's pivotal leadership role in organizing the 1963 March on Washington along with the movement's elder statesman, A. Philip Randolph.[68]

Despite such tensions, the march was a resounding success. More than a quarter of a million people of diverse backgrounds were at the event, sprawling onto the National Mall and around the reflecting pool. At the time, it was the largest gathering of protesters in the history of the nation's capital. With live television coverage of the march on August 28, 1963, Dr. King's famous "I Have a Dream" speech from the steps of the Lincoln Memorial—regarded ever since as one of the greatest speeches in American history—exhilarated the nation that day and for decades to come. Largely due to the prominence garnered by popular reception of Dr. King's speech and its impact on the successful passage of civil rights legislation, Dr. King became the youngest recipient of the Nobel Peace Prize on October 14, 1964.

By the mid-1960s, two major issues transformed the trajectory of the civil rights movement: the Vietnam War and the quest for economic justice. As the prevailing visionary of the civil rights movement, Dr. King confronted both these concerns in very profound ways during the last years of his life. Challenged by the carnage and corruption he witnessed in America's war in Vietnam, Dr. King expanded his appreciation of nonviolence as the core of the Christian way of life in global terms. On April 4, 1967, Dr. King delivered his "Beyond Vietnam" sermon at the Riverside Church in Harlem in which he boldly denounced America's bloody and immoral military involvement in Southeast Asia.[69] There were several reasons Dr. King and other civil rights leaders turned their attention to the issue of the Vietnam War as an urgent concern. First, the civil rights movement represented the moral conscience of the nation and the Vietnam War had quickly become the moral crisis of a generation. This being the case, King felt that, as a Christian, he had to bear witness against such an atrocity. Second, Dr. King was among the growing number of civil rights and antiwar activists who recognized that the billions of dollars spent on supporting and expanding the war could have been spent on improving American society. Third, equal rights for all citizens required a redefinition of the whole of American society, including foreign policy. Fourth, the racial dimensions and racist attitudes displayed by the conduct of the war placed it especially within the purview of African Americans. Finally, speaking out against the war was a way of overcoming mainstream America's desire that Black people have presence without voice.[70] Dr. King also stated in his "Beyond Vietnam" sermon that from Vietnam to South Africa to Latin America, the United States was "on the wrong side of a world revolution" and questioned why the country was suppressing revolutions "of the shirtless and barefoot people" in the Third World, instead of supporting them in any worthwhile or meaningful fashion.[71]

In 1968, Dr. King and the SCLC organized the Poor People's Campaign to address issues of economic justice. The campaign culminated in a march on Washington, D.C., and included demands for economic aid to the poorest communities of the United States. Dr. King crisscrossed the country to assemble a multiracial army of the poor that would descend on Washington—engaging in nonviolent civil disobedience at the Capitol, if need be—until Congress enacted a "Poor People's Bill of Rights." The proposed legislation called for a massive federal jobs training program in order to rebuild America's inner cities. King saw a crying need to confront a Congress that had demonstrated it was "emotionally hostile to the needs of the poor"—appropriating "military funds with alacrity and generosity," but providing "poverty funds with miserliness and grudging reluctance."[72]

In March of 1968, Rev. James Lawson invited Dr. King to Memphis, Tennessee, in order to garner greater support for a strike by local sanitation workers who had launched a campaign for union representation after two workers accidentally were killed on the job. On the night of April 3, 1968, struggling to overcome his own bout with illness and exhaustion, Dr. King prophetically told a euphoric crowd at Mason Temple in Memphis during his famous "I've Been to the Mountaintop" speech:

> It really doesn't matter what happens now . . .
> . . . some began to . . . talk about the threats that were out. What would happen to me from some of our sick white brothers . . .
> Like anybody, I would like to live a long life. Longevity has its place. But I'm not concerned about that now. I just want to do God's will. And He's allowed me to go up to the mountain. And I've looked over. And I've seen the promised land. I may not get there with you. But I want you to know tonight, that we, as a people will get to the promised land. And I'm happy, tonight. I'm not worried about anything. I'm not fearing any man. Mine eyes have seen the glory of the coming of the Lord.[73]

After roughly thirteen years of leading the Black freedom struggle in America, Dr. King was assassinated on April 4, 1968. That date has essentially come to symbolize the end of the civil rights movement for most scholars. Spurred by Dr. King's murder, a series of violent uprisings broke out in more than 110 cities across the United States in the days that followed, notably in Chicago, Washington, D.C., and Baltimore. Rev. Ralph Abernathy succeeded Dr. King as the head of the SCLC. He attempted to carry forth Dr. King's intended plan for a massive "Poor People's March," which would have united poor people of all racial and ethnic backgrounds to demand fundamental changes in American social and economic structure. Under Abernathy's straightforward leadership, the march went forward but it is widely regarded as a failure. By 1966, the emergence of the **Black Power** movement, which arguably lasted until 1975, enlarged and gradually eclipsed the civil rights movement in its focus on Black empowerment and community development, although it became more secular in its orientation.[74] Despite this turn of events, it was through coordinated, cooperative efforts between Black clergy and laity at the national and local levels that any lasting victories toward implementing the "**Beloved Community**" envisioned by Dr. King have been achieved thus far.[75]

A major reason for the movement's success was its religious leadership. Rev. Dr. Martin Luther King, Jr., is probably the most celebrated and best-known African American religious leader in American history. But many Black activist ministers played leadership roles at the local and national levels at the height of the civil rights movement. Ralph Abernathy, Fred Shuttlesworth, Adam Clayton Powell Jr., C.T. Vivian, Wyatt T. Walker, Prathia Hall, Kelly Miller Smith, James Bevel, Gardner C. Taylor, Joseph Lowery, Andrew J. Young, and Leon H. Sullivan are just a handful of these gifted religious figures. In many instances, Black clergy became the designated spokespeople for campaigns articulating the grievances of Black people, and Black clergy became the chief strategists who shaped the objectives and methods of the movement that sought to redress those grievances. Furthermore, they were able to win the allegiance of a large number of people and convince them to make great sacrifices for racial justice.

One attribute that helped Black ministers gain support for the civil rights struggle was their charismatic Black preaching style. Homiletics scholar Henry Mitchell has illustrated in his research that the power of Black preaching was used both to convey meaning and to inspire people involved in the struggle for racial equality.[76] The sacred rhetoric used by these Black activist ministers explained that the civil rights participants were engaged in a religious as well as an historic mission. Many Black preachers spoke of the "holy crusade" to force America to live up to its promise of democracy. Presumed to be moral leaders of the African American community, ministers like Gardner Taylor were able to use rhetorical tools such as imagery, verbal quickness, rhythmic cadence, and reiteration in their sermons and speeches to evoke an emotional response from their audience. These performances convinced followers that their cause was right and that God had called their pastors to a divine task. Many participants in the Montgomery, Alabama, bus boycott noted that they became involved in the campaign because their charismatic pastors inspired them. Moreover, as televisions became commonplace in tens of millions of American homes, eloquent ministers such as Dr. King soon became ubiquitous spokespeople for the Black community, as well as formative leaders of the Black freedom struggle, thanks largely to the predominantly white mass media.

But the religious leadership of the civil rights movement was not limited solely to these ministers. It encompassed lay church leaders and community activists as well, many of whom had still deeper roots in their local Black communities than the ministers. Besides nurturing charismatic Black male ministers, Black churches also helped instill and inspire key African American moral values in nonclerical leaders, most of whom were women, by emphasizing the desire for freedom, justice, and equality at the core of Black Christian beliefs.[77] The cultivation of these spiritual and moral values usually took place outside of conventional, male-dominated avenues of ministerial training such as seminaries, ministerial alliances, and denominational conventions, which emphasized a hierarchical approach to leadership. Instead, the institutions responsible for inculcating cooperative as well as democratic values in church members—clubs, choirs, missionary societies, and other church auxiliaries—were both created and operated by lay leaders and members of churches.

In church auxiliaries, most of which were created and run by women of the church, members learned to handle money, speak in public, and work on behalf of the less fortunate. Auxiliaries provided a space in which members socialized, developed strong bonds, and worked on tasks in a supportive atmosphere. Although the role of lay leaders in the civil rights movement is still a largely unwritten history, there is evidence that auxiliaries played a pivotal role in what happened. For instance, the laity of Black churches organized the carpools used during the bus boycotts in Louisiana and Alabama. Many of the civil rights workers, especially the young "Freedom Riders" and sit-in protesters during the early 1960s, willingly became "jailbirds for freedom," volunteering to be arrested as the ultimate expression of civil disobedience.[78] This willingness to make a sacrifice for the Black freedom struggle was encouraged by the collective sentiment fostered in the churches' auxiliaries. For instance, most of the Black women active in the Montgomery, Alabama, bus boycott belonged to Baptist churches and were members of those churches' choirs, missionary societies, usher boards, pastor aid societies, and other groups. Although many asserted that they became involved in the movement because of their pastors' leadership, others attributed their involvement to their belief in a religion that dedicated itself to confronting the social conditions of the oppressed in keeping with the biblical mandate that all Christians must care for "the least of these" (Matt. 25:34-46).

The collective sentiment of helping the oppressed had been a long-standing objective of these lay religious organizations, as embodied by Ella Baker, one of the movement's unsung leaders and thinkers with her work in both the Southern Christian Leadership Conference (SCLC) and Student Nonviolent Coordinating Committee (SNCC). In her work with SCLC, Ms. Baker often clashed with Dr. Martin Luther King, Jr., because she did not believe in the "one great leader" model of social change, striving instead to empower ordinary people by the thousands to speak out against social injustice. Baker later recalled her mother's involvement with the women's missionary movement of Black Baptist churches and how her mother embraced the emphasis these groups placed on cooperative nature and communal spirit, all based in Christian **Scripture** over and above the traditional folkways of Black Southerners. Those early childhood lessons in which she learned about mutual concern for oppressed individuals and communities greatly influenced Baker's thinking and political activism throughout her adult life. Furthermore, her radical and inclusive vision of democracy, based on Black Christian social teachings, enabled her to prepare an entire generation of young male and female activists, both Black and white, to continue the collective quest for social justice.[79] As a tribute to her contributions, Ms. Baker's words and philosophy have been immortalized in Sweet Honey in the Rock's "Ella's Song (We Who Believe in Freedom Cannot Rest)" penned by singer-songwriter Bernice Johnson Reagon, a civil rights activist trained by Ms. Baker.

Another influential lay leader in the civil rights struggle, who expressed the core values of the historic Black Church tradition, was Fannie Lou Hamer. Born in poverty, Hamer finished only the sixth grade and picked cotton to survive in rural Mississippi during the height of Jim and Jane Crow segregation. Ms. Hamer professed that the Black Baptist church she attended was a central part of her life, shaping her reading and interpretation of the Bible. As a deeply religious woman, Ms. Hamer proclaimed that religious convictions directly informed her politics. After she joined SNCC, she dedicated herself to improving the lives of Black families.[80] Robert Moses, head of the Mississippi Freedom Summer Campaign, noted that Hamer sang the spirituals that she had learned in the church at civil rights gatherings to help foster a genuine feeling of community among the young SNCC activists. Hamer became field secretary for SNCC, was later a founding member of the Mississippi Freedom Democratic Party (MFDP), and ran for Congress. She helped lead the voter registration campaign in Mississippi, and was arrested, beaten, and tortured by local law enforcement authorities for her activities.

Directly challenging the all-white Mississippi delegation to the Democratic National Convention in 1964, Ms. Hamer addressed the nation as a leader of the MFDP in a famous televised broadcast in which she spoke of her own plight, the murder of civil rights activists, and the daily racist terror that Black Mississippians faced for attempting to exercise their rights as citizens. When President Lyndon B. Johnson and the Democratic Party's leadership, with the support of prominent civil rights leaders such as Dr. Martin Luther King, Jr., worked out a compromise to give two seats to members of the MFDP, the group rejected the deal because not all of the members would be seated. It was Hamer who refused to compromise on the governing principles of the civil rights movement when she told the party leaders that "we didn't come for no two seats."[81] In this and many other instances, she spoke truth to power in the spirit of the historic Black Church tradition in her willingness to question the nation's overall commitment to democracy for the disadvantaged members of society.

CONFRONTING "AMERICA'S ORIGINAL SIN": THE HISTORY OF THE BLACK CHURCH'S FUTURE

Black Power and the Development of New Black Theologies

Over the last four decades, there has been a tremendous change in Black Christianity in the United States and elsewhere around the world. Increasing numbers of Black Church leaders in the National Council of Black Churches have castigated mainstream white religious groups for their complicity with racism, demanded reparations, and agitated for substantive power or leadership roles within the governing structures of American society, both sacred and secular. Out of the interracial conflict and tension have emerged various Black theologies that criticized racism and other social injustices within modern society. The foremost leader in the development of **Black Liberation theology** is theologian James H. Cone, whose early works include *Black Theology and Black Power* (1969),

A *Black Theology of Liberation* (1970), *The Spirituals and the Blues: An Interpretation* (1972), and *God of the Oppressed* (1975). Black Liberation theology asserted the importance of conjoining religious practice and faith with political activism and social change for the betterment of the Black community. In the meantime, Jaramogi Abebe Agyeman (Reverend Albert Cleage Jr.), the pastor of Shrine of the Black Madonna (Pan African Orthodox Christian Church) in Detroit, Michigan, became a passionate advocate of Black Christian nationalism as defined in his books, *The Black Messiah* (1969) and *Black Christian Nationalism* (1972). In ways reminiscent of Bishop Henry McNeal Turner, Marcus Garvey, and Malcolm X, both Black Liberation theology and Black Christian nationalism argued for the religious significance of envisioning Jesus Christ as a Black Messiah for the empowerment of Black Christians. Although Black Liberation theology and Black Christian nationalism offered powerful indictments on white supremacy, these theological perspectives did not address the reality of Black women, who were forced to confront ongoing social oppression based on both gender and race. Inspired by the term and concept of **Womanist** as defined in novelist Alice Walker's text *In Search of Our Mothers' Gardens* (1984), Womanist theology has offered intense and provocative critiques of the triple jeopardy of racism, sexism, and classism within both the Black Church and American society at large. Unlike either feminist or Black Liberation theologies, Womanism offers a self-defined and self-determined vision of community empowerment that cuts across lines of gender, race, and class towards the establishment of a more just and equitable world. As articulated by Katie Cannon, Emilie Townes, Jacqueline Grant, Delores Williams, and Cheryl Townsend Gilkes, among others, subsequent generations of Black female scholars, preachers, and community activists have galvanized themselves into a full-fledged movement that has made profound contributions to the academy, church, and community over the past twenty years.

Black Churches and Presidential Campaigns in the Post–Civil Rights Era

The political mobilization of Black churches has been a major issue that has caused much consternation amongst the growing ranks of American conservatism, especially the Religious Right, over the past four decades. A key example of this issue is evident in Rev. Jesse Jackson's national campaigns for the Democratic nomination for the presidency of the United States in 1984 and 1988. Although Jackson's presidential aspirations were never fulfilled, he and millions of his supporters across the United States strove to renew the spirit of the civil rights movement by advancing the Black Church tradition's mission of social justice as the benchmark of a more hopeful, inclusive political vision for America in the post–civil rights era. In both presidential races, Jackson ran on what many considered to be a very liberal political platform, declaring that he wanted to create a Rainbow Coalition of various marginalized groups, including African Americans, Latino/as, the working poor, women, gays and lesbians, as well as progressive whites who did not fit into any of the aforementioned categories.

However, a major controversy erupted during the early stages of the 1984 campaign when Jackson reportedly made disparaging remarks, referring to Jews as "hymies" and to New York City as "Hymietown"; amid the uproar over these slurs, he later issued an apology for the remarks and was still able to run a successful nationwide campaign.[82] Jackson, who had been written off by pundits as a fringe candidate with little chance at winning the nomination, surprised many when he took third place behind Senator Gary Hart and former Vice President Walter Mondale, who eventually won the nomination. Jackson garnered 3.5 million votes and won five primaries, all in the South. Four years later, his accomplishments made him seem a more credible candidate for the Democratic nomination in 1988, especially since he was both better financed and better organized. Consequently, Jackson once again exceeded expectations as he more than doubled his previous results, capturing nearly seven million votes and winning eleven primaries.

More than simply lending moral support and ministerial endorsements, Black churches were instrumental to Jackson's political successes because they were mobilized and directly involved in local organization of his statewide campaigns, sponsoring rallies, enlisting volunteers, leading voter registration drives, and transporting voters to the polls. In many respects, Jackson's presidential campaigns as well as the influential political careers of Rev. William H. Gray III, Rev. Walter Fauntroy, Rev. Andrew Young, and Rev. Floyd Flake, among others, have been seen as a logical continuation of the political goals of the civil rights movement, thus expanding the power of Black churches in the political arena well into the future.[83]

Formation of Full Gospel Baptist Church Fellowship

Another notable development in the Black Church tradition has been the emergence of the Full Gospel Baptist Church Fellowship. In 1992, Pastor Paul S. Morton initiated a *spiritual gifts* movement with twelve of his fellow pastors from the National Baptist Convention, USA, Inc., an undertaking that eventually resulted in the formation of the Full Gospel Baptist Church Fellowship. The first *Full Gospel Baptist Church Fellowship Conference* was held in New Orleans, Louisiana, in 1994, where the denominational headquarters remained until the devastation of Hurricane Katrina forced the Full Gospel Baptists to relocate their head-quarters to Atlanta, Georgia. The Full Gospel Baptists represent a bur-geoning set of denominations or voluntary organizations (primarily from an African American Baptist background) that accepts the operation of spiritual gifts (the *charismata*) within the church in contrast to the doc-trinal teachings of many Baptist congregations. Furthermore, whereas the Full Gospel Baptists are arguably based upon a *foundation* of Baptist doc-trine, they embrace a wide range of charismatic influences akin to the Holiness-Pentecostal movement. Such influences include that of speak-ing in tongues, prophecy, the Baptism of the Holy Ghost, the "five-fold" ministry (apostles, prophets, pastors, teachers, and evangelists), the acceptance of women in ministry in all ranks, heavy emphasis on corpo-rate praise and worship, and a denominational governmental structure based on an episcopal hierarchy. Besides North America, the Full Gospel Baptist churches are rapidly expanding their membership and influence to Africa, Asia, the Caribbean, and Europe.

The "Stained Glass Ceiling" and the Elevation of Female Bishops in the AME Church

A substantial challenge that continues to undermine Black Christianity's fullest expression of a liberating gospel as mandated in Galatians 3:27-28 is marked by the ongoing institutional sexism and gender inequality within many of the denominations of the historic Black Church tradition. This is most clearly evident in the persistence of many Black churches' disavowal of Black women's call to the preach-ing ministry, denying women the right to be ordained, and ultimately restricting any recognition for female ministers to provide pastoral lead-ership. For example, up to the year 2000, no woman had ever been appointed as a bishop in the nearly two centuries of the African Methodist Episcopal Church's existence. But, in July 2000, Rev. Vashti Murphy McKenzie finally broke that barrier with the solid support of her family, local church community, and the Delta Sigma Theta sorority. Rev. McKenzie was able to shatter what she called "the stained-glass ceiling" when she was named bishop of the 18th Episcopal District in Southeast Africa (comprised of approximately two hundred churches and ten thousand members in Lesotho, Botswana, Swaziland, and Mozambique) of the AME Church. Her four-year appointment followed a successful ten-year stint as a pastor of Payne Memorial Church in Baltimore, Maryland, during which time she increased the membership from three hundred to more than seventeen hundred. "Upon assuming her post, Bishop McKenzie declared, 'One of the things we're looking to do is to respond to the numbers of children who are being abandoned [because] of AIDS.'"[84] Toward that end, she pledged to concentrate on programs for grassroots economic development, construction of schools, and expanded health care delivery. Bishop McKenzie is one of a growing number of Black female preachers and pastors who refuse to allow either sexism or racism to hinder them from making a prophetic difference within the Black Church specifically and American society more generally. Among their number are such leaders as: Rev. Dr. Renita Weems, Rev. Dr. Cynthia Hale, Rev. Dr. Cheryl J. Sanders, Rev. Dr. Claudette A. Copeland, and Rev. Dr. Suzan Johnson Cook.

Rise of Black Megachurches and the "Gospel of Prosperity"

Finally, one of the most profound transformations in the history of the Black Church tradition has been the emergence of megachurches in the past forty years. The term *megachurch* essentially refers to any congregation with a sustained average attendance of tens of thousands of churchgoers attending weekly worship services as well as the church's overall membership. Whereas most discussions of megachurches focus on very large, white evangelical congregations—there are well over 1,200 such fellowships in the United States—there is a growing proliferation of African American megachurches gaining the national spotlight. While membership size is the most immediately apparent characteristic of these congregations, the Black megachurches in the United States generally share many other traits. A considerable number of these churches have a conservative evangelical theology with a strong tendency to preach a so-called **gospel of prosperity**. Prime examples of Black megachurches of this sort include Bishop T.D. Jakes' The Potter's House and Rev. Tony Evans' Oak Cliff Bible Fellowship in Dallas, Texas; Rev. Kirbyjon Caldwell's Windsor Village United Methodist Church in Houston, Texas; and Bishop Eddie Long's New Birth Missionary Baptist Church and Rev. Creflo Dollar's World Changers Church in Atlanta, Georgia. Despite the seeming abundance of prosperity-minded conservative megachurch pastors, there are also several examples of thriving Black megachurches that espouse a liberal or progressive theology committed to social justice. These include: Rev. Dr. Jeremiah Wright Jr.'s Trinity United Church of Christ in Chicago, Illinois; Rev. Dr. Calvin Butts III's Abyssinian Baptist Church in Harlem, New York; Rev. Dr. Gary Simpson's Concord Baptist Church in Brooklyn, New York; Rev. J. Alfred Smith Jr.'s Allen AME Church in Oakland, California; Rev. Cecil Williams's Glide United Methodist Church in San Francisco, California; and Rev. Dr. Frederick Haynes III's Friendship West Baptist Church in Dallas, Texas.

More than a century ago, W.E.B. Du Bois observed that the Black Church's key role in the local community was to provide a total support system for its members.[85] In this spirit, Black megachurches host a whole multitude of social, recreational, and aid ministries for their congregations. Likewise, most megachurches employ intentional efforts at enhancing congregational community, such as home fellowships and "cell churches" *qua* interest-based small group meetings. Megachurches also tend to illustrate the suburbanization of African American Christianity, especially in the rapidly growing urban areas in the Sunbelt region of the southern United States. These large churches often occupy prominent tracts of land with tens of acres near major traffic thoroughfares. Customarily, Black megachurches grow to their great size within a very short period, usually in less than ten years, and under the tenure of a single senior pastor. Contrary to expectations, these congregations promote intense personal commitment and loyalty in a majority of their members. They also contain a large percentage of casual and anonymous spectators of all backgrounds, attracted by the celebrity status of the senior pastor as well as the multimedia ministries (book publications, Internet, television, and radio) that are often used as a form of evangelistic outreach. Although the senior pastors of these megachurches often have an authoritative style of preaching and church administration, typically they have extensive support teams of associate ministers and often retain hundreds of employees as full-time staff.

There is a growing divide between Black megachurches advocating the prosperity gospel and those advancing a prophetic gospel of social justice, a divide that illustrates a mounting theological and ecclesial dilemma taking shape within the Black Church tradition. While the impact of the prosperity gospel's embrace of wealth and comfort can be observed within the ranks of Black megachurch pastors and congregations nationwide, serious questions seem to be forming over whether comfortable megachurches, with their glamorous worship centers and modern high-tech amenities, can also represent a truly faithful witness to the all-powerful God of liberation whose love, grace, and mercy empowered Black women, men, and children to overcome the worst horrors of the past. Thus, the ability of Black megachurches to maintain their high-powered evangelistic appeal to the churched and unchurched alike, while staying rooted to the radical dimensions of the Black Church tradition, will prove a substantial challenge well into the future.

Since the megachurch movement is still a recent phenomenon, it is unclear in a historical sense how the size, demographics, and longevity of these congregations will extend beyond the tenure of their current and/or founding pastors. Evidence suggests, however, that these churches might remain vital following a shift in leadership from the founder to a successor, as long as they stay focused on theologian Paul Tillich's notion of religion as "ultimate concern" for their gathered worshipers.[86]

SUMMARY

As this chapter illustrates, the historic experience of Black Christians in North America resists any single interpretation or monolithic definition. Demonstrated by the various phases of development of African American Christendom from the Middle Passage to today's megachurches, the historic Black Church tradition has continued to be shaped by the personal as well as collective experiences of African peoples who maintained spiritual faith in the midst of enslavement and emancipation alike. Facing the challenges of a new millennium, many Black Christians have inherited an enduring faith that saw their ancestors overcome the brutal dehumanization of chattel slavery, the tragic domination of Jim and Jane Crow segregation, and countless other nameless, unimaginable horrors. Discussing the history of Black Christianity in today's society means confronting a host of complicated issues yet realizing that the foundation of this faith remains intact: the belief that Black people are divinely created and represent God's plan of salvation for a dying world.

BIOGRAPHIES

William Edward Burghardt Du Bois (1868–1963)

William Edward Burghardt (W.E.B.) Du Bois was the preeminent African American intellectual of the twentieth century. Born in Great Barrington, Massachusetts, in 1868, and educated at Fisk University (1885–1888), Harvard University (1888–1896), and the University of Berlin (1892–1894), Du Bois studied with some of the most important social thinkers of his time. He became the first African American to receive a doctorate from Harvard University in 1896. During Du Bois's prolific career, he published nineteen books, edited four magazines, co-edited a magazine for children, and produced scores of articles and speeches. Perhaps his most outstanding work was *Souls of Black Folk* (1903), a poignant collection of essays in which he defined some of the key themes of the African American experience and the dominant motifs of his own work. Moreover, in pioneering social scientific texts such as *The Philadelphia Negro* (1899) and *The Negro Church* (1903), Du Bois offered many astute insights concerning the political, cultural, and economic impact of the Black Church as a social institution. Du Bois spent much of his adult life helping to promote social justice. Combined with his teaching career at Wilberforce and Atlanta Universities were two stints as a publicist for the National Association for the Advancement of Colored People (NAACP), of which he was a founding officer and for whom he edited the monthly magazine, the *Crisis*. On August 23, 1963, the same day as the legendary 1963 March on Washington, Du Bois joined his forebears at the age of ninety-five.[87]

Maria M. Stewart (1803–1879)

Born in 1803, Maria M. Stewart was a free Black woman from Hartford, Connecticut. Stewart felt that women who became teachers could merge their contributions to the family with work outside the home, resist male domination, and participate in all aspects of community building with full equality. She encouraged women to build schools for themselves to guarantee that they would fulfill their educational opportunities. In 1831, Stewart published a pamphlet, "Religion and the Pure Principles of Morality, the Sure Foundation on Which We Must Build," that marked her commitment to religious, feminist, and abolitionist issues as the major themes of her career as a writer and public lecturer. A year later, some speeches she delivered in Boston before the African American Female Intelligence Society were reprinted in the Ladies Department of *The Liberator*, white abolitionist William Lloyd Garrison's newspaper. On September 21, 1832, Stewart delivered a public lecture before the Anti-Slavery Society at Boston's Franklin Hall; this was a historic event because it was the first speech by an American woman of any race to a public gathering that was mixed in terms of both race and gender. In 1833, Stewart delivered a bold farewell speech to the free Black community, especially geared toward the ministers of her day, wherein she stated her ire about negative attitudes toward her for being a public lecturer. Rebuking the Black male leadership of the era for their sexism, Stewart's fiery and heartfelt defense of Black women's rights to speak in public reflected the struggle of biblical heroines and wise foremothers to overcome gender oppression throughout recorded history. Maria Stewart was a visionary committed to ending injustice based on race and gender. Although she passed away in 1879, Stewart served as a role model for subsequent generations of Womanist and Black feminists.[88]

STUDY QUESTIONS

1. What are the key elements of African Traditional Religions? To what extent were these characteristics preserved? In what ways have these beliefs disappeared?
2. How did the establishment of chattel slavery affect religion in the South? What was the relationship between the Christianity of European Americans and the Christianization of African Americans from the colonial period to the start of the Civil War?
3. Why has the biblical narrative of Exodus served as such a dominant *motif* within the African American religious experience?

4. Explain the importance of the AME Church to the emerging independent Black Church movement in the North during the nineteenth century.
5. What was the perceived relationship between religion and slave rebellions during the 1800s? How did slave masters and legislators respond to this development?
6. In what ways did the experiences of Bishop Henry McNeal Turner illustrate the concerns of African Americans as they made the transition from slavery to freedom?
7. What was the role of Christianity in Dr. Martin Luther King, Jr.'s life and in the civil rights movement?
8. Discuss the evolution of Black theological perspectives from Bishop Henry McNeal Turner to Black Liberation theology, Black Christian nationalism, and Womanist theology. What impact has the development of Black theologies had upon Christianity in the United States and worldwide? What does Black theology emphasize? Is it a radical or reactionary religious doctrine?
9. What are the general conditions that have shaped religious experience in America? How has this affected African Americans in particular?
10. What role has religion *historically* played in the African American community? In what ways has it preached accommodation to white supremacy? In what ways has it encouraged resistance to racism and other forms of social oppression?

ESSENTIAL TEXTS

- *Black Religion and Black Radicalism* by Gayraud S. Wilmore
- *History of the Negro Church* by Carter G. Woodson
- *Righteous Discontent* by Evelyn Brooks Higginbotham
- *Slave Religion* by Albert Raboteau
- *There Is a River* by Vincent Harding

*U*ntil recently, the idea of a black
Bible scholar . . . was
something of a novelty, an aberration.
The tragedy . . . is that such attitudes
totally ignore the simple fact that
African Americans have long been
students and "scholars" of the Bible.
While African Americans . . . have
been treated as second-class citizens of
both the nation and the church, they
have not infrequently been
extraordinary interpreters of the Bible,
often making profound scholarly
insights that are now being more fully
documented
and proven correct.
—Cain Hope Felder

BLACK BIBLICAL STUDIES

INTRODUCTION

U nderstanding the Black Church tradition requires that we first identify the centrality of the Bible in the history of the Black experience, especially in the formation of Black cultural, religious, and communal values. To fully appreciate the Black Church experience, it is critical to examine the way Black people read, hear, interpret, and interact with the Bible in both the church and everyday life. The Black Church tradition lives with the Bible by engaging it as the sacred text of its faith and tradition. As with most Christian communities, this means conforming the life of the institution to the patterns found within the text. Like such intentional and distinct Christian communities as the Puritans and the Amish, the Black Church goes beyond a basic use of the Bible as a guidebook to an appropriation of the Bible as a historical narrative of its own contemporary experience. This chapter will explore this dynamic engagement of the Black community with the Bible as sacred text. As biblical scholar Thomas Hoyt observes:

> Blacks tend to share a perspective on the Bible that celebrates God's liberating action in history . . . [B]ecause of the real effect of the brutality of slavery, segregation, and discrimination, blacks share a common ethos of salvation in which the biblical story speaks naturally to their

story. This is what some call "the hermeneutical privilege of the poor and the oppressed."[1]

In other words, this chapter addresses how the Black Church and Black people live with and in the Bible.

THE BIBLE AS SACRED BOOK

The **sacrality** (or "holiness") of the Bible is most evident for African American people in the treatment it receives in everyday interactions of Black families and communities. It is quite common to find a family Bible displayed in the domestic spaces of Black life—sitting on the coffee table, kitchen counter, or nightstand. The ubiquitous presence of the Bible, however, does not trivialize its significance; rather its everyday use is evidence of the reverence with which it is held in Black daily life. It is not only a text that is read for its holy message as God's revealed word but it is also a text in which Black people inscribe their own lives into holy word. Examples of these **mutual inscriptions** include recordings of extensive genealogies, dates of births, weddings, and deaths in the opening pages of family Bibles. Additionally, many African Americans will record phone numbers and addresses, and place important documents in the Bible for *safekeeping*. For instance, in the state of North Carolina, the Department of Motor Vehicles still takes inscriptions in family Bibles as proof of birth for both Blacks and whites.

In addition to these written inscriptions, African Americans *inscribe* the Bible into everyday experiences when they read happenings in their own lives in terms of the actions of biblical characters or biblical events. By way of illustration, it is fairly common to hear Black Christians using terms such as "Satan" or "the Enemy" to describe an unfair boss, or evoking the image of Moses leading the Israelites through the Red Sea in order to frame a person or group's journey from captivity and enslavement to independence and self-sufficiency. In this way, they are inscribing their story on the pages of Scripture.

In many ways, the Bible is the *Book of Life*: it links temporal, ancestral, and biblical families, making them accessible to each new generation. Just as the Black Church tradition has been the steadfast life-affirming institution within the Black community, so too the Bible has been a life-preserving instrument. The Bible, and the Black community's use of it, epitomizes the intersection of sacred and common practices in everyday life. Any understanding of the place and the role of the Bible in the Black community must acknowledge that it is the tangible threshold for encountering the spiritual and the temporal.

THE BIBLE AS SACRED TEXT

Scripture as Folk Wisdom (Inclusive)

The notion of Scripture within the Black Christian experience is an *inclusive* one. It is a common occurrence within Black Christian experience to identify *biblically derived wisdom* alongside actual biblical passages as Scripture. This biblically derived wisdom is the product of the indigenous knowledge (folk wisdom) of Black people encountering the biblical text and running it through the prism of their lives. What gives this "almost Bible" wisdom its status as Scripture is that it has proven itself in real, lived experience. The idea of Scripture within the Black Church and community encompasses all sacred wisdom that emerges from the encounter between the community and the word of God.

By way of illustration, Womanist theologian Delores Williams recalls an occasion when she preached from what she believed to be a well-known biblical passage. Afterwards, a man who was intrigued by her sermon challenged her claim that the Scripture she used was in the Bible. Williams assured the man that the Scripture was in the Bible and that she would go home, look up the reference, and call him. She went home and called her mother to inquire about the reference. Without hesitation, Williams's mother informed her daughter that the passage she had preached was not "a Bible verse, but it was certainly Scripture." Her mother assured her that there is more to Scripture than the text of the Bible. As this story illustrates, the idea of Scripture is a broad category within Black Christian experience, but its breadth is tempered by, and accountable to, the actual text of the Bible.[2]

This discussion might not seem to take into consideration the sizable **fundamentalist** contingent of the Black community, a contingent that upholds the adage "God said it, I believe it, and that settles it." Such an orientation does not actually preclude non-biblical material being deemed a component of Black Christian Scripture. Unlike the creation of **apocryphal** prose, which is rooted in the Bible in the broad context of the Black community, literalist interpretations of the Bible by certain African American fundamentalists can actually instill a worldview that directly contradicts their present realities. For instance, according to a literalist reading of the Bible, fundamentalist Black Christians would have to exclude pork and shellfish from their culinary habits because of the strict dietary mandates found in the book of Leviticus (11:7, 10-12), but such an exclusion from traditional "soul food" cuisine would be considered largely unacceptable. Therefore, fundamentalist Black Christians make deliberate and strategic decisions about how they are going to live in accordance with what they regard as the absolute and immutable word of God. This reflects the creation of another body of folk wisdom based on an alternative interpretation of the Bible that is equally steeped in the Black experience, based more on insight than on inscription. Whether viewed in a liberal or literalist sense, Scripture for Black women, men, and children is firmly rooted in their encounter and ongoing interaction with the Bible.

Canon within a Canon (Exclusive)

The dynamic that we have just identified is a case of folk wisdom being added to the text of the Bible. There is another phenomenon in the Black Church of wisdom being used to edit out text from the communal use of the Bible. Howard Thurman, the noted twentieth-century Black theologian and mystic, exemplifies this point in a story about his grandmother. Having lived much of her early life in slavery, Thurman's grandmother never learned to read. She often requested that he read to her from the Bible with one restriction: she insisted that he never read any passages attributed to Paul, because the Pauline epistles were an important justification of slavery in her lifetime (e.g., Romans 13:1-7, Ephesians 6:5-8, and the epistle to Philemon). Based on this experience and later ones, Thurman speculated that his grandmother's request exemplified a common practice in the Black Church of ignoring those texts that others used to debase Black people or to champion racial oppression, thus forming a canon within the **canon**. African Americans have also emphasized motifs in the biblical text that they deemed as **liberative**, such as the Exodus narratives; or passages that resonated with their experiences of oppression in the Western world, like Psalm 137, Daniel 3, and the Passion narratives in the New Testament. Collectively, these became the central stories in their functional canon.

Over the course of generations, Black people have found—in specific biblical themes, characters, and narratives—the wisdom they needed to overcome adversity. In similar fashion, this process of identifying the canon within the canon seeks to delimit a functional set of narratives useful for arguing for African American freedom from oppression and full equality under the law.

THE TASK OF BLACK BIBLICAL HERMENEUTICS

Defining Hermeneutics

The term *hermeneutics* describes how people interpret the Bible, as well as the theories and methods that they use to accomplish that task. Interpretation here refers to reading, studying, and engaging the Bible in order to find meaning and practical life application based on one's own particular culture, life circumstances, and worldview. Stated another way, hermeneutics is interpretation of the Bible for meaning, primarily identifiable by its location, audience, and goals. The primary location and audience for Black biblical hermeneutics is the Black community. The foremost goal of Black biblical hermeneutics has been to break the dominant society's stranglehold upon and uses of the Bible to maintain systems of social injustice—such as slavery, segregation, and colonialism—against the marginalized and the powerless. Black biblical hermeneutics envisions liberation rather than domination as the central reality of the text. Such a **critical engagement** and reconsideration of the text can be empowering for Black people as they claim their full humanity as children of God. The principal context of Black biblical hermeneutics has been the dominant society's use of Christian faith and the Bible to authorize the demonization of Blackness. That society's rendition of history expressly chronicles defeat, subjugation, and oppression as the chief inheritance of African peoples worldwide. Black biblical hermeneutics has provided people of African descent with liberative perspectives on Scripture in the hope of confronting racism and overturning other devastating social ills.

The two central approaches to Black biblical hermeneutics are: (1) to identify the ways that the Black Church and Black people have interpreted Scripture and (2) to review the work of Black scholars in religion who have worked both within and outside of the church, using largely academic tools and language, to interpret the Bible in ways that uphold Black humanity and contest oppressive readings of the sacred text.

The Black Condition as Biblical Connection

The biblical stories of principal interest for Black people are those that deal with oppression and liberation. The biblical characters, motifs, or touchstones that have primacy for African Americans are those which speak directly to the experience of Blacks as an oppressed, marginalized, and subjugated people. The stories of the Israelites leaving Egypt (the Exodus motif), or of women chafing in the bonds of sexual and household servitude (e.g., the Hagar story in Genesis), or of a blameless person being persecuted or murdered (stories of the historical Jesus as disinherited, rejected, and betrayed), have particular poignancy and resonance within the Black Church tradition. One can identify the significant biblical motifs and biblical characters of major interest to the Black Church by analyzing Black sermons, the spirituals, gospel music, and Christian rap music. Even within contemporary African American popular culture, these stories and characters are repeatedly and respectfully put to song, produced as dramas, and artistically contemporized with each new generation. While these connections are based upon a common experience of oppression, there are also streams of interpretation that appeal to a common African ancestry.

Given the role played by the Bible in modern American society and culture, it is not surprising that biblical allusions pervade African American literature and music. African American writers such as Hugh Henry Brackenridge, Philis Wheatley, and Jupiter Hammon in the eighteenth century, as well as Charles W. Chestnutt in the nineteenth century, used literary references to the Hebrew Bible within their written works. Antebellum Black intellectuals like David Walker, Maria Stewart, Robert Young, and Henry Highland Garnett used critical interpretations and subversive readings of the books of Genesis and Exodus to condemn the twin pillars of chattel slavery and anti-Black racism. During the height of American slavery, slave narratives by

Frederick Douglass, Harriet Jacobs, and Solomon Northup, as well as Negro spirituals or work songs such as "Wade in the Water" and "Balm in Gilead," were laced with biblical passages that reflected moral critiques of white Christian complicity with racism and slavery, and offered hope to enslaved Blacks seeking literal and spiritual freedom. In the twentieth century, works such as Countee Cullen's *The Black Christ*, Zora Neale Hurston's *Moses, Man of the Mountain*, James Baldwin's *Go Tell It On The Mountain*, and Toni Morrison's *Song of Solomon* incorporated biblical imagery and narratives to explore various themes within the Black experience.

Even in the highly controversial relationship between the historic Black Church tradition and the so-called hip-hop generation of adolescents and younger adults born after 1965, there is a popular recognition of the Bible as a source of enduring wisdom and critical insight about both the historic and the contemporary Black experience. Despite much criticism from their elders who question the merits of the dominant art form of the younger generation, there are numerous examples of the members of the hip-hop generation embracing the centrality of a Bible-based faith and culture in this new millennium. In the hip-hop song "B.I.B.L.E.," rapper Masta Killah of the Wu-Tang Clan defines this most cherished term as an acronym for the phrase "Basic instructions before leaving earth." The rapper KRS-ONE's song "Why Is That?" is one of the most powerful expressions of the **Afrocentric** dimension of hip-hop music and engages in an incisive **exegesis** of the book of Genesis, visualizing the intellectual and spiritual crises of Black youth as directly rooted in the misinterpretation and manipulation of biblical passages such as the infamous "Curse of Ham." In songs such as "To Zion" and "Adam Lives in Theory," singer and hip-hop artist Lauryn Hill evokes lyrics and imagery from both the Hebrew Bible and the New Testament to discuss thorny issues such as the stigma of unwed motherhood or the pain of failed romantic relationships within the contemporary Black experience. Such hip-hop songs as Kanye West's "Jesus Walks" and DMX's "Prayer" openly wrestle with the artists' theological fears and concerns based on the tensions that exist between traditional Black communitarian values that they were taught—based on the Bible—and the immediate realities of the world around them. Knowing that the Bible was written thousands of years ago by people of a vastly different culture and civilization, these young African Americans are nonetheless placing their very contemporary experiences in conversation with the biblical story.

How Blackness Became Demonized in the Church

Another key element in the context of Black biblical hermeneutics is the evolution of the dominant Christian Church's view of Blackness. The meaning of Blackness became transformed within the Christian Church during the second century, after the biblical texts were written down. Origen (185–c. 254), an Alexandrian Egyptian, was the first Christian to identify Blackness positively with divine good, as distinguished from a negative connotation of evil. He connected Blackness with Jesus Christ, though he remained ambivalent about a connection between Blackness and morality. Conversely, Jerome (342–420), who translated the Hebrew and Greek texts of the Bible into the Latin Vulgate (common language), posited that Blackness was a synonym for evil and sin, and he connected Blackness to sexual prowess and carnal lust. It is ironic that the first pope who could write Latin, Victor I (189–199), came from North Africa, and that three of the renowned Latin-speaking church scholars, Tertullian (160–c.225), Cyprian (d. 258), and Augustine (354–430), all came from North Africa, although some controversy remains as to whether they were of Arabic (white) or Moorish (Black) heredity.

Pope Nicholas V (1447–1455) issued a papal bull (rule or mandate) giving all of Africa to Portugal, while allowing dispensation for the baptizing and enslaving of Black Africans. Thus, Portugal, as a Western Christian country, was the location of the first auction of enslaved Africans in 1441. In addition to the beginning of the fifteenth-century slave trade, two other major historical events in medieval Europe *guaranteed* that Christianity and Christendom would demonize Black skin and Blackness: (1) the Muslims conquered Edessa in the twelfth century; and (2) the so-called Black (bubonic and pneumonic) Plague decimated the European population in the fourteenth century (30 to 50 percent loss of life in a two year period). Fallen Christians felt threatened by their dark-skinned, so-called infidel, Muslim conquerors and by the dark skinned Moors who had conquered parts of Christian Europe. Needing a scapegoat to deal with the overwhelming loss of life from war and disease as well as forty-eight years of famine, Blackness became implicated as the cause of suffering.[3]

BLACK PRESENCE AS BIBLICAL CONNECTION

The significance of exploring the Black presence in the Bible is that, for the historic Black Church tradition, the point of connection with the biblical stories is not only one of social condition but also one of racial connection. The types of biblical interpretation that African Americans learned from the dominant culture find practically no Black presence in Scripture. An early approach of scholars seeking to debunk this misinterpretation was to identify discrete individuals in the Bible who are undeniably linked to Black people and nations.

The identification of the lineage and historic presence of Black people in the Bible begins in the nineteenth century with the sermons of churchmen such as J. W. C. Pennington and Henry Highland Garnett, as well as Robert Lewis's text, *Light and Truth . . . Universal History of the Colored and the Indian Race* (1844). It continues in the twentieth century with scholars such as Robert Morrisey, Charles Copher, Gene Rice, Renita Weems, and Cain Hope Felder. Whether through textual analysis, or examination of archaeological, geographical, or historical evidence, these commentators have convincingly demonstrated that there is indeed a strong Black presence in the Bible, particularly in the populations of the ancient Egyptians, Canaanites, Ethiopians (also called Cushites or Nubians), Sabeans, Putim, and Hebrews. Initially, the argument focused on the presence of discrete Black individuals such as: Zipporah, Moses' Cushite wife; Zephaniah's father, an apparently Cushite member of King David's family; Ebed-Melech, the Judean court official who rescued the prophet Jeremiah; the Cushite who helped to thwart Absalom's revolt; the Christian convert who was an Ethiopian court official; Simon of Cyrene who carries Jesus' cross during the Passion narratives; and Simeon (aka *Niger*, the Latin term for "black"), a formative leader of the Antioch church.[4] Subsequent scholarship has held that it is insufficient to simply identify whether or not particular individuals and nations within the Bible are Black. In fact, the contexts and cultures of the biblical world were located on the continent of Africa in addition to being intimately related to, and significantly influenced by, an African worldview. Although seldom considered in any general discussion of the historic and modern geography of the region, the *Middle* East is the northeast corner of the African continent and the hotly contested terrain of Palestine is firmly fixed upon the African continental plate. Consequently, the peoples we would call *Black* today were ever-present in the biblical text, from the earliest stories about the Israelites' experiences in the land of Pharaoh, through the Holy Family's flight to Egypt, and finally on the road to Calvary. It is now commonly understood moreover that many of the peoples of the ancient Near East in the lands of the Bible were African. Most recently, biblical archaeology, undertaken by leading white scholars in the field, has substantiated the claims made by Copher and others two decades earlier: the biblical Garden of Eden was in a strangely undefined location, bounded by the Nile Valley to the south and west, and extending as far north and east as the Fertile Crescent (the region dominated by the Tigris and Euphrates rivers), which are all North African territory. This research reflects a considerable paradigm shift within the overall nature of biblical scholarship. By demonstrating that the dark-skinned African context was synonymous with that of the Bible, it is apparent that quite a number of key concerns and arguments posed by pioneering Black biblical scholars have moved from the margins to the mainstream. Therefore, the claim of Black biblical hermeneutics in the twenty-first century is not only that there are Black people in the Bible but also that the Bible itself is set in a strongly African context both geographically and culturally. The presence of Sunday school materials and sacred iconography that depict the biblical world as being Black, in an ever-increasing number of Black churches, reveals the growing acceptance of these modes of biblical interpretation that center on a Black presence and context. So, today, Black Christians continue to read themselves into the text relying on both hermeneutical devices—connection through condition and racial identification—in order to support their claims.

THE CURSE OF HAM

Of particular interest to the presence of Blacks in the Bible is what is referred to as the "Hamitic curse" or "Noah's curse" in Genesis 9. This particular story, which was used as the primary Christian justification for the enslavement of Africans in the Americas, and later for the racial oppression of African Americans, was for many years the only widely recognized instance of Black presence in the Bible. For much of the history of biblical interpretation in America this text has been used to depict Black people as corrupt, evil, and sexually immoral. The story, in brief, is that Ham enters the tent, sees his father Noah drunk and naked (or in some way sexually vulnerable), and leaves to tell his two brothers. The two brothers come in backwards in order to cover their father without looking at him. Noah wakes up, realizes what his "youngest son had done" and curses Canaan, Ham's son, and his descendents to perpetual servitude. This curse thus justifies the subsequent accounts of the taking of the Canaanites' land by the Israelites who are descendents of Noah's first son, Shem.[5]

While there are many interpretive traditions about what occurred in the tent, all agree that, at best, Ham demonstrated immodesty and disrespect toward his father and at worst, Ham assaulted his father's honor. Some dominant interpretations went as far as to say that he possibly raped his father or mother or that he castrated his father (see Stephen Haynes's Noah's Curse: The Biblical Justifications of Slavery, a work that explores the contested history of biblical interpretation of this passage). Likewise, most of the monotheistic faith traditions—Judaism, Christianity, and Islam—presume that the curse of servitude issued not only from Noah but also from the very mouth of God. Moreover, even though the text itself makes no explicit claims about race (this is implied based on reading race retroactively into the Genesis 10 "Table of Nations" accounts), and is principally concerned with a regional dispute over rights to the land of Palestine, the Curse of Ham has been used as the biblical rationale and theological justification for the perpetuation of racism against Black people. Gradually, slavery and race became connected in Western interpretations of the story of Noah's curse of Canaan. The work of Black biblical scholars such as Copher, Felder, Wimbush, and others has demonstrated that this interpretation has little to do with the biblical text and everything to do with the collusion of biblical interpreters with a larger project of racial oppression, economic exploitation, and territorial conquest.

OVERVIEW OF BLACK BIBLICAL HERMENEUTICS

Historical Readings from the Black Church Perspective

To fully grasp how people of African descent interpret the Bible, it is important to recognize the nature and dynamic of a biblical hermeneutic that was born in the sermons of antebellum Black Church Mothers and Fathers who, though often not allowed to go to school, nevertheless had a word for God's people. Whether enslaved or free, early Black preachers in the eighteenth and nineteenth centuries read and deciphered the Bible to the best of their abilities in order to craft messages for Black worshipers needing guidance, courage, and inspiration in a hostile world. These preachers did not exegete in the literal sense, but they did interpret "with the help of the Holy Ghost." In practical terms, the exegesis of the biblical text for many Black preachers focused on "making it plain," that is, making the word of God accessible and relevant to God's people. David Shannon and Vincent Wimbush suggest that to find lived Black biblical hermeneutics, one should go to the primary texts of Black songs, stories, and sermons. For example, in his article "'An Ante-bellum Sermon': A Resource for an African American Hermeneutic," Shannon determines to learn from African American literature how Black people have historically read Scripture. Exploring the noted poet Paul Lawrence Dunbar's "An Ante-bellum Sermon" as a sermon in verse, Shannon begins to discern certain hermeneutical principles (contextuality, correlation, confrontation, and consolation) evident in early African American sermons.[6] Similarly Wimbush, in his article "The Bible and African Americans: An Outline of an Interpretive History," reads the historical interpretive tradition of African Americans in their songs. By this means he discerns how the Bible provided a "language world" to help Africans in America, disoriented by their condition in this land, make sense of their new reality.[7] Wimbush's work continues in this trajectory in his monumental volume *African Americans and the Bible*, in which he invites scholars from various fields to explore the ways the Bible has been employed in African American songs, poems, graphic art, and literature.[8]

Contemporary Readings from Black Biblical Scholars

In general, research by Black biblical scholars has: (1) demonstrated a Black presence in the Bible; (2) challenged Eurocentric readings of the Bible; (3) assessed and reviewed how those in the Black community interpret the Bible; and (4) embraced creative, interdisciplinary scholarship by implementing various theories and methods from other disciplines outside of biblical studies (such as Charles Copher's interconnected use of archaeology, history, and biblical scholarship to discuss Black presence). Toward this end, Black biblical hermeneutics as a field of study has worked to provide a necessary corrective to traditional Western biblical research by using previously overlooked cultural and historical resources. One must also note the importance of context in interpretation, and the many dimensions of liberation as a social reality, internal and external, to the community.

In recent decades, certain Black biblical scholars have been concerned that many in the Black Church have appropriated a literalist reading of the Bible that is foreign to the mainstream of historical modes of biblical interpretation of the Black Church. New Testament scholar Cain Hope Felder argues that not only must Black people cast a critical eye on standard and traditional methods of exegesis, and the hermeneutical assumptions that go with them; they must also try to free themselves from the habit of "Bibliolatry": worshiping the Bible as the exclusive, definitive, and entire revelation of God.[9] Instead, Felder and other scholars contend that a more holistic, critical reinterpretation of the Bible is needed, one that reflects an understanding of the Bible as a part of Scripture and not a history or science textbook. Thus, in reflecting on the use of the Bible, Black biblical scholars also invite us to reclaim the goal of freedom and liberation as the central end to which all interpretation is accountable. Precisely because Black biblical scholars believe that the Bible is the most sacred text within the Black Church tradition, they contend that a rigorous engagement and examination of the text is itself an act of faith.

As a result of developing methodologies steeped in the experiences of persons of African descent, scholars use creative, interdisciplinary reading strategies to see the Biblical texts in new ways.[10] In *Yet With a Steady Beat*, Hebrew Bible scholar Randall Bailey contends that some read and approach the biblical texts with the intention of gaining insight into how the contexts of the oppressed in the Bible can speak to the current contexts of Black people in the United States. Others begin with Black folk tradition as the starting point for interpreting the biblical text, while still others focus on exegeting the passages of Scripture that are essential to Black theology. The common denominator in these interdisciplinary approaches lies in the attempt to relate the biblical texts to the existential reality of being Black in the United States. They are concerned that biblical interpretation within the Black community takes seriously its own context as well as the context within which the texts were written. This means they utilize the perspectives and products of ethnography, literary analysis, historiography, music, and drama as they relate to understanding contemporary Black existence. A similar analysis is used to interpret the biblical context. Thus, Cain Hope Felder is able to argue that oppression resulting from texts such as the Curse of Ham is not merely racism triggered by skin color but is actually embedded within the emerging tribalism and later nationalism of the ancient Israelites. As Felder and other scholars argue, the social structure of the ancient biblical realm operated in complex ways that were not defined by the imposition of systems of prejudice based on skin color and racial discrimination, as we understand them in contemporary terms. Therefore, when the Israelites favored themselves throughout the Scripture as God's chosen people, this not only reflects a nationalistic character of the biblical text that justified the conquest and domination of presumably lesser peoples (e.g., the Canaanites, the Moabites, the Philistines) but also condemns more powerful rival nations that dominated Israel (e.g., the Egyptians, the Assyrians, the Babylonians) during eras in which the Israelites' collective faithfulness was at low ebb. Far from declaring that Genesis 9 and related texts have nothing to do with race, Wimbush asserts that the nationalist and tribal views expressed in these passages have often been misinterpreted and manipulated by ruling elites who use oppressive readings of the Bible to lend credibility to racism, ethnocentrism, sexism, colonialism, and other unjust exercises of societal power over the course of human history. Taking the contemporary situation of Black people seriously leads New Testament scholar Vincent Wimbush to ask:

> How might putting African Americans at the center of the study of the Bible affect the study of the Bible? . . . Would or should the agenda of the study of the Bible then necessarily be focused around the identification of Africans as biblical characters?
> . . . With the interaction of the Bible and African Americans as case-study, how might a multidisciplinary study in the construction and re-constructions of societies and cultures in complex relationship to sacred texts be shaped?[11]

Furthermore, Wimbush argues that placing the African American experience at the center of studying the Bible is not about signaling the right interpretation, or doing a sort of racial–ethnic cheerleading, but that such a methodology is a major challenge to the racially biased way of doing biblical interpretation in the West. Such a method of interpretation becomes not only a necessary act but also an overtly political and inherently radical act. Influenced by the proliferation of negative views about Blackness in Western society, both scholars and general readers alike tend to make wrong assumptions about Black folk in Scripture as well as in daily life. Taking the interpretive traditions of African Americans seriously would require the scholar or student of the Bible to begin with intense self-reflection above and beyond reflection on cultural, socio-political, and socio-psychological issues. This strategy would open up the Bible to dispel some of the many assumptions made about what the Bible is, what is done with it, how it is read and interpreted, and how it is used, beginning with the *"whole quest [journey] for meaning (in relationship to a [sacred] text)."*[12] While challenging assumptions about biblical interpretation is a major struggle, the main purpose is to be open to studying the Bible from a different point of departure.

In terms of expanding the methods, theories, and perspectives within Black biblical hermeneutics, the contributions of Womanist scholarship have been invaluable. To a considerable degree, Womanist biblical scholars have furthered this interpretive approach by placing the experience of women of the African **Diaspora** as a central point of departure and the well-being of the Black community as the end of all Black biblical interpretation. A Womanist biblical hermeneutic recognizes the reality that the historic Black Church is in large measure an institution given birth to, nurtured, and sustained by Black women.

The types of questions raised by Womanist biblical scholars are exemplified in the work of Hebrew Bible scholar Renita Weems, who investigates the ways in which African American women have strategized their reading and hearing of the Bible. Weems questions several socio-political stances: (1) how men have become too complacent with writings that practically terrorize women; (2) how white women are in denial about the system that so oppresses non-white women, while this same system privileges white women; and (3) how the historic Black Church buys into an authoritative, male-dominated church tradition. Weems's analysis further deconstructs questions concerning why the biblical text—so laden with oppressive content and oppressive interpretation—wields such power and garners intense devotion, especially among African American women. She argues that African American women find the portraits of relationality in the biblical text credible, meaningful, and valuable. While the law forbade the enslaved to read, and misogynist tendencies in the Bible taught women to see the text as men do, Weems posits that when women in general, and Black women in particular, approach a text, they do so from social locations and using reading strategies that allow

the biblical text to speak to their deep desires for dignity, justice, liberation, and vindication.[13]

SUMMARY

In sum, Black biblical hermeneutics reflects the tremendously rich discourse in which church people and scholars engage today. It is a conversation that begins with how African Americans appropriate Scripture in
their churches, and continues with an examination of how it has been
employed in African American literature, poetry, songs, and sermons.
More important, it is a dialogue between the academy and the historic
Black Church, whereby the former places the latter at the center of an
interpretive paradigm and seeks to learn as much as possible about how
African Americans generally read the Bible. In this regard, Black biblical
hermeneutics represents a paradigm shift that places historical and contemporary African American appropriations of the texts, rather than the
historical context of the ancient Near Eastern biblical authors, at the
center of its scholarly inquiry.

To best understand Black biblical hermeneutics, the student has to
remember the necessarily subjective nature of the engagement with
Scripture. Personal experience, individual biography, and historical contexts
affect approaches to the study of biblical texts. It is necessary to show great
care in the reading of these texts and their significance for African
Americans. To take one example, translations often reflect the translators'
biases. The *King James Version* translates Song of Solomon 1:5 as "I am black
but comely"; the *New Revised Standard Version* translates the same passage "I
am black *and* beautiful (italics ours)." Those gifted in the ancient languages
can see the reality of bias as an opportunity to translate these texts and make
them available for Black people. Understanding that there are different genres or types of writing in the Bible is a way to begin to accept the complexity of biblical analysis and the difficulty of reading a work critically, when for
some only a particular version of the Bible is ever credible.

Black biblical hermeneutics has evolved over four hundred years from the
time of the hush harbor to the twenty-first century. Even so, tension still
exists between the church and academia concerning the proper role of exegesis, hermeneutics, and the place of Scripture. Some scholars view literary
analysis as the proper tool for studying Scripture and leave no room for the
faith community's contribution. Other scholars are sensitive to the question

of belief; they have engaged in artistic and creative analysis to help the text come alive for students and congregants. Some Christians engage in Bibliolatry, worshiping the Bible itself (and the wording of the *King James Version* in particular), ultimately limiting God's capacity to act in their lives due to a narrow and misguided frame of reference. Other people of faith read with healthy curiosity and questioning, to which attentive scholars and students should listen in order to strengthen the ability to communicate about biblical texts between academic and faith communities.

BIOGRAPHIES

Charles B. Copher (1913–2003)

Dr. Charles Buchanan Copher was a United Methodist pastor and served his denomination as a local pastor in several Midwestern states and subsequently as a member of the Judicial Council. In 1947, he received a Ph.D. from Boston University and became the third African American to attain a doctorate in Old Testament studies. Dr. Copher spent his life reorienting the discipline he loved, pointing it in the direction of Africa and Africans. In part, this reorientation was a result of his consideration that biblical scholarship itself had to change in reaction to the claims of the Black Power movement of the 1960s and because of the distinctive theological strides in Black Liberation theology made by James Cone. Thus, Copher recovered a brand of biblical scholarship that identified African figures in the pages of the Scripture of the Black churches in which he taught. By most estimates there would be no contemporary African American biblical hermeneutic without his input. Copher's work in the late 1960s and the 1970s provided the framework upon which subsequent works in this sub-discipline are based. In 1947, Copher joined the faculty of Gammon Theological Seminary, an African American seminary of the Methodist Church, and Clark College. Though his tenure on the Clark faculty was brief, he would remain on the faculty of Gammon throughout his career, playing a significant role in the evolution of that institution, as it became part of a union of seven historically African American seminaries called the Interdenominational Theological Center (ITC) in Atlanta, Georgia. Dr. Copher served as the first Dean of Faculty of the ITC, assuming this position in 1959. He subsequently served as ITC's Vice President for

Academic Affairs. Copher joined the ancestors on August 15, 2003, when he was ninety years old.

Renita J. Weems (1954–)

Celebrated by *Ebony* magazine as one of America's top fifteen preachers, Rev. Dr. Renita J. Weems earned her undergraduate degree from Wellesley College in Wellesley, Massachusetts, and her master and doctoral degrees in Hebrew Bible from Princeton Theological Seminary in Princeton, New Jersey. From 1987–2004, Weems taught on the divinity faculty at Vanderbilt University in Nashville, Tennessee, as a professor of Hebrew Bible. She served as the William and Camille Cosby Professor of Humanities at Spelman College in Atlanta, Georgia, from 2003 to 2005. Dr. Weems is founder and editor of *"SomethingWithin"* (something within.com), an online newsletter that explores issues of faith in the context of the challenges women face on a daily basis. Weems is the author of several widely acclaimed books on women's spirituality and wholeness: *Just a Sister Away* (1987), *I Asked for Intimacy* (1993), *Battered Love: Marriage, Sex, and Violence in the Hebrew Prophets* (1995), *Showing Mary: How Women Can Share Prayers, Wisdom, and the Blessings of God* (2003), and *What Matters Most: Ten Passionate Lessons from the Song of Solomon* (2004). Ordained an elder in the African Methodist Episcopal tradition, Dr. Weems has written about the waxing and waning of faith all believers endure on the spiritual journey. Her book *Listening for God: A Minister's Journey through Silence and Doubt* (1999) won the Religious Communicators' Council's prestigious Wilbur Award in 1999 for excellence in communicating spiritual values to the secular media. As a guest speaker for numerous national gatherings of religious, civic, and sorority organizations, local churches, community wide events, and radio and television programs, Dr. Weems has been in much demand as a speaker, preacher, and workshop leader.

STUDY QUESTIONS

1. What is Scripture from the perspective of Black biblical studies? Why is it important for churchgoers and biblical scholars to be in conversation about the meaning and interpretation of Scripture?
2. What is the significance of Black presence in the Bible?

3. In what ways is the Bible a text of liberation and blessing for Black folk? In what ways has the Bible been used as a text of curses for Black folk?
4. What have you learned about biblical scholarship and its evolution in relation to the negative impact on Black people of the so-called Curse of Ham?
5. What impact have oppressive readings and usage of certain biblical texts had on the status of the Black community today in the United States?
6. Read the first chapter of Song of Songs. What is your understanding of Blackness based upon this text?
7. What is Black biblical hermeneutics? What impact does Womanist theory have on this discipline?

ESSENTIAL TEXTS

- *African Americans and the Bible* by Vincent Wimbush
- *Just a Sister Away* by Renita Weems
- *Stony the Road We Trod* by Cain Hope Felder

*T*here is, then, a desperate need
for *a* black theology, *a*
theology whose sole purpose is to
apply the freeing power of the gospel
to black people
under white oppression.
—James H. Cone

CHAPTER THREE

BLACK THEOLOGIES

INTRODUCTION

In his book *There is a River* Vincent Harding talks about "that magnificent company of witnesses—my mothers and fathers—whose lives form the wellsprings of the black struggle for freedom in America"; wellsprings that feed a river that *"is us . . . in us, created by us, flowing out of us, surrounding us, re-creating us and this entire nation"* (italics added).[1] Harding's metaphor of the river is an apt image for the African American Christian theological tradition in the United States. It is a theological tradition that is rich and diverse and whose plurality of expression is as varied as the Christian faith itself. It is possible, however, to identify dominant streams within the tradition that reflect the **sacred worldviews** and practices of a majority of African American Christian communities. In this chapter, we will outline several of these streams and introduce the theological tenets that inform their piety and practice. This will be accomplished by an examination of what might be called the broad stream of the African American, or for the purposes of this book the theological tradition of the Black churches.

By theological tradition, we refer to what virtually every commentator on the Black Church—from J.W.C. Pennington in the 1840s, continuing in W.E.B. Du Bois at the turn of the twentieth century, and on through Carter G. Woodson, Gayraud Wilmore, Dwight Hopkins, *et al.*—has recognized as elements of an overarching framework in the midst of the diversity and plurality of African American Christian communities. This framework constitutes what Barbara Holmes terms the African American "Christian home," created in a land and in a faith in which we were treated as strangers.

Put another way, we will review those common theological ideas and commitments that are shared widely across the many discrete ecclesial traditions that in a larger sense make up what has been referred to throughout the text as the Black Church. Particular attention will be paid to the liberating or liberative dimensions of this tradition.

This chapter will identify the strands of this broad tradition by offering an interpretation that first identifies the three dimensions of Black existence that form the sources of the historical development of the Black Church's theological tradition (hereafter, Black Church theology). We will then describe the sacred worldview that emerges from this intersection and that forms the norm for theological reflection in the Black Church context. As with all traditions, Black Church theology has embedded within all of its expressions dialectical tensions between pieties (ways of understanding the contours of a faithful life) that are philosophically and theologically either more material (earthly focused) or spiritual (heavenly focused). Because this text is concerned to describe the liberative character of the Black Church, this chapter will focus on how these tensions play themselves out in Black Church piety. This will be followed by an account of how this theological tradition has been taken up in academic expressions of theology. But first, it might prove helpful to outline what exactly is meant by *theology* and the term *theological tradition*.

Theology: A Definition

The traditional approach to a definition of theology has generally been to begin with an etymological investigation of the word *theology*. The rendition has gone something like this: as a compound word of Greek origin, *theos* has been defined as the divine or God, and *logos* as words or thoughts about God. Theology is, according to this pattern, the reflective practice of construing and articulating our understanding of the divine reality, that reality's relationship to creation, and the appropriate ways in which human life ought to be ordered, individually and corporately, according to a particular theological interpretation. Understood in this way, theology is first a noetic activity from which material practices may be drawn. Theological reflection, presumptively, has been done by those who have leisure to *think*, and are not immersed in the daily toils of "making a living." In the history of Western Christianity, this has meant that the task of doing theology has been the provenance of church leaders and scholars. Theology as a term has therefore come to refer to the work done by professionals.

In recent times, this way of understanding theology has shifted to encompass recognition that whenever an individual or community reflects upon God and orders their lives according to that reflection they *are doing theology*! This recognition does not diminish the earnest service that academic theologians do for the church and the world. Rather, we see in it a profound recognition that if one is to give an account of theology as it "lives and breathes" in social and religious communities the focus must be on the doings of everyday people. This is recognition of the church doing theology, and it is the paradigmatic practice of the Black Church. Precisely because the history of the Christian tradition, as it has unfolded on the North American shores, has denied the genius and veracity of the Black Church, Black Church theology has developed necessarily without the social or institutional structures that facilitated an often dichotomous approach to theological development. Put another way, the Black Church has developed its theological tradition as primarily an ecclesial and not an academic endeavor. Thus, in this chapter, the more inclusive idea of Black Church theology will be the predominant mode of inquiry, versus a comparison of *schools* of theology that might be more appropriate to other church traditions.

Theological Tradition

A theological tradition is a sustained communal reflection on practice, teaching, experience, and a "handing on" of both the wisdom and genius of that communal reflection from generation to generation—so each generation is not *sui genera*. Understood in this way, a theological tradition encompasses the act(s) of a community as it attempts to interpret the working of God in its midst and the implications this presence has for the ways that community should structure its private and public life and form the piety of its members. A tradition is, succinctly, the practices, objects, people, and ideas that a community treasures and from which it draws its distinct character. A theological tradition is, more specifically, the web of ideas that holds this system together. To this point the idea of tradition in general and theological tradition in specific is still a bit abstract. Some examples might be in order.

Just such an example is the Bible. While most Christians never stop to think about it, the only reason they have the Bible is that previous generations of Christians have held it to be the sacred scripture of the Christian faith, and have given it to their children in the faith as such (*traditio*). So, although there may be many translations and debates about hermeneutics, the one set thing is the idea that the Bible is the Christian text. Correlatively, communities that have as their central sacred scripture the Old and New Testaments (and in some cases the Apocrypha) can be readily identified as being Christian. This is the case of the *tradition* treasuring those things deemed holy or sacred. Another example is the name Paul. Virtually any Christian community in the world, throughout time, recognizes that when this name is spoken in the context of a religious discussion, the person being referred to is the apostle Paul and some degree of reverence is immediately given to the discussion. Of course, this is the tradition revering and passing along the importance of a person. For someone unacquainted with the Christian tradition, the immediate question when the name is spoken might be "Paul who?" Similarly, in many cases a religious community is recognizable as Christian to the outside world by its adherence to the practice of centering an entire time of worship around the consumption of wafers or crusts of bread and the sipping of wine or grape juice.

In all of these preceding examples, what we have is the working of a matrix of practices, people, and things that relate to one another in ways that provide mutual meaning, making a discrete religious community internally and externally recognizable. This matrix is what we broadly mean by the concept of tradition. A theological tradition has specifically to do with the way a discrete faith community articulates its understanding of what its faith affirmations, practices, and sacred texts mean. What does the Lord's Supper mean? Who do we say that Jesus is? How do we describe the working of the Holy Spirit? These questions are all the stuff of theological tradition. So, when we ask what is the theological tradition of the Black Church, we are asking what are the theological ideas and ruminations about God, human beings, and practices that make the Black Church a distinct part of the Western tradition of Christianity. Having some sense of what is meant by tradition, let us focus on the specific character of the Black Church's theological tradition. A fitting place to begin is with some account of the existential realities that give currency to this theological tradition.

THE THREE ASPECTS OF BLACK EXISTENCE: SACRED INHERITANCE, EXPERIENCE, AND SCRIPTURE

A proper place to begin a description of Black Church theology is with the identification of the three aspects of Black existence that inform what we will call a Black sacred worldview from which distinct religious pieties and ranges of religious and cultural practices emerge. What we mean here by the term sacred worldview is that set of ideas about the divine-human relationship, human persons, and creation, that come together to form a coherent worldview, from which actions and ways of being in the world emerge.

Sacred Inheritance

The first source of this sacred worldview is the sacred inheritance that informs all African Diasporan cultures throughout the Western hemisphere. These blends of West African worldviews and distinctive religious wisdom from previous generations has echoed, with varying intensity, in the midst of Black cultural construction for the last four hundred years. Many scholars have identified these echoes as **African carryovers** in Black religion and culture.[2] These carryovers were worldviews (ways of understanding reality), cultural norms (orality), and practices (musical rhythms) that form a pre-thematic foundation for cultural construction and communal formation.[3] With the idea of sacred inheritance, we are identifying those influences (explicit and implicit) that have to do with ideas about the presence and character of the divine (God). These become an inheritance for each generation because they represent the experience, traditions, and wisdom of succeeding generations of Black Christians that are passed on as resources for contemporary existence. A significant way that this sacred inheritance manifests itself is in a premodern bent that characterizes much of the African American theological reflection. We will delineate this point more fully later in this chapter.

Experience

The second aspect of this triune source is the discrete experience of racial oppression that has characterized the history of Black people in the New World. It is well known that the crucible in which African American Christianity was formed was the system of racial oppression that has characterized the existence of African Americans since the first landing of Africans on these shores in 1619. For the first two hundred years, the system was most fully expressed by the American institution of chattel slavery. This was followed by the years of segregation (Jim and Jane Crow), and in more recent decades a cultural and economic racism that, while not as materially debilitating as in previous epochs, still leaves a majority of African Americans living on the margins of the mainstream of American economic and political life. The consequence of this situation has been that the majority of African American communities have experienced their existence as, in the words of Howard Thurman, having "their backs against the wall."[4] For this reason, questions of justice and mercy have always been at the center of African American theological reflection. For the Black Church's theological development, oppression has not just been an ancillary to **praxis** and thought of the Church; it has been at the very heart of the matter. This is a distinguishing mark of the tradition and its development in the broader stream of American Christianity that encompasses many theological traditions that were developed by religious communities who have been the beneficiaries of the general system of racial oppression.

An important dimension of the historical experience of African Americans is the reality that racial oppression has been tightly bound to the practice and proclamation of the Christian faith by the white community. That is to say, during the period when a distinctly African American Christianity was evolving, the dominant voices in the American Christian community were ones that both challenged the humanity of Black persons and explicitly supported a system of racial oppression. Black Church theology was thus born in the absurd situation in which African American persons and communities found themselves, namely: a context in which the Christian faith was the dominant justification for their subjugation.[5] Precisely because African Americans experienced white mainline Christian faith as what Fredrick Douglass aptly described as "the corrupt, slaveholding, women-whipping, cradle-plundering, partial and hypocritical Christianity,"[6] there is a notable emphasis on the person-to-person ethical practice of the Christian faith. This expresses itself in strongly developed ideas about personal sanctification and Christian love that have become inseparable in the tradition.

Scripture

The third wellspring of the African American Christian sacred worldview is the tradition's encounter with Scripture. As Vincent Wimbush has demonstrated in *African Americans and the Bible: Sacred Texts and Social Textures*[7], the African American encounter with the biblical occurred on both a literate and pre-literate level. Both the learned and experiential streams of this encounter were the grounds upon which African Americans found an expression of the faith that validated both their humanity and their quest for freedom. The Bible thus became authoritative in Black Church theology in a way that discrete religious doctrines only approximated. The *teachings* of the Black Church are frequently subjected to a level of biblical scrutiny and hermeneutical interpretation that, to the culturally naïve, may seem like a type of *Bibliolatry*. In more cases than not, however, this is the tradition expressing a suspicion of the mainline Christian *traditions*, which had too easily accommodated themselves to the culture of racial oppression that animated the larger society.

These three streams (sacred inheritance, experience, and Scripture) come together in what can be termed a *Black sacred worldview*. Before proceeding, it is important to note that, while this triune structure may bear echoes of earlier Protestant formulation—Richard Hooker's ideas about faith standing on a "three legged stool" (Scripture, reason, and tradition), or the so-called "Wesleyan quadrilateral" (Scripture, reason, tradition, and experience)—we are in fact dealing with something a bit more textured and complex than either intended.

Neither Richard Hooker nor John Wesley was working with anything as complex as what is here named *sacred inheritance*. While the idea of tradition is roughly comparable, it does not contemplate the presence a prethematic faith as the idea of an African carryover of sacred worldview encapsulates. Additionally, neither conceives of a human existence, from which experience flows, whose primary characteristic is absurdity. That is to say, Hooker and Wesley, and the traditions they represent, presumed an encounter with the faith mediated through a culture that both affirmed and added value to their humanity; not one that sought to diminish that humanity. Consequently, the triune configuration we are identifying here is something uniquely Black, and from which emerges a distinct Christian tradition—Black Church theology.

Black Sacred Worldview

The product of the triune configuration just described can be termed a Black sacred worldview—defined as the intersection of faith, thought, and action from which emerges material, spiritual, and intellectual currents that give form to African American religion and culture. This complex of creativity is what we might term the wellspring for Black Church theology. This sacred worldview then forms the commitments that express themselves through religion and culture.

The relationship between religion and culture is one of dynamic reciprocity. Culture provides the material by which religion is given meaning. Every religion relies on the larger culture to give it language, symbols, and spaces of meaning to communicate the experience of the transcendent to which that religion bears witness. Likewise, every human culture relies on the presence of religion(s) to bear witness to its existence as something more than a social contrivance. The American ideal of the United States being "one nation, under God" is an example of this relationship. Both religion and culture reciprocally benefit from the presence of the other. More important, both gain much of their form and function from the other. An example is the Pledge of Allegiance, which in its form and function is much like the covenants developed in the early Reformed communities of New England, or the confessions of the Reformed and Lutheran communities of the eighteenth- and nineteenth-century mid-Atlantic seaboard. The point is that this dynamic relationship between religion and culture is a general pattern within human societies. Before turning to a description of how the discrete commitments emerge from Black religion and culture, it might prove helpful to identify dominant ideas about the nature of reality that inform this worldview: ideas about God, humanity, and creation.

A hallmark of the Black sacred worldview is what might be termed its richly textured cosmology from which flows a very particular view of God, human beings, and the universe that they inhabit. Unlike many Christian traditions within the contemporary context of the United States, this tradition does not have a formal commitment to the scientific worldview as being the only valid description of reality. Instead, it operates with a view of the universe harkened to in Scripture that understands reality to consist of things and powers seen and unseen. "For in him all things in heaven and on earth were created, things visible and invisible, whether thrones or dominions or rulers or powers, all things have been created through him and for him" (Col. 1:16). This is what many have termed a premodern understanding of God and creation. This is not to say that the Black sacred worldview is somehow erroneous or unsophisticated. Rather, it is to suggest that the presuppositions that underlie it are primarily informed by religious interpretation and sensibility rather than simply physical observation. This has very significant implications for the character of this theological tradition—most notably, the tradition's insistence that the conduct of one's bodily life affect the condition and fate of one's spirit. We will now proceed to outline several dimensions of this Black sacred worldview.

GOD, HUMANITY, AND THE SPIRIT IN THE BLACK SACRED COSMOS

A major point of theological controversy during the modern era (from roughly the fifteenth to the twentieth centuries) has been the nature of God's existence and relation to creation. For many centuries, the presumption was that God, while essentially transcendent, was nonetheless immanent within creation in the manner of a *personal* actor. That is to say, God was conceived of *acting* in creation in discernible ways. This view changed, however, during the Enlightenment. During this period, with the rise of the scientific worldview and historical criticism, the epistemological underpinning of this view was challenged and, in many instances, replaced with a *modern* theological view. This modern view was skeptical both of a supernatural view of God's relation to creation and of the idea that Scripture gave an accurate historical account of events related to God relationship to creation.[8]

The consequence of this paradigm shift was that the authority and interpretive basis of Scripture was opened to debate, and the primary account given by Scripture of reality—one of creation peopled by angels, powers, and principalities in which God was a personal actor—was rendered largely as metaphor. Much of Black Church theology dissents from this view. There are several bases for this dissent.

Historically, the intersection of the sacred worldviews brought by enslaved Africans to these shores, and the dominant theological context into which they came—the Great Awakenings—produced a context in which the view of God and creation was decidedly *un*-modern. Neither

81

the traditional faiths of the enslaved West Africans nor the evangelical faith that they encountered on these shores were particularly sympathetic to the faith that emerged when Christianity was run through the sieve of the Enlightenment. Another basis of dissent was the troubled relationship between African Americans and the scientific revolution. Precisely because of the heavy assaults on the capacities and basic humanity of African Americans, using the latest scientific tools of every era,[9] a scientific onslaught on their life-giving religion would never be authoritative. After all, how could modes of scientific inquiry that had been so wrong about Black humanity be trusted to be right in its ruminations about God? Finally, the bent of modern readings of the biblical text—readings that seemingly preclude the possibility of reading God's liberating hand into history—created little basis for the liberative reading of the text that has historically been a cornerstone of the Black biblical interpretive tradition.

In place of a *modern* or exclusively materialist view, Black Church theology has largely held the view that not only does God *act* in history but that the action is also consonant with the character of God revealed in Scripture. So, historical figures like Black abolitionist David Walker could say definitively:

> The fact is, the labour of slaves comes too cheap to the avaricious usurpers, and is (as they think) of such great utility to the country where it exists, that those who are actuated by sordid avarice only, overlook the evils, which will as sure as the Lord lives, follow after the good. In fact, they are so happy to keep in ignorance and degradation, and to receive the homage and the labour of the slaves, they forget that God rules in the armies of heaven and among the inhabitants of the earth, having his ears continually open to the cries, tears and groans of his oppressed people; and being a just and holy Being will at one day appear fully in behalf of the oppressed, and arrest the progress of the avaricious oppressors; for although the destruction of the oppressors God may not effect by the oppressed, yet the Lord our God will bring other destructions upon them.[10]

Additionally, the premodern view allows a reading of the biblical text that can sustain a vision of God and Jesus Christ upon which to establish a personal relation. This personal relationship was the basis for a personal identity, aptly described during the modern civil rights movement as **somebodyness**. As well, the tradition has found the modern view's insistence on an exclusively "this-worldly" interpretation of the faith one that is largely incapable of providing a basis for the Christian hope of life beyond the "veil of tears." Finally, the inability of the modern view to provide an interpretive apparatus to make sense of Black Christians' real experiences of the movement of the Spirit and fellowship with Christ, borne witness to by generations of their forebears, rendered any theological system rooted in the commitments of modernity insufficient to the task of interpreting their view of God and reality.

There are several theological commitments, anchored in the Black sacred worldview, that are deeply embedded within the mainstream African American tradition about human persons, their relationship to God and to one another. The first commitment has to do with the human persons as such. The tradition has a basic commitment to the inherent dignity of all persons. This dignity and worth as persons derives solely from their status as children of God. The anti-slavery dictum of the eighteenth century—"[God] hath made of one blood all nations of men for to dwell on all the face of the earth"(Acts 17:26 KJV)—symbolized this current in Black Church theology in its earliest form. This commitment is, perhaps, the cardinal point upon which all other affirmations are built. Given the way the dominant culture has denied the personhood and human dignity of African Americans on both cultural and religious bases this commitment is very understandable.

A second commitment is that God calls to human persons, in the midst of their circumstances, another reflection of the largely evangelical character of the tradition. This offer of salvation is one that recognizes the agency of both God and of human persons. Agency, then, is near the center of Black Church theology's understanding of divine-human relations. This commitment is rooted in several grounds:

1. As a response to the historical denial of Black agency in American public and religious life (experience),
2. As a studied interpretation of the scriptural idea that we as individuals choose to respond to God (Scripture), and
3. As a manifestation of the retention of an African sacred worldview in which the primary expression of human particularity is in the encounter with the divine (sacred inheritance).

Here it is important to note that the emphasis on agency is not synonymous with the modern idea of individualism. Rather, it is recognition of the human person as being one in the many, yet being one with dignity.

A third commitment is that human persons are most fully human in their relations with one another. This is the idea that *sanctified living*, while heavenly focused, is materially expressed in the treatment of other human beings. This is embodied by the tradition's commitment to the idea of Christian love. In conceptualizing this way of approaching the idea of piety, Peter Paris observes that the Black Church tradition has held that "the moral act itself constitutes the person as person. Becoming a person, a moral being, necessitates the treating of another as a person. In such an act, being and doing are interdependent."[11] As with the other commitments, this one is also rooted in the basic foundational structure that we have identified: existential (experiential), scriptural, and sacred heredity. The motto of the African Methodist Episcopal Church encapsulates the existential moment of this piety well: "God Our Father, Christ Our Redeemer, Man Our Brother," which is by its very nature relational. We see dimension having to do with sacred inheritance and scripture in works such as *Soul Theology: The Heart of American Black Culture*. In this work, Nicholas C. Cooper-Lewter and Henry Mitchell observe the significance in the Black Church tradition of the common saying, often invoked by Martin Luther King, Jr., in his sermons, that in God's world there are "no big I's and little you's."[12]

The fundamental nature of theological anthropology within Black Church theology is twofold in that it restores and sustains the humanity of Black persons in the face of cultural and religious discourses that would deny this recognition. This nature is grounded in the divine-human relationship.

As mentioned earlier, the broad stream of Black Church theology is rooted in a very richly textured cosmology. The tradition's understanding of the universe is one in which there are two primary dimensions of reality existing simultaneously with each other—the material and the spiritual. The existence and operation of both of the dimensions of reality bring God's creation to fulfillment in the final resurrection, the time that the tradition has historically called "that great gittin' up mornin'."

The spiritual and the material dimensions of reality relate to one another in such a way that the spiritual impinges upon the material both in terms of God's presence moving and affecting creation and the working of forces that would hinder the Christian's journey to salvation. The former is the working of the Spirit; the latter is that of the adversary. The helpful and empowering forces become central to the interpretation of reality in the Holiness-Pentecostal movement, a broad swath of Baptists and Wesleyans, and a not-insignificant number of Black churches in other traditions. Like many of the currents in the broad stream of the Black Church tradition, the form and response to the centrality of the spiritual has significant connections to practices that echo back to the first Africans brought to the shores of the New World. It is beyond the scope of this chapter to detail these practices, yet it is important to notice the underlying theological commitment that undergirds them and that is central to the theological description of reality given by many of the traditions within the Black Church.

To summarize to this point, we have identified the essential dimensions of the Black sacred worldview as being informed by: (1) the existential and historical reality of African Americans; (2) the particular reading of Scripture by the tradition; and (3) the apostolic witness of the previous generations within the community. We turn now to a description of the ways that this view flows into a common commitment that nourishes Black Church theology.

Before moving on, though, it is necessary to identify what might be termed the two dialectical poles that are present in various streams of Black Church theology: the *compensatory* and the *constructivist* theological traditions. While some commentators have suggested that these represent two competing and inimical streams of thought and practice that are, hence, exclusive of one another, it is more helpful to recognize that they are both present, with differing emphases, in the variety of Black Church traditions. Thus, our approach to what has been termed the *compensatory* and *constructivist* sides of Black Church life will view them as dimensions of a larger theological scheme that we have termed a *redemptionist* interpretation of the Christian faith.

COMPENSATORY AND CONSTRUCTIVIST DIMENSIONS OF BLACK CHURCH THEOLOGY

In his work *The Negro's God as Reflected in His Literature*, Benjamin Mays identifies what he terms the *compensatory* and the *constructivist* views of God and the Christian faith as two primary ways that Black Church theology expresses its faith.[13] The first, as the name may betray, is an interpretation of the faith whose primary purpose is to provide sustenance to communities chafing under seemingly intractable oppression. This stream of the tradition roots both the significance and point of existence in the achievement of eternal salvation, a vision from which to draw strength for present living. A biblical theme strongly emphasized here is that echoed by Paul: "I consider that the sufferings of the present time are not worth comparing with the glory about to be revealed to us" (Rom. 8:18). Several commentators have disparagingly identified this view of the faith as an "over-yonder" or "otherworldly" faith.

The constructivist interpretation emphasizes those aspects of the faith that bear most directly on the material condition of Black persons and their communities. A substantial concern of this stream of Black Church theology is with the issue of justice in the contemporary context. The various political and social movements that have emerged from the Black Church have been an expression of this reality. The modern civil rights movement is a prime example of this theological trajectory.

It would be misleading to assign the distinction between these two theological approaches to a spiritual/material dichotomy. As Dwight Hopkins observes in *Black Faith and Public Talk*:

> The black community has a long tradition of practicing faith as a total way of life. It has shown that faith is not limited to certain areas of being human then absent in others. In fact, faith covers all of reality, secular and sacred.[14]

What is at work here are different ways of expressing and recognizing one's humanity precisely through some form of enacted agency. The first emphasizes the self as a *moral* agent, the second as a *social* agent. To better get a handle on these differences, a review of the way each expresses piety will prove helpful.

Compensatory/Accommodationist Piety

Two significant dimensions of the first stream piety are its compensatory and accommodationist character. The foundations of this understanding of piety are rooted in the triune structure earlier identified (experience, scripture, and heredity), yet the character of experience has a distinct reality. The vast majority of the Black Church traditions that evidence this compensatory/accommodationist piety and theological view were born and nurtured in the antebellum and Jim and Jane Crow

(post–Reconstruction) South. The historical reality of these religious traditions was one in which racial oppression was particularly virulent and
violent.[15] In fact, this theological view and the piety associated with it are
very compatible with the African American politics of the era in that
region. In essence, this accommodationist view is the religious corollary
to Booker T. Washington's social and economic politics, which relied on
the admonition to self-development as having primacy over a politics of
social and political empowerment.[16] The churches most closely associated with this theological view have historically been the Wesleyan traditions, the Baptist traditions, and the Pentecostal traditions. On the
contemporary scene, the Charismatic non-denominational movements
can be added to this list.

This focus on the eternal fate of the individual Christian has led to an
emphasis on sanctification and personal holiness. It is here that we can
see a strong connection between this stream of Black Church theology
and the Wesleyan tradition. The manifestation of this focus was in a religious practice that was only liminally concerned with matters of politics
and protest. The strength of this tradition was that it endowed the
believer with an agency and significance largely denied in the larger
world. In essence, this view recognized the believer as a moral agent in
his or her own destiny. It also provided a vision of existence, albeit on the
"other side of the Jordan," when God would reward the Christian's perseverance and remove the yoke of suffering so endemic to Black life in the
context of American cultural and public life. A further point to be
noticed is that even though this stream of the tradition was, itself, not
primarily involved with political and social protest, it was the seedbed for
a sense of Black agency, that would animate the modern civil rights
movement in the mid–twentieth century, precisely because the movement was cast in moral terms.

The Constructivist Piety

A tenet of much of the African American tradition is that all of God's
children find themselves born into a world of sin. This is not a statement
about the goodness, or ferocity, of God's creation. It is only recognition
that people are born into a personal and social context in which they are
beset by sin. Sin is, of course, precipitate of suffering. In their historical
and contemporary reality African Americans have never known a time in
which they have not suffered greatly because they find themselves mired

in the midst of abominable social structures of sin that have continually assaulted their humanity and well-being. The constructivist stream of Black piety has largely focused itself on the ways Black **moral agency** should combat the material and social structures that deny the humanity of Black persons and further our oppression. As noted by Gayraud Wilmore, this stream of Black Church theology has existed as a "radical thread" for as long as there have been Africans facing oppression in the Americas.[17] The salient point of this piety is that the Christian faith is here understood to encompass one's cooperation with God's *acting* to mitigate the suffering caused by the destructive presence of sin by bringing down the structures of sin and giving the Christian strength and hope in their midst.

For much of the nascent period of the independent Black Church movement (late eighteenth and early to mid–nineteenth centuries), this theological piety was developed by Northern Black Church leaders such as J. W. C. Pennington, Martin Delany and others. While facing systemic racial oppression, these leaders were spared the decidedly deadly form of racism that characterized life in the Southern states.

The Eschatological Vision

What has animated much of the theological streams just reviewed is a strong **eschatological vision**. It has been a vision of wholeness and peace and the manifest presence of God. This vision is most fully formed in the book of Revelation's reflections of the *eschaton*. That is to say, the vision of redemption in eternity—God making it right—is the controlling metaphor. This is the vision of when God will make right that which is wrong, sinners will receive their due, and the righteous will dwell forever with God in the New Jerusalem. An important but certainly subsidiary vision is that put forth by Isaiah of a time when "the wolf shall live with the lamb, the leopard shall lie down with the kid, the calf and the lion and the fatling together"(Isa. 11:6). These two visions are dimensions of the Christian eschatological hope as reflected in Black Church theology. The first vision is authoritative for both streams in this tradition but stressed more in the compensatory/accommodationist piety. The second vision, with its manifestly social implications, places greater emphasis on the material redemption of persons and communities and is emphasized by the constructivist piety.

As we conclude this section, it would be helpful to draw attention to a figure who synthesizes the two streams of Black Church theology just outlined, Dr. Martin Luther King, Jr. Two aspects of King's public ministry exemplify the union of these two streams of Black Church theology. The first is evident in his pastoral pronouncements and, to a degree, in his absolute commitment to nonviolence. His concern for the spiritual welfare of civil rights activists and segregationists alike—because violence scars and deforms the soul—reflects the emphasis that the compensatory/accommodationist tradition places on the eternal fate of the soul. His program of nonviolent direction action, however, *materialized* this commitment. Far from the quietism often attributed to the compensatory stream, protests and boycotts led by King reflect a commitment to social and economic transformation that expresses the constructivist stream of the tradition. King's example teaches us that these two streams of the tradition are not diametrically opposed. Both are concerned with issues of freedom and liberation: the first with spiritual liberation from the bondage of both personal and social sin, the second with material liberation from sinful systems of oppression, and finally both with the well-being of God's children. What separates them are circumstance and emphasis. Yet, there are instances in which the common commitments to freedom and to the well-being of God's children create the conditions under which they may be fused with a powerful force. The modern civil rights movement was just such an occasion.

Having reviewed the currents that form the broad stream of Black Church theology, it is now possible to turn to a brief review of the two dominant academic theologies that emerge from this tradition: Black theology and Womanist theology. While it is certainly the case that there are additional theological currents within the field of Black Church Studies (e.g., Pan-Africanist theology) these are the dominant schools that emerge from and constructively deal with the Black Church's theology.

BLACK LIBERATION THEOLOGY

Beginning in the mid 1960s, in the period often referred to as the era of "Black Power" there emerged a theological movement closely related to the rising militancy of that age. We can trace the Black theology movement to two sources: the church and the academy. With the publication in 1966 of the Statement by the National Committee of Negro

Churchmen on Black Power,[18] a dimension of Black ecclesial discourse long on the margins of the public proclamation of the Black Church reappeared. This theological stream was the strident and militant demand for justice and empowerment for Blacks in America and for a cessation of the larger Church's collusion with oppressive power structures. The vision of justice raised by this and subsequent documents was not that of the then extant vision of integration, which in reality was little more than assimilation, but rather one of Black humanity being accepted on its own terms. A seismic shift occurred in 1968 with the assassination of Rev. Dr. Martin Luther King, Jr. As Gayraud Wilmore put it: "The King of love was dead and with his death an era of interracial church social action and theological innocence came to an end."[19] In the wake of this shift, James H. Cone published what would become the two touchstones for the Black theology movement: *Black Theology and Black Power* and *A Black Theology of Liberation*.[20] With the publication of these works, Black Church theology's focus on freedom developed another dimension. This dimension focused sharply on the idea of liberation. The praxis model of theological discourse informed both the method and content of this model. This, of course, meant that the ways that the movement arranged and expressed its theology differed from earlier renderings. To these descriptions we now turn.

Oppression as Context

The starting point for Black theology has been the situation of oppression that has characterized Black existence in America. This priority of context meant that for Black Theology all theological reflection was accountable to the project of liberating African Americans from the system of racial oppression that animated much of American social, economic, cultural, and religious public life. While the project of freedom was a significant part of earlier streams of Black Church theology, the placement of liberation as the primary measure of the Christian faith was new. As well, the explicit use of the idea of Blackness as a theological category was an innovation.

An animating principle of the Black theology movement was that the mainline Christian faith in America, was presumptively the faith of white supremacy. That is to say, the movement made plain what was the implicit reality of the faith in the American context: that the entire normative structure within which the faith operated had at its center the experience and needs of white Americans. This meant that in American religious life, only those expressions of the faith that reflected a Eurocentric character were deemed authentic. So, liturgy and preaching were only Christian when they reflected harmonies and structures that emerged from European classical and folk traditions. More important, only images of Jesus and other biblical figures rendered as white were acceptable. In light of this, the Black theology movement contended for an expression of the Christian faith that not only challenged the truth of this faith of white supremacy but also that placed the needs of Black people at its center.

The primary affirmations that emerged as the center of the Black Theology movement were:

1. God as revealed in Scripture and in Jesus Christ (the Oppressed One) works primarily for the liberation of oppressed people;
2. God takes on the identity of those on whose behalf God is bringing about liberation;
3. In the context of racial oppression in America this means God is Black and;
4. The authentic expression of Christian faith is one that works with the purposes of God, which in the American context is the liberation of Black people.

These are the core affirmations that the branches of the Black theology movement shared in common. Among the adherents of the movement, however, there were many differences in aims and expressions.

From its inception, streams existed within the Black theology movement that demanded that the project of liberation ultimately be held accountable to a vision of reconciliation. Theologians such as J. Deotis Roberts and Cecil Cone contended that without this aspiration toward reconciliation the Black theology movement would be little more than the dark twin of the white theologies and traditions that it so harshly critiqued. Another expression of Black theology was linked to Black Christian nationalist thinkers such as Jaramogi Abebe Agyeman (Albert B. Cleage, Jr.), the founder of the Shrine of the Black Madonna, who contended that the only acceptable faith for Black people was one that contributed to the building of a Black nation.[21]

By the 1990s the movement had developed to an extent that there were significant works not only in the area of theology but also in Bible, ethics, liturgy, practical theologies such as Christian education, liturgy, and worship. A movement that developed from and in many ways as a response to the Black theology movement is Womanist theology.

Womanist Theology

In the mid–1980s the voices of Black women began to be heard on the theological scene. Theologians such as Jacqueline Grant and Delores Williams and ethicists such as Katie Cannon sought to illumine dimensions of oppression not taken seriously enough by the first generations of Black theologians. Specifically, these thinkers sought to identify the intersections of race, class, and gender in creating systems of oppression unique to Black women. By highlighting this particular form of systemic evil, these theologians and ethicists sought to give voice to the experiences of Black women who had been silenced by the **patriarchy** of the dominant society and the Black Church, and by the racism of the larger society and the contemporary feminist movement. This theological stream also sought to demonstrate the significance of the Black woman's struggle against oppression in giving an account of the Christian faith and to reframe the way theology and ethics were approached. This reframing would, as Cannon puts it, recognize that contending against and surviving "tyrannical systems of oppression," *is* witnessing to the power of God and the "true sphere of moral life."[22]

The name *Womanist*, which has been broadly taken by the thinkers in this project, comes from the writer Alice Walker in her work *In Search of Our Mothers' Gardens*[23] in which she claims for Black women a space of agency and meaning that was/is often denied to them by their larger cultures (society and church). While the earlier chapters introduced the Womanist movement, it is important here to contextualize Womanist thought in the flow of the Black Church's theological tradition. As with Black theology, Womanist theology emerged from the experience and work of scholars—who were formed by, and place a significant part of, their identity in the Black Church. This is what places it in the broad stream of Black Church theology. Womanist thought has offered several unique contributions to the larger theological landscape of the church and the academy.

Beyond the already mentioned inclusion of the witness and wisdom of Black women—the undeniable foundation of the Black Church—Womanist thought brings communal well-being to the center of theological discourse. Emerging from the unique vantage point of women who have been responsible for the welfare of many in the society, Womanist theology is—unlike many dominant expressions of the Christian tradition—concerned with the welfare and wholeness of the entire community. This understanding of communal welfare necessarily manifests itself as the cultivation and expansion of human dignity, living into the fullness of life as a witness to God's power and a radical and inescapable commitment to contend with, and on behalf of, "the least of these." Thus, the works of Womanist thinkers have sought to *humanize* every aspect of the broader Christian theological tradition and, specifically, the traditions of the Black Church tainted by patriarchy. In this work they have reflected the commitments that emerge from the broad stream of Black Church theology, which has at its core a strident commitment to passing on the experience of God's power, through witness and testimony, as the balm for the dehumanizing and annihilating workings of oppression.

SUMMARY

This chapter has sought to identify the currents that run through a broad stream of theological reflection that give rise to an ecclesial and ethical tradition committed to the ideals of liberation and human wholeness. While we have recognized that there are many ways this commitment reflects itself, it is undeniable that, in the final analysis, the theological tradition of the Black Church has, at its best, exemplified the Christian faith's commitment to bringing the message (*kerygma*) of hope to those chafing under systems of oppression and evil. The continuing challenge within the church, and in the larger society, is making real this unique expression of the Christian faith.

BIOGRAPHIES

Martin Luther King, Jr. (1929–1968)

Martin Luther King, Jr., was the pre-eminent African American voice during the modern civil rights movement. Born in 1929, King came from a long line of Baptist preachers and thus frequently referred to the Black Church as the mother in whose bosom he was nurtured. Best known for his role as the paramount African American public theologian of the twentieth century—using public oratory to give a Christian theological grounding to the civil rights movement—King was also a leader within the Black Church. He and other progressive clergy joined to form the Progressive National Baptist Convention in 1961. Educated at Morehouse College, Crozier Seminary, and Boston University, Dr. King had the opportunity to study with several giants of the Black intellectual tradition such as Benjamin Mays, George Kelsey, and Howard Thurman. In his work, King exemplified the genius of the Black Church and the academy. In 1964, he was awarded the Nobel Peace Prize—the youngest person to receive that award in its history. Beyond his many speeches and addresses, King also authored several books: *Stride Toward Freedom, The Measure of a Man, Strength to Love, Why We Can't Wait, Where Do We Go From Here: Community or Chaos,* and *The Trumpet of Conscience.* Martin Luther King, Jr., was assassinated on April 4, 1968, while working with striking garbage workers in Memphis, Tennessee.

James H. Cone (1938–   )

James H. Cone is widely credited as the founder of the Black Theology movement with his publication of *Black Theology and Black Power*. Raised in the Jim and Jane Crow South, Cone came to know not only the breadth of racial injustice but also, and more importantly, the depth of the Black Church's religious resources to combat oppression and sustain the humanity of Black people. After his graduation from Philander C. Smith College in 1958, Cone went on to do graduate work at Garrett-Evangelical Seminary and Northwestern University. Since 1970, he has taught at Union Theological Seminary in New York City. Through his work there, he has trained several generations of Black and Womanist theologians. Cone is credited with the development of the first organic North American liberation theology. Beyond the establishment of this field of study, which was done in dialogue with theologians such as J. Deotis Roberts, Cone has brought Black theology into dialogue with other liberation theologies (e.g., Minjung theology and South Africa's Black theology) and influenced their development. Among his many writings are: *A Black Theology of Liberation, God of the Oppressed, For My People: Black Theology and the Black Church, Martin & Malcolm & America: A Dream or Nightmare,* and *Speaking the Truth: Ecumenism, Liberation and Black Theology.* James H. Cone is a dominant figure in the field of North American theology and continues to be an influential voice in the Black Church's theological development.

STUDY QUESTIONS

1. What are the elements that inform the Black Church's theological tradition?
2. What is the coherent sacred worldview that is the foundation of Black Church theology?
3. What are the faith commitments that emerge from this sacred worldview?
4. Distinguish the dominant ways that these commitments express themselves in African American Christianity.
5. What is the vision of redemption that is the culmination of this theological tradition?
6. What are the three academic schools of thought that emerge from the tradition?

ESSENTIAL TEXTS

- *A Black Theology of Liberation* by James H. Cone
- *Introducting Womanist Theology* by Stephanie Mitchem
- *Jesus and the Disinherited* by Howard Thurman
- *Sisters in the Wilderness* by Delores Williams

Your country? How came it
yours? Before the Pilgrims
landed we were here. Here we
have brought our three gifts and
mingled them with yours: a gift of
story and song . . . the gift of
sweat and brawn . . . the third, a
gift of the Spirit . . . Actively we
have woven ourselves with the very
warp and woof of this nation, —
we fought their battles, shared their
sorrow, mingled our blood with
theirs, and generation after
generation have pleaded with a
headstrong, careless people to
despise not Justice, Mercy, and
Truth, lest the nation be smitten
with a curse.
—W.E.B. Du Bois

CHAPTER FOUR

THE BLACK CHURCH,
CULTURE, AND SOCIETY

INTRODUCTION

This chapter will discuss the social significance of the Black Church as the single most autonomous Black institution in North America, one that has historically played a major role in response to social, political, and cultural changes within Black communities and their relationship to the broader society—and continues to play that role. Any consideration of contemporary Black community development, and the place of Blacks within the wider social fabric of U.S. society since the Second World War, must take into consideration:

- The role of the Black Church,
- Its historical legacy rooted in resistance to slavery,
- Liberative action for Black people's human rights within the context of the United States as a liberal democracy, and
- International movements for Black liberation such as Pan-Africanism.

The Black Church here, as elsewhere in this book, is understood to comprise diverse forms of church organization, theologies, and worship experiences. There is no single "Black Church"; rather, as sociologists C. Eric Lincoln and Lawrence Mamiya note, the term *Black Church* serves as a kind of "sociological and theological shorthand reference to the pluralism of Black Christian churches in the United States."[1] Based on extensive research on Black congregations in different regions of the United States, Lincoln and Mamiya's study presents a comprehensive overview of the contemporary development of the Black Church. It is clear from their pioneering research that there are many different expressions of Black Christian religiosity, collectively referred to as the *Black Church*. The Black Church, then, is comprised of recognized cultural traditions and practices that have contributed, in historical and contemporary contexts, to the development of Black community life.

Drawing on perspectives from sociology and anthropology, this chapter will outline a critical approach to the study of the Black Church as a dynamic social institution. From this perspective, the Black Church is connected to larger processes of social change in regional, national, and international contexts. The first section will suggest that the study of the Black Church must necessarily take into consideration societal and cultural changes as integral to its emergence. In other words, the Black Church is dynamic and is reflective of as well as influenced by changes in Black communities and the wider society as much as it, in turn, is also influential in societal development. This dialectical relationship between the Black Church and Black communities and the wider society is critical in the study of the Black Church's development. Thus, the Black Church is understood to be both informed by, and constituted of, dynamic social and cultural practices.

The second section, on Black congregational studies, will extend this discussion of a dynamic and changing institution by examining important trends and changes in the contemporary development of the Black Church in Black community life over the latter half of the twentieth and early twenty-first centuries. Specifically, the discussion will focus on the role of women and challenges to normative gender ideology in the Black Church by exploring issues of sexuality and sexual diversity. These issues have emerged as some of the most controversial and crucial in the development of the contemporary Black Church.

Once we have discussed issues of gender and sexuality within in contemporary Black Church development in the United States, the third, and final, section of the chapter focuses on the importance of understanding the Black Church's participation in global religious pluralism. That is to say that the Black Church is understood here as one expression, and not the sole, all encompassing and definitive religious tradition of all Black people in the United States, specifically, and in the Americas, broadly.

CRITICAL PERSPECTIVES FOR STUDYING BLACK RELIGION, CULTURE, AND SOCIETY

Understanding Black Culture and Faith

This chapter takes up the study of the Black Church, culture, and society as social relationships expressed in dynamic tension in the life circumstances of individual Black people and Black communities. Thus, rather than viewing the Black Church and the social contexts in which it is embedded as being static and fixed, the perspective employed here sees the Black Church as fundamentally dynamic. Lincoln and Mamiya express this idea of tension as a "dialectical model of the Black Church," which is fundamental to Black Church development.[2] Black faith and culture are understood as being necessarily linked and contentious areas in which social meaning is constructed, interpreted, and reinterpreted. In other words, Black faith and culture are conceptualized as encompassing multiple ways of being religious and Black: within the Black Church, in other religious traditions practiced by Black people, and in wider social, political, and cultural contexts. Differences, too, in location between urban and rural churches, as well as social class have also historically contributed to diverse experiences of Black Church development. This diversity accounts for the variety of Black churches and **Black Christian worship** experiences. Thus the widely accepted axiom of Black Christian experience: that no two churches are exactly alike, even within the same denomination, nor are any two church worship experiences alike within the same church.

Important, too, is the need to contextualize the Black Church as one form of religious expression of Blacks in the United States. The tendency to construct African American religious experience as a monolithic category called the *Black Church* obscures the variety of Black religious expression, including non-Christian traditions. The final two segments of this chapter address the importance of situating the Black Church within the context of the plural religious experiences of Black people within the United States and locating the United States, itself, as part of a larger African Diaspora.

Doing Research in Community

Social science researchers seek to pay attention to the politics of conducting research. That is to say, an integral part of the research process is to bring into question research methods as well as relationships between researchers and the individuals and communities on whom they conduct research. In disciplines such as sociology and anthropology (which began as a part of the modern western academy in the nineteenth century as literally a "science of society" and "study of man," respectively), these issues have particularly been addressed as related to the development of systems of knowledge that are in themselves inherently value-laden. That is to say then, that the scientific notion of *objectivity*, which situates the researcher outside and apart from the communities and topics of study, has been critiqued. Feminist and anti-racist researchers have been particularly vocal in their critique of the biases in knowledge production that privileged male and white, western, Euro-American experiences as the norm.[3] They call, instead, for an account of social experiences that takes into consideration the intersection of race, class, gender, and other aspects of social difference (such as sexual orientation, age, and ability), in differentially shaping the lives of men, women, and children in the United States. In Black social contexts, social class, access to education and issues of *color* or "shadism" (intra-group distinctions based on a positive assessment of lighter skin tones and eye color as well as straight hair), have had a long history of differentiating experiences of being Black in the United States as well as status within Black communities. This chapter suggests that a research approach that takes into consideration an individual's subject position, in relation to the Black Church and Black community life, is not only insightful but a necessary part of the research and teaching and learning process about the Black Church.

In *The Souls of Black Folk*, an influential collection of essays on Black culture, politics, and society, W.E.B. Du Bois introduced the concept of **double consciousness** as a way of expressing the contradiction of being both Black and American in a racially segregated United States, which had historically—through law, custom, and practice—not recognized the humanity of Black people.[4] As Du Bois famously noted, to be both Black and American was to simultaneously experience an authentic sense of self through the mores, values, and practices of Black communal life, while at the same time having an acute awareness of the ways in which the dominant, mainstream, Eurocentric American culture viewed Black people as subordinate and radically Other. Du Bois expressed this tension as "two warring ideals in one dark body."[5]

Double consciousness, which pervaded the ways in which Black people in America saw themselves and represented their own experiences, was also expressed earlier in the writings of formerly enslaved Africans, such as Olaudah Equiano[6] who chronicled their experiences of enslavement in the written form that became known as slave narratives. More than a century later, the concept of *double consciousness* is still salient for the production of research on and about Black Church and society. Though expressed in ways that differ from previous eras, the massive societal and cultural changes of the post–civil rights era brought in new forms and variations on old racial stories and stereotypes. Du Bois's analysis suggested that all Black people confront this doubling in various arenas of social life. Thus, as discussed in the following, Black researchers—many of whom are cultural insiders in some ways, and in others, cultural outsiders to their communities—must necessarily confront double consciousness.

Insider/Outsider Participant Observation in Black Church Studies

How then do researchers who are members of the communities that they study negotiate their relationships with those religious communities? What are the roles, responsibilities, privileges, and challenges faced by researchers who simultaneously occupy insider and outsider positions? In the twenty-first century academy in which questions of the politics of knowledge have center stage, these are important issues to consider. These questions will be addressed by looking at two related issues: (1) the tension between academic study of religion and religious practice within the academy and (2) the notions of voice and representation often expressed in questions concerning the legitimacy of individuals or groups to represent and discuss the experience of religious groups and individuals.

With roots in the nineteenth century and Christian theology, the academic study of religion is one of the newest humanities disciplines in the modern western academy. The academic study of religion is primarily distinguished from theological inquiry through the fact that the study of a particular tradition is not in itself a religious path or "way of being religious."[7] However, the academic study of religion and theological studies as separate disciplines that engage in the study of religious experience often overlap. This is readily apparent in Black Church studies, in which a significant proportion of scholars who conduct research on Black Church traditions are themselves insiders, because the scholars are also congregants and church leaders. With theological seminaries and divinity schools one of the main arenas of higher education for Black people in the twentieth century, it is not surprising then that a significant component of Black intellectuals in the twentieth century were affiliated with churches. Historical examples include Alexander Crammell, Daniel Payne, Benjamin E. Mays, Howard Thurman, and Martin Luther King, Jr. Contemporary scholars who continue this tradition include Emily Townes, Cheryl J. Sanders, Katie Geneva Cannon, James Cone, Cornel West, Gayraud Wilmore, Robert E. Franklin, and Cheryl Townsend Gilkes. These scholars have been able to bring the expertise of their scholarly training and the commitment of their religious vocation both to the study of the Black Church and to their work in confronting issues such as racism, sexism, economic, and political disempowerment in Black churches and communities. An ethic of care and responsibility guides the work of such scholars.

Adding to this tradition of engaged, socially conscious scholarship by scholar-theologians is the work of social scientists such as sociologist C. Eric Lincoln and anthropologist Arthur Huff Fauset. Both scholars contributed influential studies on Black religious experiences in the mid–twentieth century. Fauset's *Black Gods of the Metropolis: Negro Religious Cults of the Urban North*[8] was based on anthropological fieldwork on Black religious experience in 1940s Philadelphia. His pioneering scholarship laid the groundwork for understanding the development of Black religiosity in Northern cities to which Black people had emigrated in massive numbers during the Great Migration. C. Eric Lincoln's *The Black Muslims in America*[9] was the first sociological study of the Nation of Islam in the United States. The study provided the first scholarly work on Islam and the Black experience in the United States. Lincoln's work was significant in providing a detailed overview of the development of the Nation of Islam in the United States locating the movement in the socio-historical context of Black people's lives in the United States. Decades later, Lincoln and Lawrence Mamiya conducted and published an exhaustive sociological analysis of the historic Black Church tradition, *The Black Church in the African American Experience*.

Oral/Aural Culture and the Study of the Black Church

The conditions of forced capture and transportation ensured that enslaved Africans brought scant, if any, physical materials with them to the Americas, through the Middle Passage, and very few personal objects of enslaved peoples have survived. Oral traditions, thus, became important repositories and modes of transmission of Black religious and cultural traditions.

The oral traditions of the Black Church were crucial for the development, maintenance, and transmission of knowledge in Black communities. Law, custom, and practice prohibited the vast majority of Black people, for most of their history in the United States, from acquiring literacy and reading and writing texts. As such, oral culture became a significant repository of knowledge and mode of critique about Black experience. It is crucial that any study of Black religion, culture, and society should take into consideration *orality*—acts of utterance, and *aurality*—acts of listening and attentiveness, as integral to understanding the richness of Black religious experiences. Failure to do so would result in missing a large part of the story of Black religious experience in socio-cultural contexts.

Preaching, praying, testifying, and singing remain the cornerstones of the Black worship experience in the Black Church. Tempered and refined through Black people's experiences of slavery and racial injustice, these oral traditions are not static and fixed; they are open to interpretation and reinterpretation. As singer and historian Bernice Johnson Reagon noted in the documentary of the same name, "the songs are free." Accordingly, contributions from fields of study explicitly concerned with performance, such as ethnomusicology and the history of Black popular music in the United States, offer insights to understanding orality that highlight the importance not only of the *content* but also of the *performance* of Black oral cultural traditions.

The oral traditions of the Black Church include Black sacred music in the form of spirituals and gospel music. Black sacred music is a major influence on the development of American popular music such as blues, rhythm and blues (R&B), and jazz. Many noteworthy contemporary Black musicians and performers (such as soul and R&B greats Patti Labelle, James Brown, and Aretha Franklin) note the importance of Black Church music, and the experience that they received from performing it in Black Church contexts, as the training ground in which their talents were honed.

Visual Culture and the Study of the Black Church

There has been an overwhelming focus on the oral/aural contributions of Black cultural traditions to the exclusion of visual culture. Art historian Lisa Gail Collins suggests in *The Art of History*,[10] that this exclusion came about through the influence of Du Bois who, while he lauded the contribution of the spirituals as significant, was generally dismissive of the artisanal work of Black people during slavery. The lack of comparable focus on visual traditions continued throughout the twentieth century. The result has been the virtual ignoring of the significance of visual cultural production as a main strand of the study of Black cultures. This lack of focus also has extended into the study of religion. The inclusion of visual culture in the study of Black religion, however, would add to the examination of the richness of expressive culture.

BLACK CONGREGATIONAL STUDIES

Community, Church Work, Culture, and Crisis

The historical Black Church, from its early days in the eighteenth and nineteenth centuries, in the United States, served spiritual, political, economic, social, and cultural needs. As the single most autonomous institution in Black communities to emerge from slavery and racialized segregation, the Black Church served important civic and political functions. The Black Church was the only space in which Black people could define their spirituality on their own terms. Importantly, too, the Black Church provided social and cultural spaces for the broader community such as schools and libraries, and afforded Black men, women, and children the opportunity to develop leadership skills otherwise denied in the broader society. During the civil rights era, from the mid 1950s to the early 1970s, the Black Church, especially in the South, was an important mobilizing force in Black community political activity. The political leadership and ministry of Dr. Martin Luther King, Jr., himself a Black Church leader, serves as an important symbol of the American civil rights movement. However, the Black Church of the civil rights era has given way to a variety of different forms of church community organizations that have emerged in response to the shifts and changes within Black communities and in the wider society. These include:

- Desegregation in the post–civil rights eras
- Increased social disparity between rich and poor in Black communities
- Urbanization
- Secularization
- Increased immigration of Black people from the Caribbean, Africa, and Latin America and the re-establishment in the United States of African Diasporan religious traditions (including forms of Black Christianity, traditional African, and African-derived traditions)

These changes, as will be discussed in the conclusion of this chapter, have had profound impact on the contemporary development of the Black Church.

Gender and Sexuality in Community/Church Leadership

Questions of authority, leadership, gender, and sexual identity and the role of women have emerged as critical in contemporary Black Church development. How can the Black Church be so politically assertive on questions of race and representation yet remain conservative (and, in some cases, reactionary) regarding gender, the role of women, and sexual orientation as they relate to church membership and leadership? The answer to these related questions is complex and is rooted in the intersection between conservative theologies and wider Black community mores and values and perspectives on race, gender, and sexuality.

Sexism within the Black Church continues to be a major issue of concern. The term *sexism* refers to systemic discriminatory practices and attitudes that devalue and denigrate women within society. Sexism is related to *patriarchy*, a term derived from Latin for "rule of the father." Patriarchy is a complex system of social relations that operate in private and public contexts and across social institutions in which power is allocated to men over women and children. Patriarchal social relations are characterized not only by an unequal share of power that privileges men over women but also by ideologies that justify these practices as either inevitable and/or natural. Religion is one of the areas in which sexist practices have been reinforced with the authority of sacred text. These same practices and the attitudes that support them have also been challenged. The Black Church, like other religious traditions, has been the site of both sexist practices and attitudes that support them as well as a place in which the same have been challenged.

In many Black churches, women constitute the majority of regular congregants and yet are relatively few in number in positions of leadership within their churches. Some Baptist, Pentecostal, and Holiness congregations specifically prohibit women from preaching in the pulpit and serving as pastor of a church. Nevertheless, while there are formal and informal proscriptions in these congregations that inhibit Black women's participation in church leadership, Black women have contributed to the development, organization, and growth of Black Church life in multiple capacities as theologians, musicians, educators, and organizers.

For example, Cheryl Townsend Gilkes's discussion of the role of Black Church mothers underscores the importance of Black women's leadership roles within the church context and their impact in the wider community.[11] As "mothers of the church" Black women have been able to **nurture** Black congregational and community life through the performance of tasks and duties, such as the preparation and serving of communal meals, fundraising, and children's education, which have often been undervalued in their importance to sustaining Black religious and communal life.

Relatedly, Black Womanist theologians such as Katie Geneva Cannon and Delores Williams have challenged sexism within Black Church life by calling for a reevaluation of methodologies and assumptions about Black Christianity from the perspective of Black women's historical and contemporary experiences. Their work has opened a space for critical inquiries of gender and its intersection with race and class as an important focus for theological discourse. However, Womanist discourse remains largely silent on explicit discussions of issues of sexuality and sexual orientation.

Kelly Brown Douglas's groundbreaking work *Sexuality and the Black Church: A Womanist Perspective* called for concerted Black theological reflection concerning sexuality and gender.[12] In this work, Douglas used a Womanist approach to understand the silence around Black sexuality in the Black Church and community. In doing so, Douglas aimed to break the silence and contribute to discussions about sexuality within the Black Church and wider community with particular attention to homophobia and sexism. The ideologies of *heterosexism* and *homophobia* support the silence around sexuality. Heterosexism is an ideology that assumes the naturalness of male-female sexual relations while relegating all other relations as abnormal or unnatural. Homophobia is the hatred and fear of homosexuality and homosexuals, and indicates the harboring of prejudicial attitudes and behaviors. For Douglas continued silence couched in the ideologies of heterosexism and homophobia are tantamount to condemning Black gay, lesbian, bisexual, and transgendered persons to marginality within the Black Church. Douglas notes that the reticence for dealing with HIV/AIDS by the Black Church is related to the association of the disease with homosexuality. Thus, silence about HIV/AIDS is part of a larger theological silence about sexuality.[13]

Responses to the call for bringing questions of gender and sexuality to the fore in Black Church contexts range from greater inclusivity of individuals of diverse sexual orientations in already-established congregations to the creation of Black churches that primarily address the needs of gay, lesbian, bisexual, and transgendered members. Unity Fellowship Church, founded by Archbishop Carl Bean, is a church in which African American gays, lesbians, bisexuals, transgendered, and intersexed people are explicitly welcomed in a worship context that situates itself within Black Church traditions. The first meetings of Unity Fellowship Church took place in the Los Angeles home of Bean in 1982. By 1985, the church was meeting in a public space and had received governmental non-profit status. In 1990, the Unity Fellowship Church Movement was established as a non-profit organization. Since then, Unity Fellowship Churches have been established in other major U.S. cities. In addition to the Los Angeles Mother Church, there are Unity Fellowship churches in: Riverside, Long Beach, and San Diego in California; Newark, New Jersey; Baltimore, Maryland; Washington, D.C.; Brooklyn, New York; Charlotte, North Carolina; Detroit, Michigan; and Atlanta, Georgia. The aim of the church is to provide a welcoming space for African Americans whose sexual and gender identity has historically been unwelcome in the Black Church. As expressed in its mission statement on the church's website: "The primary work of the UFCM [Unity Fellowship Church Movement] is to proclaim the SACREDNESS OF ALL LIFE, thus focusing on empowering those who have been oppressed and made to feel shame."[14] The Unity Fellowship Church Movement is devoted to carrying out a variety of social programs that engage the broader community. These include the establishment of a mass choir, and urban outreach ministries that address social issues such as providing education about HIV/AIDS.

DIASPORAN STUDIES AND THE BLACK CHURCH

The Black Atlantic, the Middle Passage, and Religious Experience

The term *diaspora* originates from Greek and refers to "dispersal." It has historically been used with reference to Jewish history and the multiple ancient and modern migrations of Jews throughout the world. The term has more recently been applied to discussions of experiences of migration of peoples, cultures, and technologies associated with the growth of modernity and capitalism as a global economic system. Black religion and culture in the Americas can be seen as one of the *modern diasporas*, involving notions of community and identity that are trans- and multinational.

Multiple migrations formed Black identities in the Americas. As discussed in the first chapter, the Middle Passage serves as a central metaphor of dislocation, exile, and intercultural contact. The Middle Passage takes its name from the term used to refer to the second leg of the trans-Atlantic ocean voyage, by ship, of the triangular trade system that linked the economies and cultures of Western Europe, Africa, and the Americas. The first leg of the triangular trade system was comprised of ships that left the ports of Western European cities such as Liverpool in Northern England and sailed down the coast of West Africa where manufactured goods were sold. The second leg of the voyage, the infamous *Middle Passage*, was the forced transportation of Africans purchased for slavery in North, Central, and South America, and the Caribbean. The final and third leg of the triangular trade system was the return voyage from the Americas to Western Europe with the agricultural produce such as cotton, indigo, sugar, and its byproducts such as rum and molasses, for Western Europe. The Middle Passage, however, has become a metaphor for more than the trans-Atlantic ocean voyage.

British sociologist Paul Gilroy proposed an influential example of the use of this metaphor with his notion of the **"Black Atlantic."**[15] For Gilroy, the Black Atlantic represents African Diasporan experiences through putting an emphasis on the centrality of movement, migration, and cultural exchange. Regarding the latter, Gilroy argues against what he calls "ethnic absolutism,"[16] which is the tendency to conceptualize social and cultural development in one area of the world as occurring in relative isolation from influences of other cultures. Instead, Gilroy calls for a perspective that takes into consideration the ways in which people from diverse areas of the world influenced each other historically, and continue to do so today.

Even in conditions of enforced separation such as racial segregation during slavery and colonialism, people of African and European descent influenced each other's linguistic, religious, and other cultural traditions. The idea then of a "European" history that developed separately and autonomously from "African" and "American" histories is refuted. Anthropologist Eric Wolf[17] made a similar point in his call for perspectives on the study of culture that take into consideration the impact of cultural exchange and adaptation, and the interrelatedness of events in different areas of the world. The title of Wolf's study, *Europe and the People Without History*, was an ironic critique of the idea that global history is essentially a European enterprise into which non-Europeans are drawn through their contact with Europe.

Migration and Reconstruction of Religious Traditions

One of the main questions that have preoccupied scholars of Black religion and culture in the Americas is the question of origin and the autonomy of these traditions. Simply stated: Are New World African cultures a continuation of traditions that originate in Africa? If so, which ones in particular? Or, are New World African cultures entirely *new* phenomena? Anthropologists Sidney Mintz and Richard Price,[18] in their essay exploring the origins of New World African cultures, suggest that the point of origin and the subsequent development of these traditions is a result of the slave trade and the Transatlantic Middle Passage. To exemplify their viewpoint, Mintz and Price suggest that the originating moment of New World African religion was when an African aboard a slave ship offered ritual assistance to another African from a different ethnic group. This metaphorical starting point emphasizes the intercultural interactions not only between Africans and Europeans but also between Africans themselves, as well as the impact of race and racism and their interplay with political and economic relations of power on the development of Black religion and culture. Thus, the traditions created by Africans and their descendants in the Americas were new traditions involving new forms of identity and community formation that referenced multiple cultural, social, and geographic locations.

Because of post–Second-World-War migration of people of African descent, religious traditions that developed in Africa, the Caribbean, and South America have been brought to major cities in the United States, Canada, and Western Europe. These transported traditions include African traditional religions and African-derived traditions such as *Yoruban* **Orisha** as well as forms of Christianity, such as the African nativist churches developed in Africa, and indigenous Christianities of the Caribbean and Latin America.[19]

Included among the latter group are the Converted and Spiritual Baptist faith, two related African Caribbean religions that originated in the Caribbean island nations of St. Vincent and Trinidad and Tobago. Practitioners of these traditions have emigrated from the Caribbean, in the post–Second-World-War era, to large metropolitan cities such as New York City, Boston, and Washington, D. C., in the United States; as well as London, England, and Toronto, Canada.[20] The Converted religion, like the Spiritual Baptist faith, developed out of enslaved Africans' and their descendants' interpretation of Christianity under conditions of enslavement and colonialism in the Caribbean. Both religions can be viewed as forms of African Caribbean Christianity that incorporate ritual practices, beliefs, and symbols from both African and Euro-American Christian traditions. Such religious adaptation is indicative of the ways in which Black people, in response to the repression of traditional African religion and culture by law and custom, responded in creative ways to express their religiosity by borrowing and reinterpreting beliefs and practices from Euro-American Christianity on their own terms.

The Politics of Pluralism

The recent emigration of practitioners of traditions such as the Spiritual Baptist faith and the Converted to major urban centers has changed the landscape of Black religious experience, and Black Christianity in particular. All-encompassing characterizations of Black religious experience as the "Black Church" are inadequate to account for the religious diversity that actually exists. In particular, the existence of these faith communities challenges definitions of the Black Church as specifically a Southern, Black, United States-based phenomenon.

For example, Grant African Methodist Episcopal Church is a historic Black Church in the city of Toronto whose initial congregation in the nineteenth century was composed exclusively of African Americans who had escaped slavery on the Underground Railroad from the United States to Canada, and their descendants. Its contemporary twenty-first century congregation, however, is reflective of post–Second-World-War migration trends to large North American cities like Toronto, Canada, and Brooklyn, New York, in which the Black population is linguistically, ethnically, and culturally diverse, including those with recent origins in the Caribbean, Latin America, Western Europe, and Africa.

Why does the overwhelming tendency to locate Black religious experience in the United States as fundamentally rooted in the Black Church exist in the first place? Three related reasons link the tendency to characterize African American religious experience under the rubric of the "Black Church."[21] First, until recently, African Americans and African American culture received very little attention in the main areas of knowledge production and dissemination, namely the mainstream media, education, academic disciplines in the humanities and social sciences, and what Baer and Singer term, "polite society," or the cultural elite in the United States. Second, when mainstream white institutions focused upon African Americans and African American culture, the emphasis was on the production of a singular representation of Black experiences, reinforcing racial stereotypes. This, in turn, served to support dominant power relations in which Blacks were subordinate to whites, economically. Third, Baer and Singer point to the role of African American intellectuals in contributing to a monolithic image of Blackness out of the need to respond "to threat and slander from the dominant society" by stressing Black "unity and commonality" and not emphasizing the diversity of Black experiences.[22] All three factors have contributed to a tendency to characterize African American religion as the "Black Church." This characterization, however, created a monolithic image of Black religious experience that obscured the reality of religious diversity in Black communities, historically, and in contemporary contexts.

Pan-Africanism, as expressed in the early-twentieth-century by scholar and activist W.E.B. Du Bois and United Negro Improvement Association founder Marcus Garvey, focused on the liberation of peoples of African descent through concerted political activity that challenged the *status quo* of Black subjugation and disenfranchisement based on the racist ideology of inherent Black inferiority. It also included linking the political aims of Black people for self-determination and human dignity in the United States with Black people elsewhere in the Americas, and indeed the wider world, including continental Africa. What can be called neo–Pan-Africanist sentiments are expressed in the outreach activities and ministries of Black churches that specifically espouse theologies of liberation; these theologies advocate not necessarily Black *unity* but *solidarity* with social justice movements across regional, ethnic, geographic, and cultural boundaries.

SUMMARY

Historically, the Black Church was the most autonomous institution in Black community life. As such, it was the institution through which Black people could achieve affirming definitions of self in the face of a wider culture in which they were denigrated by custom and law during the Jim and Jane Crow period. This historical legacy has extended to the present day making the Black Church a vital component of contemporary Black community life.

The chapter has presented an approach to the study of the Black Church that grounds it in social and cultural contexts. That is to say, rather than seeing the Black Church as separate and apart from everyday life experiences, including political and social questions, the Black Church is viewed as being shaped and informed by responses to these issues. Thus, the Black Church is a dynamic social institution that has changed through its evolution in response to shifts in the Black and wider communities. In the past, the Black Church was at the forefront of the struggle for civil rights in the United States.

Today, one of the biggest challenges faced by the Black Church concerns issues of gender and sexuality, specifically the role of women and gay, lesbian, bisexual, and transgendered persons. The Black Church has historically been silent on the issues of sexuality; adopting, for the most part, a variation of "don't ask, don't tell," with respect to sexual identities other than heterosexual. There is, however, a growing challenge for the Black Church to break the silence on issues of sexuality and gender. Theologians such as Kelly Brown Douglas have called for the inclusion of discussions of sexuality and gender as an integral part of theological reflection on Black religiosity. As well, the founding of churches, such as the Unity Fellowship Movement, provides a worship experience based in the traditions of the Black Church.

The chapter concluded by situating the Black Church as part of a larger African Diaspora. This innovative approach to studying the Black Church suggests it is part of a Black Atlantic world shaped by interactions between Africa, Europe, and the Americas. Studies of the Black Church from this perspective must extend beyond the continental United States to take into consideration the migration and the development of Black religiosity that includes other experiences of Black Christianity.

In summary, the Black Church is a dynamic institution that has been an integral component of Black community development in the United States. Contemporary developments in the Black Church reflect the emergence of transnational migration and challenges for inclusion of gender and sexual diversity.

BIOGRAPHIES

Zora Neale Hurston (1891–1960)

The author of the acclaimed novel *Their Eyes Were Watching God*, African American folklorist, novelist, and anthropologist Zora Neale Hurston was born in Notasulga, Alabama, in 1891. Hurston's undergraduate education included studies at Howard University in Washington, D.C., and Barnard College in New York City, from which she received a B.A. in anthropology in 1927. Hurston studied with acclaimed anthropologist Franz Boas at Columbia University. Her work concentrated on Southern African American cultural traditions. Her pioneering anthropological work in the study of Southern African American cultural traditions and folklore is notable for its sensitivity to, and valuation of, these traditions as worthy and valuable contributions from African Americans. Although she died in obscurity and poverty, interest in her work revived in the 1970s largely through the efforts of writer Alice Walker.

C. Eric Lincoln (1924–2000)

Charles Eric Lincoln was born in 1924 in Athens, Alabama. A sociologist, ordained Methodist minister, influential educator, and prolific writer, Lincoln was dedicated to studying African American religious and cultural experience. An author or editor of more than twenty books, he is famed for his sustained and detailed study of the Nation of Islam and the Black Church in the United States. Utilizing sociological analysis, Lincoln's pioneering book, *The Black Muslims in America* (1961), discussed the Nation of Islam as a social and religious movement. His work in this area was the first sustained study of Islam and African Americans and paved the way for legitimizing the study of Black religious experience in the academy. Lincoln's other well-known work, *The Black Church in African American Experience* (1990), was co-authored with former student Lawrence Mamiya.

STUDY QUESTIONS

1. Why is it more appropriate to characterize the Black Church as a social institution rather than a denomination?
2. Identify the key elements of a critical approach to understanding the Black Church in the context of Black religion, culture, and society.
3. What impact does a Womanist approach to religion and society have on the study of the Black Church?
4. Citing specific examples, discuss the ways in which the Black Church is shaped and influenced by its interaction with events and trends that take place in Black communities and the wider society.
5. What has been the impact of changes in U.S. society in the post–civil rights era on the Black Church?
6. In what ways has social activism in the Black Church influenced Black community development and in turn the wider society?
7. Identify and discuss the challenges of pastoring a church with a diverse ethnic, cultural, and linguistic population. How do such

churches challenge and expand conceptualizations of the Black Church as a Black community institution?

8. How would a consideration of visual cultural elements influence your understanding of the worship experience in the Black Church?

9. In what ways do issues concerning gender and sexuality challenge the future development of the Black Church? How do these issues mirror wider social concerns?

ESSENTIAL TEXTS

- *The Black Church in the African American Experience* by C. Eric Lincoln and Lawrence Mamiya
- *Black Gods of the Metropolis: Negro Religious Cults of the Urban North* by Arthur Huff Fauset
- *The Negro Church* by W.E.B. Du Bois
- *The Negro Church in America* by E. Franklin Frazier

What, then, is the word of the religion of Jesus to those who stand with their backs against the wall? There must be the clearest possible understanding of the anatomy of the issues facing them. They must recognize fear, deception, hatred, each for what it is. Once having done this, they must learn how to destroy these or to render themselves immune to their domination. In so great an undertaking it will become increasingly clear that the contradictions of life are not ultimate. The disinherited will know for themselves that there is a Spirit at work in life and in the hearts of [human beings] which is committed to overcoming the world.

—Howard Thurman

AFRICAN AMERICAN CHRISTIAN SOCIAL ETHICS

INTRODUCTION

This chapter explores the nature of **African American Christian social ethics** as it relates to the moral tradition of the Black Church within the context of the Black community. As the previous chapters have illustrated, the Black Church has instilled a deep belief and comfort in Black people that God has the power, if need be, "to part the waters" and reveal the way to freedom. Equal to that belief, however, is an ethic within the Black Church that people must do their part by entering into a new field of moral vision. This new way of thinking, being, and doing must be such that people realize that they are actually expected to be moral agents who find the willing courage to proceed on the path of liberation that God has set before them.

African American Christian social ethics is the study of the essential virtues, moral approaches, and liberating vision unique to African Americans that aid in preserving and promoting the community by making visible the foundational role that identity (who one is) plays in one's thoughts (what one thinks) and actions (what one does). Simply put, it is the study of this liberating faith in action.

Although African American Christian social ethics concerns itself with a liberative agenda, this is not to say that the Black Church has acted consistently in this fashion. While the actual customs of Black Christians and the moral practices of the Black Church often have been liberative, to say so is not to claim that it describes the totality of the Black Church's practices in the past or present. Thus, social ethics in the

Black Church tradition must be prescriptive in character. Unlike the sociology of the Black Church, whose aim is principally to describe, African American Christian social ethics draws upon Black theologies to envision practices and perspectives that are liberative and to suggest how the Black Church can embrace them more wholeheartedly. Thus, African American Christian social ethics is both a constructive endeavor that focuses on the moral formation and social transformation of Black people on an individual and communal basis, as well as a resistance movement that continues the liberating agenda to correct American society's oppressive tendencies and its continued efforts to dictate the moral rules and ethical practices of Black people. We will fully explicate this endeavor by looking at three major approaches within African American Christian social ethics: (1) **Virtue ethics**, (2) **Liberation ethics**, and (3) **Womanist ethics**. For the Black Church, ethical meaning is a critical tool for self-reflection that is grounded in the contextual realities of the African American experience. Before introducing the three approaches within this field, therefore, we must take a closer look at the early African American moral context as experienced through and shaped by chattel slavery.

CHATTEL SLAVERY AND THE AFRICAN AMERICAN MORAL CONDITION

To understand African American Christian social ethics, one must first confront the moral crisis posed by chattel slavery. As historian Albert Raboteau attests, when Africans were brought into slavery, they were not merely transported from one world to another—one culture to another— but rather they and their humanity were transformed. They were torn away from the structures and systems that had ordered their lives along the lines of African tradition and tribalism and forced into being subjugated people of doubtful human status.[1] Because culture helps people to unify, resist, and thrive, all of the actions of the white enslavers—severing linguistic groups, breaking up tribes, tearing apart families—had as their goal the dehumanization of African persons and the erasure of their culture. Nevertheless, the African ethos persisted, and enslaved Africans passed it on to their descendants. One of the indestructible yet adaptable characteristics of enslaved Africans' culture was linking their African past to their American present through their religion.[2] Since the Middle Passage, the interplay between slavery and Christianity has been the most central and critical moral dilemma of the modern era. This is especially important to the Black Christian tradition because the African holocaust (referred to as *Maafa*—the buying, selling, and extermination of human beings of African descent) is a crisis of epic proportions that still has not been adequately or largely attended to by white mainline Christianity or white American society at large. In this most crucial example taken from the experience of African peoples, if white Christianity was not, in fact, synonymous with the culture of white slave control and domination, it most clearly followed this white supremacist culture in the way it condoned and was complicit in the dehumanizing of Black peoples. Consequently, white slave traders found no moral or spiritual contradiction in professing a Christianity that extolled a God of love and peace while at the same time engaging in the heinous and violent white supremacist culture of enslaving African peoples. In contradistinction, this not only has historical significance but ethical significance as well for understanding the formation of Black Christianity in America. Since it is necessary to nourish people by a communal ethos in order for them to become fully human, an imposed exile necessitates the formation of a substitute community, and, as we have seen, that has been one of the major functions of the Black Church.

THE BLACK CHURCH AS A SURROGATE WORLD

As a social institution, the Black Church has often been the moral cement for the Black community.[3] Whereas we have previously described the Black Church's origins in terms of the *hush harbor* and the *invisible institution*, let us now introduce the concept of the Black Church as a *surrogate world*, a place that encourages **human flourishing** in the midst of seemingly insurmountable odds. Having a profound concern for the painful realities of white supremacy and American racism, the Black Church extols an abiding faith in a bright future where racial justice will replace racism. This faith not only represents an eschatological vision but also a lived reality of surrogacy. Where society has rendered Black people virtually invisible, the Black Church has instilled in them a sense of somebodyness.[4] When things have been bleak, the Black Church has been an instrument of hope. Where Black people have often been left hungry and homeless, the Black Church has provided food and shelter. Where society created social divisions for Black people, the Black Church has formed a base of solidarity.

However, there is still much for the Black Church to address in order to claim its surrogate status in both the private (matters of Black family dynamics, gender politics, sexuality, and identity formation) and public (societal concerns such as government, education, healthcare, the marketplace, and prison) realms of the African American experience. Toward this end, the visionary work of ethicist Peter Paris's exploration of the social teaching of Black churches considers how Black Christianity optimally "encourages, sustains, and promotes (in varying good ways) political action as a necessary corollary, that is, as an action aimed at the creation of a good public realm." Paris argues that the Black Church serves as a surrogate world that emphasizes the quality of life and human fulfillment in "which all of its citizens have the experience of freedom and the necessary resources for the full actualization of their potentialities."[5]

As ethicist Samuel K. Roberts has noted, because the life of slavery was contingent and dependent on the white slave master, the enslaved Africans' establishment of their own system of virtue was both community affirming and liberative.[6] Although it may not have freed them from their physical bonds, it freed them from the degraded and demoralized moral state that trapped them in radical uncertainty. It gave them a new identity and ethos that permitted a surrogate world and community to flourish. Realizing the oppressive context in which the African American community finds itself, the ethical framework of most Black people is rooted in a double consciousness that pervades their worldview. From such a perspective, African Americans seek to identify and cultivate a set of **virtues** that reflect who they are and how they yearn to be treated. Therefore, African American Christian social ethics provides the means by which Black people's consciousness and sense of virtue work together to inform ethical judgments that might result in the best life choices available to them and that will to lead to their liberation. Nevertheless, the Black community faces a paradox: while the code of ethics professed by the Black Church tradition is simple, it is by no means easy.

Unlike African life, which was concerned primarily with the preservation and flourishing of community, African American life was mired in the bondage of slavery. For that reason, the defining characteristic of

African American Christian social ethics has been a quest for liberation. Whereas, Black theology in general regards liberation as a sacred end, for ethics, liberation is merely a moral means that is vital for the attainment of our flourishing. As a system of moral guidance cultivated by Americans of African descent, the origins of African American Christian ethics lie in the African heritage of our ancestors, as modified by their enculturation of Christian beliefs and American ideals and their rejection of the *status quo*—with its explicit assertions that people of African descent were inferior, subhuman, and unworthy of being regarded as part of the moral universe. Unfortunately, every social device available has been used to make the moral exclusion and social devaluation of African Americans normative and, thus, an implicit civic duty. Philosopher of religion Cornel West has named this process "institutionalized terrorism,"[7] among the many tools of which one finds slavery, rape, lynching, segregation, economic exploitation, cultural appropriation, unlawful imprisonment, racial profiling—and, to top it all off, the misuse of Christian sacred rhetoric as the divine legitimization of such acts. Yet, with great consistency, white supremacy has been met with the **moral wisdom** of the Black Church declaring Black people to be children of God and governing themselves accordingly.[8] Consequently, Black moral wisdom has often led to massive social action in the forms of Black-led revolts and Black Christian protests against slavery, legal segregation, racial discrimination, and Christian racism. Based on the liberating teachings of Jesus, the Black Church has cultivated an ethical system that inspires all people of good conscience and deep faith to act on behalf of social justice.[9]

Central to this African American moral perspective is the common belief that the origin and humanity of all individuals is sacred and equal. This is the real meaning of the Black Christian principle, "the parenthood of God and the family of humanity." This belief is consistent with the African American understanding of Christian faith as illustrated in the Bible and implicit in the American ideals expressed in the Declaration of Independence and the U.S. Constitution.[10] Though reformed in an American context, African American Christian social ethics is rooted in an African worldview and moral tradition. The ethics of Christians of African descent were formed by their African heritage, even prior to their encounter with white racism and white Christianity in the Western world. It is this syncretized African American worldview that makes sacred rhetoric become sacred reality, because it inspires the oppressed to struggle even harder for the freedom, justice, and equality that have been promised to them not only in the Word but also through their experience of God. This dimension of African American **moral reasoning** "mediates an understanding of God as a God of freedom and not of slavery, while at the same time mediating a logic that recognizes African traditional religious sensibilities and the larger struggle of the black community to shape its own culture."[11]

THE BLACK CHURCH AND THE AFRICAN AMERICAN MORAL DILEMMA

A central component of any culture, and especially African American culture, is its notion of morality. For African American Christians, morality and religion are synonymous, or at least inseparable;[12] therefore, central to the Black Church tradition has been its concern with lived morality—its ethics. At its most fundamental level, this African American Christian social ethic "is a search in part for a new style of moral being, a new consciousness about black folk that can reshape the old values and stereotypes of the past in light of current ethical reality."[13] Indeed, what makes the Black Church tradition exceptional is its ability to take seriously the ethical queries: "What ought I/we do?" and "How do I/we know (what, how, when, and why)?" In his analysis of the African American moral tradition, Samuel Roberts challenges us to concentrate on the concept of virtue as a historic benchmark with African American social and spiritual consciousness. Roberts states:

> African Americans who were engaged in the struggle against slavery and in the struggle to affirm racial uplift in the years after slavery held to a concept of virtue that may be defined in this way: virtue became a vision of a divinely ordered life that impelled its adherents to struggle against the injustice of slavery and to forge communities and structures that could ensure the development of the furthest moral and material possibilities of African Americans.[14]

Roberts believes that by understanding ourselves as people of virtue, African Americans are resisting white supremacy rather than merely reacting to it, thus forging our own individual and communal identity.

The African Moral Sphere and Our Modification of It

Because they derive from the virtues of African cultures, many of the moral characteristics of the African American community are unique within the North American context. The similarities between the morality of the African American community and the African moral tradition lie not only in shared virtues but also in the framework of ethical reasoning. For example, "[t]he basic building blocks for an African and African American social ethic are derived from and reflective of the dynamic structural unity among the four constitutive spheres of African experience, namely: God, community, family, person."[15] These four foundational spheres of experience inform the moral thought of both African and African American peoples, in that they arise out of the problems of daily experience. This function is consistent with the African ethical framework, for "[t]he preservation and promotion of community is the paramount goal of African peoples in all spheres of life."[16] Thus the moral dilemma—or problem of theodicy, if you will—that faces African American people, past and present, is how to reconcile the vision and understanding of a loving and liberating God with a lived experience in America that challenges their humanity and confronts them with racism and discrimination at every turn.

To appreciate the severity of this moral dilemma, it is necessary to survey the troubled nature of what it means to be both African and American—coined "double consciousness" by W.E.B. Du Bois. For the overwhelming majority of Blacks living in a society and culture that systematically dehumanizes and vilifies them, the ethical queries—"Who should I be?" and "What must we do?" —become hauntingly urgent questions that must be answered for the sake of their safety, sanity, and survival. Because of the devastating effects of the **normative gaze**, double consciousness often gives way to various expressions of Black nihilism (a perpetual sense that life is meaningless). It is only by exposing and confronting such racist ideals that the first, and most crucial, step to Black liberation can be realized.[17] African Americans must first correct their ethical orientation by turning away from the normative gaze of white supremacy—the preoccupation with how white people see them. Moral theologian Howard Thurman explains the consequences of failing to adopt this new ethical orientation:

> If an individual allows his/her worth to be determined by others, or by his/her own inadequate self-image, then one loses the freedom,

guidance, and power that comes from the self. One forfeits one's life to another, and in losing this control a person's condition changes from freedom to slavery, and one's definition changes from human too.[18]

Thurman is correct in insisting that we must define ourselves. The contribution of African American Christian social ethics is that it rejects the racist projection of white supremacy and the overly particular tribalism of traditional African worldviews. Though African and American, we are also the children of God and part of the human family, therefore properly valuing ourselves in a way that transcends culture, context, and condition.

The Moral Agency of the Oppressed

Caught in a social predicament that denies African American humanity and a religious framework that takes as central the *working power of God*, it seems that reflecting on our own moral agency—the human capacity to act or exert power over one's life—makes futile both the social survival and soul salvation of African American Christians seeking liberation. However, to think that these questions are futile is to miss the core of Black Christian moral agency. The answer to "Who is God?" (theology) and "What ought we do?" (ethics) for Black people does not deny the need to survive social oppression, nor does it reject the need for divine intervention. Rather, the answer to these questions focuses on the ethical responsibility of Black Christians to link divine justice to social justice. According to James Cone, the divine liberation of the oppressed includes in it God's election of African American people as the oppressed to fully participate with God in the struggle for freedom. Wherever social oppression and injustice are present, a need for justice is provoked. It is in those situations that an "ethic of liberation" evoked by a "God of freedom" becomes embodied by those who are otherwise considered to be weak, unworthy, and helpless.

Deep within the soul of the Black Church community, there is not only faith in a God of freedom but also commitment to exercise and practice that faith, making of it an ethic of liberation. For African American Christians, ethics is implied in theology, and, conversely, theology is made evident in ethics; to be right theologically is to be right ethically. As the Black Church moral adage goes: "You've got to talk the talk and walk the walk." For many African American Christians, God's revelation in Jesus Christ is indistinguishable from the presence of God's Spirit in Black people's struggle for humanity, from the time of slavery to the present. Preaching and practice coexist in such a way that the tendency of Black Christians has been to believe that divine revelation and the practice of ethical obedience are characteristic of a people who are determined to change their social conditions.

AFRICAN AMERICAN VIRTUE ETHICS

Turning to our first major approach, let us look more closely at virtue ethics. European American ethics and its paternalistic paradigms of theological and moral virtue have often dismissed and/or devalued Black people's experience, humanity, and character. As a community that has often been defined by a racist dominant culture, socially and morally, African Americans have responded by rejecting the labels of *inferior, amoral,* and *immoral* and created new values that align with the moral virtue necessary to survive and live. Unlike the tendency of dominant European ethics to remain within the realm of the theoretical, the study of virtue within the Black community invariably becomes linked to the practical. Thus, the preservation and promotion of the African American community is the ultimate goal of the Black Church moral tradition, while the task of African American virtue ethics is to accentuate the positive aspects of African American life rather than its limitations, and to question the contradictions evident in the pursuance of its communal goal.

The study of virtue within the Black community can be best understood when contextualized within the field of African American virtue ethics. Whereas **dominant/normative ethics** requires action driven by guidelines alone, virtue ethics requires that our action also be driven by how it reflects our moral character. In short, "there can be no good people apart from the doing of good actions."[19] Virtue ethics not only creates synergy between thought and action, but also judges the quality of action insofar as it represents the moral excellence of both person and community. As Peter Paris contends, "[I]n virtue ethics the quality of a person's character determines the quality of that person's actions and vice versa. The circularity of this argument is important because it demonstrates the relation of being and doing."[20] Whereas the classical virtue tradition (i.e., Aristotelian ethics) values thinking and doing, African American virtue ethics claims that our thinking and doing are intrinsically linked to the essence of our very being, in that we are fearfully and wonderfully made in the image of God (the **Imago Dei**).

The unique contribution of African American virtue ethics is its insistence that theological virtue take into consideration the role that the essence of one's *being* plays in one's ethical formation. African American virtue ethics is the study of the essential virtues and moral vision unique to African peoples that aid in preserving and promoting the community by making visible the foundational role that identity (who one is) plays in one's thoughts (what one thinks) and actions (what one does). Indeed, doing virtuous things or thinking virtuously is not necessarily conclusive of one's moral virtue. Rather, one who is virtuous will do these things because it is his or her very nature.[21] In spite of the claims of inferiority and deficiency by white society, African Americans continue to love themselves, respect themselves, and value themselves as virtuous because "God don't make no junk."[22]

One of the projects of African American virtue ethics is the redefining, and, in some instances, the defining of being for the Black community. Virtue ethics develops this moral formation by focusing on the virtues necessary for sustaining the excellence of African Americans in their relation to God, community, family, and their own personhood. This approach is not essentialist; it values the dignity of African American people as a whole without negating the diversity of their cultural and religious expression and varying strides for human flourishing and self-actualization. Virtue ethics also becomes a method that allows ethicists to ascertain the particularities of Black communities' and individuals' moral character outside the normative standards of the ethical system of the dominant white society.

For those in power, all people possess the ability to freely choose their course in life. Thus everyone, regardless of social location or racial difference, is considered a self-directing agent possessing freedom and a wide range of life options and choices. Within this perspective, everyone possesses both the agency and the means to achieve desired ends that would allow them to be considered virtuous. For example, dominant Eurocentric ethics tend to define as virtues such qualities related to economic success as self-sufficiency, frugality, and efficiency. It also makes short-term suffering a desirable norm because it is believed to help build character.[23]

In contrast to this approach, African American virtue ethics argues that communities of the dispossessed (people of color, white women, poor people, and other marginalized groups) are not afforded equal opportunities to achieve social freedom or economic success, relative to their white male counterparts. Similarly, whereas the *universalizing* virtues of industry and suffering may be means that bring about desired ends for members of the privileged class, these attributes do not result in the desired ends of success or freedom for members of communities of the dispossessed. Indeed, a double standard is imposed on African Americans, since what is seen as virtuous for the privileged class (i.e. suffering and/or sacrifice) is considered vice by the oppressed when endured by members of the communities of the dispossessed. New standards must be developed that explore and legitimate the peculiar virtues of the African American community and churches.

Africans were taken from their native land and brought to the Americas under severe physical and social conditions of dehumanization; thus, freedom became the primary ethical imperative. Within this context, hear Roberts again:

> [V]irtue became a vision of a divinely ordered life that impelled its adherents to struggle against the injustice of slavery and to forge communities and structures that could ensure the development of the furthest moral and material possibilities for African Americans.

Thus, during slavery, living a life of virtue became one of the greatest tools enslaved Africans had in their struggle against a system that sought to deny them full humanity. A life based on the virtues of freedom and justice "held out the promise of a life of self-possession, a life lived in pursuit of actions consistent with a free person's conceived good end or purpose in life."[24]

As the enslaved Africans worked and made a home in this land of oppression, the Black Church became the primary center not only for community development but also for self-identification. Meeting in the woods under the secrecy of night, the first Black churches became the only place in which the humanity of the enslaved was affirmed. Eventually, groups of Blacks organized and formed their own congregations and denominations, and these Black churches became paramount in the Black community. As the central institution of African American life and culture, Black churches became the crucible and model of character and virtue for the entire Black community.[25] The Black Church guided its community in the struggle for justice through the development of the moral virtue of its members. How are we to understand these moral virtues? One thorough and prominent way of doing so is to examine the six virtues of people of African descent as identified by Peter Paris and to ask the extent to which the Black Church has been a conveyor and nurturer of these virtues in its mission of promoting and preserving the community.[26] As the following chart indicates, Paris's six virtues of

African peoples are inextricably linked to contemporary moral practices of the Black Church, historical examples, and the sacred rhetoric of the Black Christian community at large.

Moral Virtues in the Black Church Tradition[27]

Moral Virtues	Definition	Moral Practice	Historical Antecedents	Sacred Rhetoric
Beneficence	Goodwill and Hospitality	Benevolent offering and Food pantry programs	Mutual Aid Associations	"Give and it shall be given back to you." (Luke 6:38)
Forbearance	Patience and Tolerance	Cross-cultural worship services	Nonviolent resistance	"Behold, I send you forth as sheep in the midst of wolves: be ye therefore wise as serpents, and harmless as doves." (Matthew 10:16)
Practical Wisdom	Common sense and Spiritual discernment	Rites of passage and Youth training programs	African Proverbs	"Train up a child in the way s/he should go, and when s/he grows old s/he will not depart from it." (Proverbs 22:6)
Improvisation	Ingenuity and Invention	Sermonic styles and Musical adaptations	Signification of spirituals	"Making a way out of no way" (Black sacred idiom)
Forgiveness	Unity and Reconciliation	"Love feast"	Public repentance of public sins	"All have sinned and fall short of the glory of God." (Romans 3:23)
Justice	Common good	Public forum for social activism	Underground railroad	"You reap what you sow." (Galatians 6:7)

Beneficence

When encountering the Black Church community, no virtue is more readily apparent than **beneficence** because it is an extension of the African and African American ongoing imperative of building community. Beneficence is the extension of hospitality to people both within and outside of the community. "Benevolent offerings" are routinely collected during Black Church worship services and used to provide direct financial support to those in dire need. "Food pantry programs" are a crucial element of Black Church ministry, formed to feed the elderly, college students, and struggling families. Black communities have practiced self-sustaining beneficence throughout their history, as exemplified by the formation of informal mutual aid societies and formal social maintenance organizations designed to provide economic support, social services, and human resources that otherwise would be unavailable. The scriptural foundation of beneficence is grounded in the Christian expression of mutuality wherein that which is given will ultimately be returned, thus ensuring ongoing replenishment for and restoration of the entire community.

Forbearance

Forbearance is the African American practice of patience and tolerance, in order to preserve and express appreciation for life in the midst of life-threatening realities. Given that African Americans function and exist in a racist society, the practice of forbearance as a mode of survival is an ongoing reality. As it has fulfilled its role as mediator between the African American community and white society, the Black Church has extolled forbearance as a virtue vital to promoting both racial harmony and Black welfare. Cross-cultural worship services, which, for the Black Church, are often designed to bring together white and Black congregations in the wake of racial tensions in order to promote racial tolerance or reconciliation, are examples of an organized practice of forbearance by the Black Church. The practice of nonviolent resistance, as a form of forbearance, was fundamental for the realization of desegregation during the civil rights movement. Forbearance should not be misconstrued as passivity or complacency, but rather as an illustration of the ability of the Black community, when necessary, to heed scriptural wisdom by being "wise as serpents and innocent as doves" (Matt. 10:16).

Practical Wisdom

Practical wisdom is the virtue that serves as the basis of African American moral reasoning. It is the extraordinary knowledge of ordinary

African American people, typically referred to as "common sense," "spiritual discernment," or the "wisdom of the elders." Practical wisdom plays a vital role in the religious upbringing of children. The Black Church conveys practical wisdom to its children and youth through intentionally designed rituals and mentoring programs, such as rites of passage ceremonies and youth religious training programs such as: BTU (Baptist Training Union), YPWW (Young People Willing Workers), and YPD (Young People's and Children's Division). As they learn basic Bible beliefs and religious doctrine, build social skills, and mature spiritually through these events and programs, the young are molded as future leaders of the church and society, and benefit from the teaching and guidance of older, more experienced church members. African proverbs convey from one generation to the next the accumulated knowledge of life gained through cultural experience. The scriptural assurance of practical wisdom as a virtue is that the soundest investment the Black community can make is in the development and formation of its youth.

Improvisation

Improvisation represents the "something out of nothing" ethos exhibited through the ingenuity and creativity of Black people necessary for meeting the community's needs. The virtue of improvisation is the mixing of the old and the new, tradition and novelty, for the sake of communal survival, inspiration, and flourishing. Improvisation can also be considered as the driving force behind much of African American culture, in that the community has had to rely upon its own ability to respond immediately and urgently with spontaneous solutions that verge on the miraculous. The sacred reference, "making a way out of no way," is used not only as a motivational phrase but as a moral imperative for evoking this virtue in action as commonly illustrated in Black sermons and music. The sermonic styles and musical adaptations found within the Black Church display how an art form can simultaneously serve not only as artistic expression of Christian worship but also as political rhetoric or social commentary used to evoke social awareness or political protest. The spirituals sung during chattel slavery are historical illustrations of improvisation because these songs not only expressed spiritual transformation and transcendence but also communicated instructions for revolutionary acts with the utmost urgency for obtaining freedom.

Forgiveness

Forgiveness is the habitual exercise of fostering relationships with others while attempting to resolve the tensions of a divided community. As an effective means for seeking restoration and spiritual balance, forgiveness is synonymous with reconciliation. Instead of being a goal in and of itself, forgiveness is a vital process for moral growth and communal transformation within the Black Church community. The giving and obtaining of forgiveness are important aspects of life in the Black Church as a reflection of good standing, right relationship, religious piety, and social conscience. While private forgiveness is valued within Christian life, public forgiveness is crucial within Black Christianity due to its communal emphasis. The "love-feast" serves as a suitable example of this virtue. During a special worship service scheduled prior to taking Communion, the object of the love-feast service within the African Methodist Episcopal (AME) tradition is to have members examine their hearts and then seek forgiveness from members toward whom they might have any discord or ill-will. They do this so they may partake of the Lord's Supper with a clean heart. Certain acts have historically necessitated public acts of contrition in order to receive a sense of pardoning from the community. Because teenage pregnancy is a result of fornication, for example, such acts have historically been considered as public sins and thus bring an obvious reproach to the cause of Christianity and the politics of respectability prized by conservative, traditional Black Christian communities. In such instances, the congregation would require that a public confession be made before the entire church so that the "sinner could be restored into the fold." Knowing that each person is fallible in his or her own right, Black Christians take seriously the scriptural mandate to forgive in hopes that they too shall be extended the same measure of grace.

Justice

Justice is not only akin to all of the aforementioned virtues; it is actually the culmination of them all. Justice is the ultimate virtue that has as its goal the preservation and promotion of Black communal life. Because, more than anything else, African Americans have been denied justice, the Black Church has rendered itself as a central site for discerning, articulating, and facilitating justice. By serving as a center for the advancing of literacy and education, the fostering of Black businesses, and providing advocacy on behalf of civil rights and political concerns for the Black community, Black congregations have served as refuges for Black people who were overwhelmed by an unfair and unequal world. The enactment of justice is not a request for understanding or love, but rather a demand for what is affirming of humanity and necessary for the common good. In confronting the great social ills of a particular era, such as slavery, segregation, apartheid, the prison industrial complex, and the devastation caused by Hurricane Katrina, the Black Church continuously acts as a public forum for social activism and political mobilization. Of all the aforementioned virtues, justice is the highest. Indicative of Black moral excellence, the religious expression, "reaping what you sow," resonates with what it ultimately means to be responsible for one's own actions as well as being accountable to God and community.

APPROACHES TO LIBERATION ETHICS IN THE BLACK CHURCH

Turning toward our second major approach, liberation ethics, let us look more closely at the variations of liberation found within Black churches. As previously mentioned, from its genesis the Black Church, regardless of community or context, has been intimately concerned with liberation. However, it is impossible to speak intelligibly or experientially about the Black Church, whether past or present, without also addressing its various expressions and understandings of the concept of liberation. Even within the field of African American Christian ethics, liberation has been understood in a multitude of ways, which we will examine here briefly. For example, George Kelsey believes liberation is the promise of renewal, redemption, and ultimate release from racism.[28] E. Hammond Oglesby equates liberation with social freedom.[29] Cheryl Sanders defines it in terms of spiritual and material empowerment.[30] Robert Franklin and Darryl Trimiew identify liberation as human fulfillment through social justice. In general terms, however, African American liberation ethics can best be defined as a practical moral inquiry that is centered on more than freedom from oppression; rather it is a system of moral reasoning that looks for ways to develop a just, sustainable, and participatory Black community.[31]

Outside the academy, public figures and liberation movements have also understood liberation to mean different things, including everything from emancipation to integration, human rights to civil rights, and Black power to economic power. Liberation, thus, is not only a definitive characteristic of the ethics and theology of the Black Church, but of its view of God as well. As James Cone claims, "God's election of Israel and incarnation in Christ reveal that the *liberation* of the oppressed is a part of the innermost nature of God. Liberation is not an afterthought, but the essence of divine activity."[32] From the Black Church perspective, the belief and/or faith that God not only desires freedom for the oppressed but also that God works toward this end informs not only the Black community's thoughts but its actions as well. "Thus we can say that Christian ethics is meaningless apart from God's election of the oppressed for freedom in this world. Indeed, apart from divine liberation, there would be no community and thus no Christian ethics."[33]

As essential as freedom and liberation are to the purpose and goal of the Black Church, we must understand them. If misinterpreted, they may actually hinder the ethical maturation of the Black community. As ethicist E. Hammond Oglesby has discerned,

> One of the perennial problematics inherent in the structure of Black theological discourse is the tendency by some Black thinkers to define the essence of Black Theology in terms of freedom *from* . . . "freedom from white control," "freedom from oppression and exploitation," "freedom from white racism and injustice," . . . It is my basic contention and ethical conviction that freedom is more than the absence of restraint. Indeed, the search for a unified theory of freedom would suggest to all of us that while freedom *from* is a necessary condition for human dignity and the realization of human potentiality; it alone is not sufficient. [Black Theology needs a broader] perspective of freedom which embraces . . . a freedom *for* . . . a freedom *to*; and [a] freedom that expresses itself as freedom *in community*.[34]

We should not understand liberation in the passive voice, according to which the Black community was *liberated* from racism, discrimination, sexism, and injustice. Rather, we should construe liberation in an active sense, in which the Black community is forever *liberating* in order that it may do more and be more than it has done or been before.

Forms of Liberation

As mentioned previously, since its inception, liberation has been an essential element in the belief and teachings of the Black Church, and the pursuit of liberation has taken a multiplicity of forms and methods. The following chart, informed by Robert Franklin's analysis of the typology of the political ministry of the Black Church, articulates the various ways in which liberation ethicists have interpreted the Black Church's pursuit of liberation. Even though the demarcation between these groups is often blurred because many Black leaders and groups demonstrate tendencies in more than one tradition, the differentiation between the traditions is helpful in understanding the varying approaches to achieving liberation.

MORAL APPROACHES FOR LIBERATION IN THE BLACK CHURCH TRADITION[35]

Moral Approach (Historic Figure)	Practical Means	Ultimate Ends	Scriptural Basis	God as . . .
Pragmatic Accommodationists (Joseph H. Jackson)	Assimilation	Social Order	Romans 13:1-2	Sovereign
Redemptive Nationalists (Albert Cleage)	Incidental Separatism	Ethnic Purity	1 Peter 2:9-10	Redeemer
Grassroots Revivalists (C.H. Mason)	Indifferent Separatism	Individual Salvation	Romans 12:2	Savior
Positive Thought Materialists (Daddy Grace)	Opportunism	Health/ Wealth/ Success	1 Chronicles 4:10	Provider
Contemplative Communitarians (Howard Thurman)	Reconciliation	Common Unity (Beloved Community)	Matthew 5:44-48	Love
Prophetic Radicals (Martin Luther King, Jr.)	Confrontation	Racial Equality	Luke 4:18	Liberator

Pragmatic Accommodationists

Pragmatic accommodationism is a moral approach that uses assimilation to attain social order. The accommodationists contend that the status quo is the natural order predestined by a Sovereign God, and one's civic responsibility is to yield to that order. Instead of agitating the social norms and confronting social ills (i.e., racial prejudice, class inequality, and sexual oppression), pragmatic accommodationists believe it is necessary to yield to the social and political systems in order to secure a role within society. For example, using this approach, liberation is attained by gaining economic independence through social conformity.

Redemptive Nationalists

Stemming from the Black Nationalist movement, **redemptive nationalists** seek to reclaim a separate nation (either on the North American or African continent) in order to achieve total liberation from the dehumanizing conditions of racism and discrimination that plague the American political system. This redemptive nationalist approach reflects many Black religious traditions, from Black Christian Nationalism to the Nation of Islam. This unapologetic approach aims to retain Afrocentric aesthetics and ideals, and emphasizes economic autonomy through the ownership and control of businesses in Black communities by Black people and for Black people. With God as Redeemer, redemptive nationalism claims such activity affirms and redeems Black people through empowerment. Redemptive nationalists interact with mainstream American social and political systems as little as possible in order to maintain ethnic purity.

Grassroots Revivalists

Unlike pragmatic accommodationists and prophetic radicals who often use social organizations and political mechanisms for promoting their message, **grassroots revivalists** constitute a moral approach that aims to reach the urban masses through face-to-face spiritual interactions and powerful conversion experiences. Believing in a God who wants to save the world through belief in Jesus Christ, these grassroots revivalists are primarily concerned with the salvation of the persons they are trying to reach. Since the primary goal is to meet the spiritual needs of those struggling to survive in a system of social and economic oppression, grassroots evangelists are often indifferent toward agendas of Black pride, Afrocentric ideals, or political activism. Instead, they concern themselves only with personal salvation as linked to the formation of character, disregarding the roles of politics, economics, and even the church, in society.

Positive Thought Materialists

Commonly known as *prosperity gospel*; the health, wealth, and success movement of **positive thought materialists** focuses on a morality of material prosperity. This tradition, believing that God's primary role is that of Provider, often appeals to those in economic crisis because it gives hope that God will provide them with their earthly desires. Unconcerned with concepts of justice, personal salvation, or ethnic purity, these materialistic practitioners merely seek to advance in individual prosperity. Uninterested in the sources and causes of social and economic hardship, materialists rarely join the other liberation ethic traditions in confronting racism and injustice, and thus find themselves alienated from the other traditions.

Contemplative Communitarians

Unlike the above-mentioned traditions, that do not make wholeness and the restoration of the broken relationships a priority, **contemplative communitarians** believe that true liberation will come only when reconciliation has occurred with God, neighbor, and enemy; and all are restored to a common unity in what Dr. Martin Luther King, Jr., called the "beloved community." This spirit of unity is not bound by race, class, gender, or nation, but exists "wherever the heart is kind and collective will and the private endeavor seek to make justice where injustice abounds."[36] Contemplative communitarians believe social transformation begins with individual transformation through contemplative moral reasoning. The ethical insights gained from religious encounters will instruct faithful living and obligate individuals to strive for social transformation.

Prophetic Radicals

Prophetic radicals represent those within the Black community who believe that by assimilating to the political structures of oppression one contributes to one's own oppression, and that liberation and justice will come only through confronting the systems of oppression. Understanding God primarily as Liberator, the prophetic radical tradition contends that in confronting injustice, they are acting as tools of divine justice. Epitomized in the person of Martin Luther King, Jr., the prophetic radicals have been catalysts for social change in slave rebellions, and the Black power and civil rights movements. Prophetic radicals believe that it is their duty to confront social sin in order to insure the realization of social justice and liberation.

WOMANIST ETHICS

The third major approach in African American Christian social ethics is Womanist ethics. Because Black women's realities are not only plagued by racist oppression and economic exploitation but by sexist abuse and gender bias as well, Black women's relationship with suffering has been all encompassing. Womanist ethics brings together virtue ethics and liberation ethics to liberate Black women from **interlocking systems of oppression**. Heretofore, the other schools of African American ethical thought (virtue ethics and liberationist ethics), because of their patriarchal roots, have disproportionately focused on the preservation and promotion of Black men. This painstaking reality has necessitated that Black women cultivate moral resources that can help them negotiate histories of enslavement, colonization, Jane Crow segregation, sexual harassment, domestic abuse, and other debilitating forces experienced outside and within the Black Church community. Consequently, Womanist ethics is best understood as an inter-structured analysis of the interlocking systems of oppression as they uniquely shape the moral condition and moral agency of Black women.[37] To engage in Womanist ethics is to name the oppressions that disrupt lives, wounds souls, destroys communities, and forestall liberation. It is to honor the reality of God in Black women, their call for justice, and the Christian love that values Black women's lives, striving to generate what is needed for such reflection, restoration, and renewal. Womanist ethics is the most contemporary and revolutionary discourse within African American Christian social ethics. It merges virtue ethics and liberation ethics as a means to preserve and protect the entire Black community by dismantling interlocking systems of oppression. Womanist ethics proposes that Black women can provide the wisdom and resources necessary for the survival and thriving of the entire community. Womanist virtues and liberation practices are dependent upon Black women's unique ability to facilitate them. Though focused on Black women, Womanist ethics is an inclusive endeavor that traditionally views liberation and virtuous living as that which promotes "the survival of an entire people—male and female."[38] As the following chart illustrates, Womanist ethics focuses on certain moral principles epitomized by the moral wisdom (herein referred to as **Mother Wit**) demonstrated by specific moral practices. This wisdom reflects specific moral virtues that are characteristic of Black women, the moral exemplars in the Black Church and the larger society.[39]

WOMANIST ETHICS AND THE BLACK CHURCHWOMEN'S TRADITION[40]

Moral Principles	Moral Virtue	Mother Wit	Moral Practice	Moral Exemplars
Radical Subjectivity	Unshouted Courage	"God don't like ugly."	Women's Day	Nannie Helen Burroughs
Traditional Communalism	Quiet Grace	"Lifting as we climb."	Club Movements	Harriet Tubman
Redemptive Self-love	Invisible Dignity	"God don't make no junk."	Sister Circles and Retreats	Vashti McKenzie
Critical Engagement	Unctuousness	"Hitting a straight lick with a crooked stick."	Ordination of Black Women	Sojourner Truth

Radical Subjectivity

Radical subjectivity is the foundational moral principle that guides the liberation of Black women. It dictates that Black women must assume a defiant posture and audacious, inquisitive nature in order to rise above their circumstances and experience that which otherwise would be denied. By being both fearless and savvy, Black women exhibit the corresponding virtue of "**unshouted courage**," which enables them to take control of their lives in ways both bold and cautious.[41] Radical subjectivity is manifested in the *womanish* ways of Black girls as they imitate the behavioral patterns of their mothers and older Black women. Such behavior commonly elicits the wise retort "God don't like ugly," which cautions one to be mindful to act always in a manner pleasing to God. For instance, "Women's Day," the brainchild of Nannie Helen Burroughs, is a special day within the Black Church tradition in which all church activities are oriented towards and predominately performed by Black women.

Traditional Communalism

Traditional communalism is the way in which the practical wisdom and common sense of Black women support the survival and success of the Black community. Characteristic of this principle is the virtue of **"quiet grace,"** the exercise of functional prudence gained through lived experience. [42] As they fulfill their role as culture-bearers and caretakers of the community, Black mothers, church mothers, and "other-mothers" are compelled by the moral adage "lifting as we climb." In so doing, Black women create familial networks that galvanize resources and produce results for those unable to do so for themselves. Through their emphasis on Christian moral values, members of the African American women's club movement demonstrated the principle of traditional communalism. They were created to empower women, develop social skills, promote economic empowerment, and foster racial pride for the entire Black community.[43] The most notable exemplification of traditional communalism is Harriet Tubman's heroic work as *conductor* of the Underground Railroad, through which she emancipated not only herself, but also two hundred other enslaved African Americans.

Redemptive Self-love

To possess **redemptive self-love** is to esteem and reclaim the unique aesthetic aspects of Black femininity that normative society usually disparages. It is the moral attribute of **invisible dignity** that allows Black women to turn these supposed aesthetic vices into self-affirming virtues, as expressed in the Black Christian aphorism "God don't make no junk."[44] Black churches are guided by the principle of redemptive self-love when they sponsor "sister-circles" and women's retreats, which attend holistically to the social and spiritual needs of women. As the first female AME bishop, Vashti McKenzie refused to diminish her femininity, typically expected of women who serve in leadership positions traditionally reserved only for men. Rather, she proclaimed that her femininity was, in fact, the very embodiment of the divinity within her, and as such the very source of her ministerial authority.

Critical Engagement

As the final Womanist principle, **critical engagement** is the assumption that Black women possess the unique capability to transform society by imparting a liberating vision of a just and inclusive world. Black women display the virtue of **unctuousness** (i.e., the ability to be both deliberate and discerning[45]) when they bear prophetic witness to oppressors and allies alike by confronting racism, sexism, and other forms of social injustice in their midst. As an abolitionist, women's suffragist, and itinerant preacher, Sojourner Truth was doubly stigmatized by racism and sexism, yet refused to conform or succumb to these dehumanizing forces in word and deed. Because she was confident in her ability to "hit a straight lick with a crooked stick," she single-handedly changed the discourse on gender, race, and power for generations to come.[46] In similar fashion, Black women who have struggled to answer their divine call to preach and become ordained to pastor, have shattered the "stained glass ceiling" of ecclesiastical hierarchy to pave the way for other Black women called to ministry.

SUMMARY

The urgent moral crises for the Black Church in the twenty-first century continue to revolve around the challenges presently confronting the Black community. They require further examination by the three major approaches discussed in this chapter. First, we have to clarify our identity as a people of African descent, which means that we must accept our African identity in history and rehabilitate our image of Africa, as well as how it is perceived in the world. Second, and closely connected to it, we have to participate in intergenerational dialogues wherein we may discuss different paths and approaches to liberation in order to have a shared understanding of our historical strivings, our present options, and our future possibilities for communal empowerment. Last and most important, we must celebrate the diversity of Black people and their religious expressions, so that Black liberation may be better understood as the proactive stance of human flourishing (self-determination) rather than exclusively the defensive response to white supremacy (self-defense). This is the attempt for Black people to define who and what we are in order to wrest our identity from white assimilation in addition to affirming ourselves as the people who are "fearfully and wonderfully made" (Psalm 139:14)—equal and unique in beauty, culture, and intelligence just as God intended. We must no longer fall prey to "**ontological Blackness**" that deems the efforts and experiences of African Americans as "the Blackness that whiteness created." [47] We must avoid falling into the same moral pitfalls by recognizing that our mores, virtues, and values as Black people are not just reactions or compensations for the prior (and often negative) actions of whites but we are actually human beings, self-defined and self-determined. If acted upon, such an ethical trajectory would restore and reconcile the Black community while allowing for viable examples of more loving and humane relations by which this society can focus on the necessary work of "liberating the oppressed" and "making the wounded whole."

BIOGRAPHIES

Katie G. Cannon (1950–   )

Katie Geneva Cannon is credited with a long list of firsts as a preacher, scholar, and teacher. The first African American woman to be ordained to the ministry in the United Presbyterian Church (U.S.A.) denomination, she is also the first African American woman to earn the Doctor of Philosophy degree from Union Theological Seminary in New York. Born in Kannapolis, North Carolina, during the height of Jim and Jane Crow racial segregation, her approach to preaching, teaching, and research departs from the experience of the interlocking systems of oppression and is committed to "debunking, unmasking, and disentangling" those forces. Her most notable contribution is her development of Womanist thought within the religion academy. Accordingly, she is considered the progenitor of the Womanist movement in the religion academy and the scholar to whom the field of Womanist ethics is most often attributed. She is the author of numerous articles and books including the classical texts *Black Womanist Ethics* and *Katie's Canon: Womanism and the Soul of the Black Community*.

Peter J. Paris (1933–)

Peter Paris is the Elmer G. Homrighausen Professor Emeritus of Social Ethics at Princeton Theological Seminary and an ordained Baptist preacher. A naturalized African American citizen who was born and reared in Nova Scotia, he is a descendant of Africans who migrated from slavery in the United States to "freedom" in Nova Scotia over two hundred years ago. Having served as president of the American Academy of Religion (AAR), Society of Christian Ethics (SCE), and the Society for the Study of Black Religion (SSBR), Paris's scholarly work and mentorship has inspired and shaped the field of African American religion and social ethical thought in unprecedented ways. His lifelong and intense collaboration with and scholarship of the disparate peoples of Africa and the African Diaspora have been modeled and studied by scholars in several of the humanities, social science, and theological disciplines. His examination of the foundations and moral implications of the leadership, social teachings, and spirituality of the peoples, as represented by his classical texts, *Black Religious Leaders in Conflict*, *The Social Teachings of the Black Churches*, and *The Spirituality of African People*, are vital to the study of African American Christian moral tradition.

STUDY QUESTIONS

1. What are the definitive characteristics of the Black Christian moral tradition? How and why are they different from dominant ethical traditions?
2. What are the three major approaches of African American Christian social ethics? Define and show how they have functioned within the Black Church tradition.
3. What virtues and virtue theories dominate the African American Christian social ethics tradition and why are they different from those of normative ethical traditions? How do virtues function differently within the Black context, and specifically, how do the virtues function differently regarding the experiences of Black women?
4. What are the different moral approaches to liberation within the Black Church tradition? How has morality and God been interpreted and pursued differently within these traditions?

5. What are the greatest challenges facing the Black Church in the twenty-first century and how may the heritage of the African American Christian social ethics tradition address these challenges?

ESSENTIAL TEXTS

- *African American Christian Ethics* by Samuel K. Roberts
- *Black Womanist Ethics* by Katie Geneva Cannon
- *Mining the Motherlode: Methods in Womanist Ethics* by Stacey M. Floyd-Thomas
- *The Social Teaching of the Black Churches* by Peter J. Paris

*A*ll education ultimately is for
either domination or
liberation, it cannot be for both . . .
Spirituality and personal salvation
not withstanding, a major and
controlling responsibility of the
(B)lack church has been, is, and
will continue to be the
humanization of the dehumanized
and the liberation of the oppressed.
—Grant H. Shockley

CHRISTIAN EDUCATION IN THE BLACK CHURCH TRADITION

INTRODUCTION

African American Christians must learn to negotiate the death-dealing dilemmas of a racist, classist, sexist, homophobic, and hegemonic society, even as they struggle to be faithful to the gospel of Jesus Christ. Taking seriously the need to teach its people to survive and to be faithful in the face of oppression and domination, the Black Church has become a problem-solving institution assisting its people in survival, resilience, faithful living, and hope. As a problem-solving institution, the Black Church articulates, rekindles, heals, and innovates its religious tradition and cultural identity for the present age while looking toward a hopeful future and coming generations. Christian education in the Black Church fosters the cultural and religious identity of its membership while equipping its people and healing them from the ravages of oppression. Living together as a community of faith is the way the entire congregation learns and matures in its faith journey. It is in community that strategies of survival and hope are passed from generation to generation. Teaching and learning occur as the problems of survival and faithfulness are negotiated and solved. Christian education is not simply a church program or ministerial department. Christian education is the work and life of the whole congregation as it grows as a community of faith, a community of oppressed people seeking liberation, a community of persons dedicated to **discipleship** of Jesus Christ.

As a way of establishing the conversation concerning the entirety of congregational life as being Christian education, this chapter begins with the notion that discipleship is a central way in which Christian education occurs in the local church. Then this chapter gives definition to Christian education as a **practical theology**. The conversation then moves to describing and illumining ways Christian education functions in the Black Church. The next section cites compulsory **mis-education** as the historic context out of which education in the Black Church is fashioned. The section after that looks at the pedagogical theory as an interlocutor with Black Liberation theology and discusses Black Liberation pedagogy and some of its foundational and constitutive elements. The final section, while quite brief, is a look at the challenge of Black Church Christian education in the twenty-first century.

In sum, this chapter engages several rudimentary questions that assume that liberation is a significant aspect of education. These foundational questions provide perspective and necessary vocabulary as a way of assisting the reader in beginning to think about Christian education as a practical theology in the context of the Black Church tradition. The foundational questions for this chapter are:

- What does it mean for the Black Church to renew the "passing-on" of tradition?
- What most renews the experience of Black Church and Black Christians?
- What is distinctive about Black Church teaching and learning?
- What does it mean for the Black Church as a problem-solving institution to educate its people for the myriad of social ills that threaten survival?
- If Christian education is a tool of liberation, what are the structures and practices of Christian education in the Black Church that keep the church resilient?

Discipleship as Aim and Means

While education is a tool of liberation, discipleship is both the aim and the means of education. Christian Education in the Black Church continually calls children, youth, adults, and older adults to be **disciples** of Jesus. Christian education in the Black Church, acknowledging and tending to the needs of the people beset by an oppressive environment,

152

strives to link the social, theological, and emotional with the cultural, economic, and political aspects of Black life. Unlike white churches who delay responsibility or create strata of expectations based upon longevity, Black Church culture believes that long-term disciples and new disciples are disciples—all with equal value, worth, and expectation. For example, in many Black Church contexts, children (as new disciples) preach, usher, sing in choirs, and teach. There is little to no "waiting period" for responsibility if one demonstrates a particular aptitude or call to specific ministries of the church.

As disciples, persons are thought to be lifelong learners who participate in the educational purpose and mission of the congregation with the intent of gaining new knowledge, insight, spiritual growth, and faith maturity. This belief is the basis for the local congregation as a whole being the primary place of faith education as well as the approach that learning happens *intergenerationally*, that is, through nurturing relationship across the generations rather than the generations being isolated one from another or compartmentalized into age-level roles and responsibilities. Intergenerational activities are paramount to the Black Church for the passing on of tradition. Christian education assists disciples in vocation—a lifetime journey of learning, working, playing, and growing in faith maturity. Education is the way that disciples challenge the culture of domination/*status quo* in an effort to transform, empower, restore, and resist, bringing about liberation and healing. The task of discipleship, clergy or laity, is to learn to be faithful and to keep the tradition of hope and survival alive.

What Is Christian Education?

Approaches to Christian education vary, as do definitions of what the term *Christian education* means. Christian education is a term used in the local church; it is also an academic discipline taught in colleges, universities, and seminaries. Christian education may seem ambiguous or fluctuating in the way that it is talked about or in the ways that its theories and aims are understood because the term is used in different ways in varying settings. Although it includes Sunday school, it is more than Sunday school; though it includes moral education, it moves beyond moral conservatism; as well, the academic field is larger than the study of practices for teaching the Bible. This chapter uses the approach that Christian education, as an academic discipline, is a practical theology, more specifically, a practical theology rooted in liberation theology.

What Is Practical Theology?

Practical theology has many meanings.[1] The most common definition is that it is a study of institutional activities of Christianity including Christian education, preaching, church administration, pastoral care, liturgics, and spirituality. Another meaning is that practical theology is that branch of Christian theology that seeks to construct action-guiding theories of Christian praxis in particular social contexts.[2] In this regard, practical theology focuses upon "how to"—how to pray, how to preach, how to teach, how to parent, how to transform society, how to liberate a people, and so forth. This *doing* of theology is strongly informed by and undergirded by theories of "why to," for example, why Black Christians practice the way of life and the ways of faith in particular and distinct fashions.[3]

While thinking about the definition of practical theology, we must not mistakenly associate the word *practical* with busyness, convenience, or that which is sensible. Contemporary society asserts that to have value any truth should reduce to that which has application or that which can quickly be seen as relevant or that which is without ambiguity. Mistakenly, it is often thought that if ideas cannot be *applied* or if conceptual or abstracts thoughts are not immediately pertinent or useful, they should be disregarded, dismissed, or seen as valueless. Rather, practical theology is our human response to the call of God in which we come to realize our purpose in the will and way of God. Practical theology is the action and reflection of a lifetime of commitment to a Christian journey of faith in ways that we are stretched, challenged, and changed into mature followers. Practical theology then is vocational work—work that is a lifelong journey of Christian discipleship.[4]

Christian Education as Practical Theology in the Black Church

While a variety of Christian theologies are operative in Black churches, Christian education as a practical theology is rooted in Black liberation theology—a theology that espouses that God is the god of the oppressed and God wants liberation for all God's people.[5] Black

Christians, as oppressed and faithful people, want the obstacles of oppression removed or surmounted, as well as guidance in acting upon their value and purpose in God's world. Working at being faithful disciples, Black Christians are concerned with the liberative as well as vocational aspects of discipleship.[6] As a way of acting upon this concern, Black people have demonstrated historically the profound capability for innovative and creative solutions to the multiplicity of difficulties and challenges foisted upon them as oppressed and marginalized people. Lawrence W. Levine echoes this outlook:

> Upon the hard rock of racial, social, and economic exploitation and injustice, Black Americans forged and nurtured a culture: they formed and maintained kinship networks, raised and socialized children, built a religion, and created a rich expressive culture in which they articulated their feelings and hopes and dreams.[7]

With the entire local congregation as the living laboratory of liberation and survival, the Black Church has fashioned and molded itself into a problem-solving institution where education is paramount. Being faithful disciples has demanded radical ways of living, risking, and learning. Education has been the avenue for radical change in individuals, neighborhoods, and the larger society. Moreover, education has been a means by which the prophetic message of the gospel was made available to the people in tangible, life-giving, life-sustaining ways. A lifetime of discipleship is understood to be a lifetime of learning and the entire local church, including all the experiences that take place there, is the central gathering place for that learning.

UNDERSTANDING WAYS CHRISTIAN EDUCATION FUNCTIONS IN THE BLACK CHURCH

With the notions of liberation and vocation in mind, the church is to be the body of Christ in the world. Therefore, the primary purpose of education is to build up that body. The building up of the body in and of itself is the challenge of an entire lifetime. When oppression is an inherent dimension of life for multiple generations, the task of building up the body becomes a formidable one. Perhaps the creation of communities makes the building up of the body in an oppressive context possible, even joyful.

Building up the body of Christ creates communities incarnating God's love to participate in God's transformation of the world to emancipate all creation from bondage. Christian education in the Black Church is a communal act of teaching and learning throughout the entire congregation. As a tool for liberation, it is not relegated to a classroom, a ministry, or a program. For our purposes, it is not simply part of the assignment for an associate ministry. The entire local church, as a faith community, is the place of teaching and learning for vocation and liberation. All persons, clergy and laity, as participants in the communal activities, are engaged in experiences that shape, form, inform, and transform concerning liberation and vocation.

To understand the ways education functions in the Black Church it is important to:

1. Consider the historic context out of which Christian education was formed, that is compulsory mis-education,
2. Understand the role and identity of the pastor as the primary teacher in the congregation, as well as the role of the laity as teachers,
3. Understand the structure of the church, and
4. Consider the multidimensional and prophetic ministry of the Black Church as an educational force for its people as well as the larger society.

Compulsory Mis-Education: The Historic Context

The origins of Christian education in the Black Church are rooted at the intersection of Christianity, North American slavery, and the struggle for survival and liberation. Although the signing of the Emancipation Proclamation on January 1, 1863, virtually ended slavery, the psychological, social, economic and spiritual effects remained with the subsequent generations. In this day and time, it maybe difficult to imagine what slavery was like. W.E.B. Du Bois described slavery in this way: "Oppression beyond all conception: cruelty, degradation, whipping and starvation, the absolute negation of human rights . . . It was the helplessness. It was the defenselessness of family life."[8] The educational commitment of the Black Church was shaped by several agendas: healing the generational scars of slavery, teaching life-lessons for survival, and personal salvation through Jesus Christ for all people. Noted Black scholar, Carter G. Woodson, coined the term "mis-education," which captures the context out of which the Black Church's educational philosophies and ministries have been fashioned. By mis-education, Woodson meant that white elites and educators intentionally prohibited African Americans the right to formally learn the skills of reading and writing. By example, enslaved Africans were not allowed to speak to one another in their own African languages, nor were they allowed to practice the African religions of their faith. Consequently, this prohibition meant that the enslaved were not permitted to read and interpret the Bible for themselves. Compulsory mis-education, as a form of oppression, stripped enslaved people of their dignity. As Woodson wrote in *The Mis-Education of the Negro*:

> If you control a (person's) thinking, you do not have to worry about his (/her) action. When you determine what a (person) shall think, you do not have to concern yourself about what he(/she) will do. If you make a (person) feel that he(/she) is inferior, you do not have to compel him(/her) to accept an inferior status, for he (/she) will seek it for himself (/herself). If you make a (person) think that he (/she) is justly an outcast, you do not have to order him (/her) to the back door. He (/she) will go without being told; and if there is no back door, his (/her) very nature will demand one.[9]

Christian education in the Black Church strives to re-educate those oppressed by compulsory mis-education during slavery and the subsequent oppressive era of Jim Crow/Jane Crow and segregation.

The Role of the Pastor as Primary Teacher; the Role of Laity as Teacher

Pastor's Role: Theology and Function of Ministry

The pastor of the Black Church is a critical interpreter of the Black experience. The pastor interprets the life of Black people in light of God's revelation in Jesus Christ and thereby provides for, teaches, and inspires the moral dynamics needed for everyday living, as well as the theological ideals and cultural wisdom needed for commonsense survival and sanity. This role as interpreter extends to political commentary, economic analysis, social critique, and all of the discourses that influence the existence of Black persons in, and beyond, the local faith community. The authority of pastor as interpreter is derived from the communal affirmation that this person is called to ministry by God. As the theologian in residence, the pastor is charged with the enterprise of teaching the congregation to access the cultural wisdom and sacred traditions of the community in ways that are life giving and life sustaining. By drawing together these various threads of Black communal creativity, the self-doubt, self-hatred, and inferiority foisted upon Black people by a racist society is squelched, and their imaginations are fueled for change.[10] Thus, pastors are far more than managers of ministry; pastors are the primary teachers of the congregation. As such, the pastor is the mediator of mystery who provides vision and hope. He or she is an "agent of transcendence beyond human experience and rational comprehension"[11] able to translate and make meaning from the mystery and transcendence into the tangible and needy reality.

Laity as Teachers—Koinonia in Action

Christianity is inherently a communal religion. As the body of Christ, the laity play a critical role as teachers who are bearers of the tradition and experience. Passing down the tradition and religion from one generation to the next, the laity rekindle tradition, while at the same time tending to the issues of survival and vocation in the current context. With the leadership of the pastor, laity teach one another and the next generations the lessons of survival and hope. As a learning community, laity and clergy create a context in the local church where people encounter and experience the redemptive and liberating activity of God at work. Additionally, they take the experience of liberation and hope out of the bounds of the local church and into the larger society.

Typical Structures That Provide Experiential Education in Congregational Life

The teaching and learning opportunities of the institution function both implicitly and explicitly to educate members about liberation and hope. The explicit educational structures of the church (e.g., Sunday school, Bible study) provide Christian education opportunities in very traditional ways. The focus of this section is upon the structures of the local church that, through tacit socialization, immerse church members in an ecology of learning and teaching liberation. By participating in the activities, responsibilities, opportunities, and duties of discipleship, church members learn, grow, and mature in faith. While there are structures of the church beyond those described below that contribute to the education of members, we will focus on only those structures that are typical and basic in churches. The principal educational arena in the local church is the worship service. In addition to the worship service, other significant venues of learning in the structure of the church are: holy days and holidays, leadership offices of the laity, schools at churches—religious and secular, and the prophetic and political ministries.

Worship

The gift and genius of Black Church worship is, in part, its educational purpose for the congregation. Worship informs and re-informs, shapes and re-shapes the congregation in shared identity as Christians, as African Americans, as men, women, and children of God. For Black churches, the sanctuary at times of worship is the central gathering place for faith and cultural formation, moral discourse, vocational imagining, and the rekindling of the shared gospel story. The congregation routinely grapples with the complex notions of salvation, forgiveness, suffering, redemption, liberation, and the like through song, prayer, offering, sermon, and response. For example, the ritualized practices and behaviors of worship—communion, baptism, praying, testifying, singing, and preaching—teach the community the priorities, the values, the mores, and social codes of the congregation. The significance of worship is brought to bear as the majority of churches establish and maintain membership roles by worship attendance. The majority of active members attends no other arena in the church as consistently as worship, giving worship the continuous occasion for educational, communal experience. Worship as a place of communal education challenges the mis-education of the people.[12]

The Sermon: The sermon is the apex of the worship service. The preacher, then, is the primary teacher in this communal experience of learning. The preacher assists the congregation in making sense out of those things that have challenged them, and, in some cases, bested and conquered them. Preaching assists worshipers with the complexity of learning survival in a racist society that would otherwise confound, confuse, and devastate the community of believers. Preaching interprets biblical truth, providing meaning concerning such critical issues in the human life cycle as marriage, birth, death, the meaning of adulthood, and the challenges of parenting. Meaning making and the unraveling of conundrums is the stuff of great sermons. Good preaching, as good teaching, finds people where they are; provides insight and elucidation; challenges and strengthens resolve; nurtures and instills resilience; places new endings on old stories to create hope; and dispenses wisdom for mind, body, and soul, moving forward with the next generation in mind.

Laity, as worshipers and thus learners, expectantly participate in the sermonic moment by actively listening—anticipating insight, wisdom, "a word from the Lord." During worship, the learner looks to the teacher to frame the important questions, to assist with prioritizing all that they must deal with on a day-to-day basis if oppression is to be survived, and to give guidance regarding moral judgment. Persons in the pews as learners look to the sermonic moment to enlighten and nurture their imaginations—their souls. Learners do not sit uncritically or unthinking in the pews. If the teacher is preaching without insight, it is common for someone to say aloud, "Help Him (Her), Holy Ghost."

Holy Days and Holidays—Formative Events

Holy days and holidays are days when significant moments of the Christian story, the Black Church tradition, or the life of the individual local church are marked and celebrated.[13] These festival days are encounters with others, our selves, our ancestors, and the revelation of Jesus Christ for the purpose of nurturing the congregation and deepening the sense of community. As formative events,[14] the days are the best kind of teaching and learning, as they are experiences of belonging and somebodyness. These events order the congregational life and reinforce the sense of mission. They create excitement, anticipation of celebration, and strengthen the renewal and/or transformation of shared living. They are an impetus for the revitalization and sustaining of the congregation. Special days are days that the church recognizes as days for fundraising, but more importantly, they are days that help to remember and celebrate the past and at the same time honor the present for a hopeful future.

While Black congregations celebrate the typical Christian holy days and holidays of Advent, Christmas, Epiphany, Lent, Easter, and Pentecost, the festival days go beyond these liturgical events. Examples of events that are significant beyond the liturgical calendar include the church's anniversary, the pastor's anniversary, usher's day, trustee day, women's day, men's day, mother's day, and school graduations. A typical special day would include innovative worship, guest preaching, special music, a communal meal or banquet, fundraising, and gift giving.

Most significant in the Black Church tradition are those holidays that mark the cultural story of survival and hope. An example of this kind of event is watch night service. As discussed in the first chapter, these services originated in the Methodist tradition. Watch night was a church meeting that had singing, praying, and preaching that began late in the evening and continued until shortly after midnight, taking the congregation into the new year. December 31, 1862, took on ultimate significance for every member of the African American community with the anticipation of President Abraham Lincoln's signing of the decree (later known as the Emancipation Proclamation) conferring freedom to all enslaved African Americans. Since the first so-called "Emancipation Day," watch night services on New Year's Eve are a staple within countless Black churches, as a commemoration of the event that marked the *beginning* of slavery's end in the United States.

Another example of the particular way Black churches mark events is with the communal celebration of birthdays. It is quite common on the first Sunday of the month for persons whose birthdays will fall in that month to be asked to stand during the worship service and be acknowledged. Often, the congregation sings "Happy Birthday" to those people, and the church gives a small gift to them. In neighborhoods where there are little economic means, high crime, and rampant drug use, and where the death of children is a common occurrence, the birthday as the rite of passage becomes a great celebration. The celebrations often include inviting the pastor and the congregation to house parties or outdoor picnics. These are heralded moments of thanksgiving to God for sparing the life of the child thus far and for encouragement to the child. The pastor is asked to offer a special prayer and sometimes preach during the home celebration.

These examples demonstrate formative events as Black congregations seek meaning and understanding in a volatile and uncertain environment. The examples point to the necessity of communal celebrations as events that are life-acknowledging, life-sustaining, and life-affirming activities.

Educating Laity for Leadership
Mentoring Children, Youth, and Adults: An emphasis on mentoring, a modified form of **apprenticeship**, is prevalent in Black Church tradition in both informal and formal ways. Mentoring is a practice of teaching and

learning that is part of the fabric of congregational life due to the focus on discipleship. Discipleship encourages communal engagement and involvement through multiple levels of intimacy. The communal relationships resemble familial relationships or kinship bonds. Churches will often operate like extended families of people who are kin or fictive kin. Informal mentoring occurs naturally between persons as they live together in church life. Formal ways of mentoring are a means of educating laity for discipleship; specifically, as a way of discerning call to ministry (ordained and lay), apprentice relationships are nurtured between laity as well as between clergy and laity. Mentoring relationships happen in structured ways, as in junior choir or junior usher board, as well as in unstructured ways, as when members sing in choirs or attend and organize events such as church retreats or serve in clothing drives. The relationships occur also when the pastor encourages laity toward licensed ministry or ordination. Discerning a call to ministry and preparation for ministry often takes many years. During such time, the person is assisting with preaching, teaching, visiting the sick, and other duties of church administration.

Children and Youth: Leadership education in the Black Church begins during childhood. Children and youth participate in the leadership life of the church by membership in guilds and clubs that have responsibility for certain aspects of communal life. By participating in these clubs, children and youth learn, experientially, the obligations and responsibilities of church leadership. The guilds and clubs can include: junior usher board, junior trustees, children choir, youth choir, drama groups, dance groups, mime groups, and teaching Sunday school to younger children. As participants in these groups, the children do not learn *about* the leadership responsibility in hopes of participating in the leadership life of the church "at a later date" or at an older age. The groups are not perfunctory in the life of the church. Junior ushers serve in worship on a regular schedule. The junior choir is needed in the worship service as a necessary dimension of praise and worship. Participation in these guilds teaches children and youth that they are welcomed, essential parts of the body of Christ, and that, as part of the body, the community looks to them with the expectation that they will contribute to the life of the church in meaningful and significant ways. These guilds and clubs are a way for the children and youth to learn, by experience, their place generationally in the community. While children and youth have genuinely needed responsibilities in communal life, they are not expected to shoulder the burden of an adult's responsibility. It is not uncommon to encourage teenaged members to begin teaching Sunday school in the lower grades as a way to teach teaching. Also, many Black youth have their first public speaking opportunity in worship service, or in the Christmas play or spring drama. Additionally, it is typical for local churches to have annual days where the children and youth *take charge* of the worship service. These are days when, under the watchful eye of adults, children and youth conduct the entire worship service, including all aspects of liturgy, preaching, and singing. In learning their generational place, youth are not expected to preach as well as the pastor or to teach as well as seasoned, elder teachers. It is understood that they are learning, maturing, and growing.

Adults: Though Black Church leadership emphasizes a pastor-centered approach to leadership, the leadership of the laity is critical to the life of the institution and to the life of the people. In congregations of persons with low socio-economic means (more generally known as the working poor), participation in leadership of the church is a humanizing experience. People who spend their workdays being told they are inferior or mindless find solace and rejuvenation when the congregation looks to them for leadership in positions such as the chair of the deacon board or the Sunday school superintendent.

Educational Enterprises and the Black Church Tradition

Seen by Black Church leaders as a tool for removing the social and emotional shackles of bondage, it has been and continues to be typical for local churches and denominations to establish schools of various descriptions. Like public boycotts, lawsuits, and social protest, establishing and maintaining schools is a strategy of resistance and survival. Historically, schools were established as enterprises that would empower and re-educate the mis-educated. Examples of such educational enterprises are Historically Black Colleges and Universities (HBCUs). While the different Black denominations vary in their educational enterprises and approaches, a great majority of Black churches has acknowledged education for its capacity to equalize social and economic inequities. In the early AME church, for example,

> [T]he church leaders were not educated people, but they had a clear perception of what education would mean to the interests of the church and the advancement of the African people then held in abject slavery. Bishop Daniel Payne, who had been a schoolmaster in Baltimore, set the educational goals for the fledgling institution by insisting upon a trained ministry, and by encouraging AME pastors to organize schools in their communities as an aspect of their ministries.[15]

Denominations have established HBCUs and local churches have established nursery, elementary, and secondary schools.

HBCUs (Historically Black Colleges and Universities)

With the help of white allies, African American churches and denominations established schools, colleges, universities, and seminaries before, during, and after slavery. The first HBCU was established in 1837, twenty-six years before the end of slavery. Richard Humphreys, a Quaker philanthropist, founded the Institute for Colored Youth to train free and freed Blacks to become teachers.[16] Humphreys, born on a plantation in the West Indies, bequeathed ten thousand dollars, one tenth of his estate, to design and establish a school to educate the descendants of the African race. During his life, Humphreys witnessed the struggles of African Americans competing unsuccessfully for jobs due to the influx of immigrants and the blatant racism that excluded and exploited freed Blacks. In 1829, race riots heightened; it was the same year that Richard Humphreys wrote his will and charged thirteen fellow Quakers to design an institution "to instruct the descendents of the African Race in school learning, in the various branches of the mechanic Arts, trades and Agriculture, in order to prepare and fit and qualify them to act as teachers . . . "[17]

Following his instructions, the institute, founded in Philadelphia in 1837, successfully provided free classical education for qualified young people. In 1902, the Institute moved to George Cheyney's farm, twenty-five miles west of Philadelphia. In 1913, the name was changed to Cheyney State Teachers College; in 1921, the State Normal School at Cheyney; and in 1959, Cheyney State College. In 1983, Cheyney joined the State System of Higher Education as Cheyney University of Pennsylvania.[18] Since 1837, with the establishment of the first Institute, 104 institutions have been listed as HBCUs on the U.S. Department of Education website concerning the White House's Initiative on HBCUs. Containing both public and private institutions, the list includes Lincoln University, Florida A&M University, Spelman College, Fisk University, Morehouse College, and Interdenominational Theological Seminary.

Local Church—Educational Offerings and Schools

Many local churches have an ethos that encourages education. Local churches will typically have congregational programs that support and affirm the educational aspirations and achievements of members. Churches provide scholarships to college and graduate students, provide tutorial programs, SAT training, and weekend trips to visit colleges and universities for young people trying to decide which schools to attend. In the spring, many churches have a celebration during Sunday worship (sometimes called Recognition Sunday or Education Sunday) where graduation from elementary, high school, and college is recognized. During this service, graduates receive scholarships and tuition assistance from the church and celebration for academic accomplishments.

It is quite common, in addition to supporting persons achieving in school, for local churches to establish schools for children and youth. Churches have nursery schools for pre-school aged children with an emphasis on supporting working and single mothers. This educational ministry, usually housed in local church buildings and sharing classroom space with the local church's Sunday school, provides a service to the parents in the congregation as well as the parents in the neighborhood. Further, many churches develop private elementary schools for the children of the congregation and the children of the neighborhood. Particularly those in underserved and underprivileged neighborhoods (e.g., Concord Baptist in Brooklyn, pastored by Gary V. Simpson, and The Greater Allen Cathedral of New York, pastored by Floyd Flake), serve as alternatives to deficient public schools with meager resources and little availability of Black-centered curricula. In multi-staffed churches, it is common to have elaborately structured educational programs for children, youth, and adults for educating in issues of faith and discipleship as well as for issues of basic survival skills. An example of this is Trinity United Church of Christ in Chicago, pastored by Jeremiah Wright. The table below, using information from Trinity's website,[19] provides a small sampling of the plethora of educational opportunities offered by the church. This sample gives an indication of the expansive definition of education that the church employs.

Model of Church-sponsored Educational Services
A Sampling of Educational Ministries at Trinity UCC, Chicago

ADOPT-A-STUDENT MINISTRY
Focused on trying to retain college students who have gone away from home and are studying at universities and colleges out of the city and state. Importantly, this ministry assures our college students that they: (1) belong to God, and (2) have a church home that cares about them.

CAREER DEVELOPMENT
Provides information, training, and job fairs to enable unemployed and underemployed members to compete and upgrade their employability for jobs with employers seeking "good" employees.

CHURCH IN SOCIETY
Continually seeks ways and opportunities to educate, inform, and empower the congregation and community to understand, identify and to be effective advocates for social justice policies that better our lives and our world.

DANCE MINISTRY
Includes children, youth, men, and women who are taught the principles of modern dance, ballet, and interpretive dance. They are also taught the African roots of dance in worship and the biblical basis for praising God with dance!

DRILL TEAM
Promotes an understanding of Scripture, encourages academic excellence, heightens cultural awareness, fosters self-discipline, and develops self-esteem.

TRINITY COMPUTER LEARNING CENTER
Trinity Computer Learning Center (TCLC) is a faith-based training facility for Trinity United Church of Christ and the community at large using computer technology to help cross the digital divide.

AFRICA MINISTRY
Promotes, educates, and advocates issues concerning Africans in Africa and the Diaspora. Opportunities shall be provided for education, travel, fellowship, economic development, missionary work, financial support, and health education.

CARIBBEAN CONNECTION
This ministry is our Afrocentric congregation's attempt to educate our North American members about the many aspects of the Caribbean culture. These aspects include the cuisine, the peoples, the countries, the customs, and the religion of our Lord as practiced in the various Caribbean places.

CHURCH SCHOOL
Meets Saturday mornings and provides Bible instructions in classes for pre-school through adults.

DRAMA MINISTRY
Nurtures the innate abilities of expression present in all of our children and youth as they learn to communicate on the stage to the world.

HIV/AIDS MINISTRY
Offers comfort through support, education, and training for individuals, families, and friends impacted by HIV and AIDS. Training required.

YOUTH CHURCH MINISTRY PARTNERS
Committed to teaching children ages 3–10 years of age about the Gospel of Jesus Christ. Through the use of Christian education materials, music, prayers, and crafts, your child can participate in an atmosphere that is designed to teach them all the elements of worship. Three-year-olds must be potty-trained and not wearing pull-ups. Space is limited to a first-come first-served basis at the 7:30 am and 11:00 am services. The space is also limited by the capacity of the classrooms for your child's particular age group.

Prophetic and Political Dimensions of Ministry

Political activism is another common feature in the life of the Black Church that is a venue for education. It is common for church leadership, both pastor and laity, to move beyond the local church and into local and regional (and in some cases national and international) politics. By actively participating in political causes, members learn prophetic dimensions of ministry as ways of liberation and hope building.

The best example of this is the civil rights movement as it was led by Christian pastors and laypeople. Dr. Martin Luther King, Jr., as the key leader of the movement, was acting out of a calling to the gospel of Jesus Christ and out of obligation as pastor of Dexter Avenue Baptist Church in Montgomery, Alabama, and Ebenezer Baptist in Atlanta, Georgia. The overwhelming majority of laity and clergy persons who assisted King engaged the struggle for human rights out of a sense of Christian duty and Christian love. Leaders of the civil rights movement like Rev. Jesse Jackson, Rev. Ralph David Abernathy, Rev. James Lawson, and Rev. Andrew Young were ordained clergy. But the role, significance, and impact of the laity as key leaders and activists in the movement cannot be overstated.[20] Leaders and members of SNCC were, for the most part, "everyday folks." Countless numbers of college students and persons such as Diane Nash were the heart and soul of the movement. Diane Nash was involved in most of the major civil rights demonstrations of the 1960s. As a college student at Fisk University, Nash became a founding member of the Student Nonviolent Coordinating Committee before working alongside Martin Luther King, Jr., in the Southern Christian Leadership Conference (SCLC). King referred to Nash as "the driving spirit in the nonviolent assault on segregation at lunch counters."[21] Evelyn Parker, author of *Trouble Don't Last Always*, poignantly captures the significant role of the laity:

> Many neighborhood churches joined in the struggle for freedom. I remember the laypeople from neighborhood churches, more than the clergy, providing the leadership for the Movement in Hattiesburg and Forrest County (Mississippi). They served as officers in the NAACP, the Southern Christian Leadership Conference (SCLC), and the Student Nonviolent Coordinating Committee (SNCC). Clergy at the heart of the Movement proclaimed freedom and justice from the pulpit on Sunday mornings and participated in protest marches alongside members during the week. Even if a pastor was removed from the

center of the Movement, laypeople continued midweek civil rights mass meetings in their churches.[22]

Dr. Parker goes on to describe the educational centrality of activism in her church and how it was embodied:

> On occasion our congregation of fewer than sixty people hosted mass meetings, with an overflow crowd standing along the walls of the sanctuary, in the choir stand, and clustered down the steps of the front door. Issues related to the Movement were heard in Sunday school, worship services, committees, boards, and auxiliary meetings. Prayers, songs and sermons focused on the theme of hope—God making a way out of no way amidst the struggle for freedom and justice. I do not recall the explicit Sunday school curriculum focusing on justice. However, the implicit curriculum, which is the tacit socialization in the church, bathed the (members) in a social theology of involvement and confident expectation. The people of the congregation saw the threads of their spiritual selves woven together with the threads of their political selves.[23]

In more recent times, the tradition of local Black churches' involvement in activism and politics remains steadfast, as well as the tacit socialization of members teaching and learning issues of liberation and hope through political involvement and activism. See the chart for examples of well-known local Black church pastors and laypersons who participate in politics as part-and-parcel of their ministerial duties.

EXAMPLES OF POLITICALLY ACTIVE LOCAL PASTORS

William Gray	Pastor of Bright Hope Baptist Church, Philadelphia, 1972–2007, former president and CEO of the NAACP, 13-year tenured U.S. Representative and at one time, was the highest-ranking African American in Congress
Floyd Flake	Pastor of The Greater Allen Cathedral of New York, Jamaica, Queens, New York since 1976; served as an elected member of The House of Representatives from 1986 to 1997
Calvin Butts	Pastor of Abyssinian Baptist Church since 1989, is known for actively participating in the politics to uplift Harlem, New York, establishing a development corporation, organizing boycotts and civil protests—appointed president of the State

| | University of New York College at Old Westbury in 1999 |
| Yvonne Delk | The first African American woman ordained by the United Church of Christ, former executive director of the Community Renewal Society (a Chicago-based mission agency related to the United Church of Christ—CRS works to empower people to dismantle racism and poverty in order to build just communities), former moderator of the World Council of Churches Program to Combat Racism working group |

EXAMPLES OF POLITICALLY ACTIVE LAYPERSONS

Barbara Jordan	The first Black woman to serve in the U.S. Congress from the South
Shirley Chisholm	Served in the U.S. House of Representatives and was the first African American woman to seek candidacy for President of United States from the Democratic Party
Marian Wright Edelman	Founder and President of the Children's Defense Fund
Condoleezza Rice	Secretary of State and former Assistant to the President for National Security Affairs (commonly referred to as the National Security Advisor) for George W. Bush]

EDUCATIONAL THEORY INTERSECTS WITH BLACK LIBERATION THEOLOGY

Black Liberation Pedagogy

In previous sections of the chapter, we have alluded to the fact that pedagogical theory helps us understand the ways in which Black Liberation theology, in its practical expression, forms, informs, and embodies within the context of the Black Church tradition. With this in mind, we want now to discuss Black Liberation pedagogy. Though a relatively new genre in the field of Christian education, the notion of liberative pedagogy appears in the scholarly work and teachings of: Paulo Freire, bell hooks, Anne Streaty Wimberly, Nancy Lynne Westfield, Evelyn Parker, and Yolanda Smith (see the bibliography for specific resources).

Simply put, pedagogy is the art and science of teaching; the study that involves the principles, theories, and practices of teaching. Liberation pedagogy—sometimes referred to as engaged pedagogy, incarnational pedagogy, or *emancipatory* pedagogy—is an essential part of Black Liberation theology in the mission of the church to transform the world.

Black Liberation Theology and Black Liberation Pedagogy

Black Liberation theology espouses that God is the god of the oppressed and the yearning of God's heart is for all the people of creation to know freedom, justice, and peace. James Cone said, "Black Theology is that theology which arises out of the need to articulate the significance of Black presence in a hostile white world. It is Black people reflecting religiously on the Black experience, attempting to redefine the relevance of the Christian Gospel for their lives."[24] As with Black Liberation theology, the context and center point of Black Liberation pedagogy are the suffering and dehumanization of the Black people. Black Liberation pedagogy assumes that the educational enterprise of the church is the way disciples grapple with the issues that have seized the Black community and that threaten to annihilate the present generation, making extinct the coming generations. With transformation as the keystone, Black Liberation pedagogy takes seriously the identity, culture, and traditions of Black Christians in the struggle for liberation. Education is a practice of freedom.[25] Education as a practice of freedom would be null and worthless if it were not for its dependency upon and fostering of community. A hallmark of Black Liberation pedagogy is that learning is a communal act.

Learning as a Communal Act

The uniqueness of this pedagogical approach in Black Church education as compared to those institutions that employ the **banking system** is not that the Black Church has abandoned the banking system of education. In many instances, Sunday school classes, Bible studies, and youth ministry programs are steeped in memorization, rote work, and competition such as Bible verse drills. The uniqueness is that the Black Church has recognized that learning, by nature and necessity, is a communal process that has the power to influence values, identities, hearts—entire societies. This communal nature of education means that education is never morally or politically neutral, so that teaching and learning are risky endeavors that have the possibility, even expectation, of transformation and healing. For Black people, the personal is political when considering the racial realities of this country, the makers of public policy, and the national politics foisted upon the poor, marginalized, and disenfranchised. Education, politically charged and politically necessary, strengthens the faith community for liberation.

No Longer Other

The communal aspect of this approach to education in the Black Church creates a context where Black persons and Black perspectives are no longer the *other* in the sight of non-Blacks. Learning in classrooms, and learning that happens beyond classrooms, are experiences where Black students and the worldview of Black theology is normative (i.e., the Black aesthetic is what is typical, valued, and honored). Students do not have to explain themselves, make excuses for their vantage point, or participate in the psychological difficulty of what W.E.B. Du Bois called "double consciousness."[26] With the awareness that discussion and conversation are politically charged, the world is brought to bear on the teaching and learning moments. Teaching and learning then become rich opportunities for engagement and meaning making between the gospel message and the contradictions and confusions of the hegemonic reality.

Desire for Change

This pedagogy against domination and imperialism acknowledges that people desire change and assumes that transformation is possible. Liberative pedagogy requires more than giving students new ideas about change. The powerful process of education transforms both students and teachers. Teaching is a sacred act where students and teachers learn together rather than students being passive recipients of the teacher's ideas. The teachers and learners are co-learners and work in partnership, motivating one another to accomplish new insight and deepen faith maturity. Teaching and learning are passionate, life-changing, life-affirming pursuits where the confounding circumstances of life and survival are met with meaningful engagement. Teaching/learning encounters (in classrooms and beyond) are experiences of excitement, risk, and relevance.

Humanization

From this perspective, education is about creating space for persons to transgress[27] the dehumanizing boundaries of oppression and move toward liberation and hope. The moments of learning become moments when humanization returns to those dehumanized by suffering and oppression. Real learning toward change and liberation is a profoundly human drama of dignity, courage, fear, loss, accomplishment, and sometimes surprise. Learning from this perspective is hard work, requiring engagement of the body, mind, and soul. It challenges Black people to resist complicity in their own oppression, and instead utilize creativity, wisdom, imagination, intuition, wonder, and intellect for transformation. This kind of learning fosters wisdom expecting the presence of God—revering the arrival of the Holy Spirit.

Tradition

Black Liberation pedagogy fosters a strong sense of *tradition*, which connects the present challenges with the actions of past generations, while offering a critique of *traditionalism* as a way of keeping persons passive and uninformed. Teaching tradition in healthy, life-affirming ways means nurturing appreciation of the questions, challenges, circumstances, and decisions of the past generations that inform and illuminate the lives, practices, and thinking of the present generation. While many claim that they are teaching tradition, they are, in actuality, teaching traditionalism. Traditionalism requires that persons be unthinking, non-questioning, and careless. Decision making is simply repetitious duplication of past decisions with little regard for the changed and changing context and circumstance. Teaching traditionalism is unhealthy for congregations as it stymies the process of change and celebrates stagnation. Indicators of traditionalism in local churches are the phrases "We've never done it that way before," and "We've always done it that way." Honoring and teaching tradition in healthy ways means fostering creativity, nurturing critical thinking, and encouraging questioning.

Education Is both Caught and Taught

To say that education is both *caught* and *taught* means that there are informal, unstructured ways that assist people in learning, as well as formal, structured ways for learning. While education transforms community, community does not just happen and it cannot be taken for granted. It requires commitment and the effort of its leadership and membership to nurture, support, and sustain healthy community. As discussed earlier, those structures of the Black Church that are educational venues for liberation are critical because they also support and sustain community.

Ministries specifically structured as teaching/learning opportunities (e.g., Sunday school or Bible study), in tandem with the broader life of congregational activities (worship, activism), are equally powerful educational events for formation and the shaping of identity. Black Liberation pedagogy has a holistic approach to communal education. It does not privilege lessons in the classroom as more educationally valuable than revelations in the worship service. It relies on the tenet that "education is caught and taught."

People learn from the curriculum of structured Sunday school and Bible study lessons held in classrooms. Equally valuable is the learning that occurs when people participate in leading worship, in serving as a trustee, or while helping in the soup kitchen. The Bible is taught through traditional classroom settings where the teacher instructs the student, and the Bible is caught when the larger congregation participates in the annual Christmas pageant that retells, in vivid portrayal, the story of the birth of Christ. Persons learn by instruction about faith, but as importantly or more importantly, persons learn the lessons of faith through the experiences of faith.

The Challenge for Black Church Education in the Twenty-first Century

While education is still perhaps the most powerful and most underutilized resource for the eradication of oppression and the healing of racism, classism, sexism, and homophobia available to the Black Church in the twenty-first century, there are many obstacles to valuing and prioritizing education. The current embodiments of oppression threatening Black people and the Black Church have compromised the potency of past strategies such as boycotts and public protests (with the possible exception of the **Million Man March**). Rampant materialism and greed as common values in the United States now complicate the struggle to heal or annihilate the "isms." Immigration and globalization add a kind of complexity to the racist identity politics of this country that the Black Church has yet to address.

The civil rights movement took us all radically closer to a better way of life (higher income levels, access to higher education, more available job sectors, and the like), but the movement's accomplishments feel as if they are slipping away. Without concerted effort to maintain the intellectual legacy of the great prophet, scholar, and activist, Dr. Martin

Luther King, Jr., the most enduring symbol of his achievements would be the streets and boulevards bearing his name in countless North American cities and a national holiday celebrated by Black local churches with "preach-offs." When Dr. King's accomplishments are recounted and assessed honestly, he should be depicted as a scholar, theologian, and intellectual. There should be emphasis that Dr. King earned a doctorate in theology, and as such was a brilliant theologian. Dr. King is rarely noted for the influence of Howard Thurman, Benjamin E. May, and W.E.B. Du Bois as much as mention of his study of Ghandian nonviolence. Furthermore, little is mentioned about his deep participation with African American intellectuals and theologians. His "Letter from a Birmingham Jail," extemporaneously written without use of a library or reference book due to his incarceration, articulated the complex genius of the moral and theological insights that he had gleaned from these forbears as it also crystallized his vision of social justice.[28] King was the leader and prophet of the civil rights movement, while he was also its great intellectual. The brilliance of King was his ability to move effortlessly from scholarly prose and theory to inspirational sermonic rendering. King's ability to be a prophet, preacher, teacher, politician, and minister came—at least in part—from his abilities to think theologically and philosophically. Perhaps King's great legacy is his insistence on critical thinking as a tool for liberation. Now, in the earliest years of the twenty-first century, the Black Church is suspicious of intellectuals, while at the same time needing well-educated clergy to lead its very educated laity. Gripped by prosperity gospel and the insatiable appetites for megachurches; education, as it was for our foreparents, might be the best way out of the confusion of ignorance and out of the grip of the more recent incarnation of this soul-robbing oppression.

SUMMARY

The Black Church renews the *passing on* of tradition through the understanding that education occurs through congregational life and the nurture of resilient disciples. All learning occurs in context. For Black Christians, learning to be faithful occurs in a societal context of hatred, bigotry, and oppression. Christian education in the Black Church, informed by Black theology, understands that God is passionately, eternally, vigorously concerned about the flourishing[29] of Black people. God as the "god of the oppressed" is concerned about souls, but of equal importance, God is concerned about the personal well-being of Black bodies and minds. Out of a communal sense of hope in God and a cultural sense of somebodyness, Black congregations solve problems for the myriad of social ills foisted upon them in the hegemonic society, and this problem solving is the particular approach to Christian education. Out of the necessity of survival as well as out of grace-filled imagination Christian education in the Black Church tradition creates and maintains practices of teaching and learning that are foundational to congregational life and visa versa. While education is done in the midst of the life of the congregation, it is understood that the life of the congregation moves beyond the walls of the church building and into the larger society. Thus, teaching and learning in the Black Church tradition are not politically neutral. Education is fundamentally political as well as culturally imbued for continued assurance of the survival of future generations.

BIOGRAPHIES

Grant Shockley (1919–1995)

Grant Shockley, considered by many to be the preeminent African American religious educator of the twentieth century, was Professor of Christian Education at the Divinity School of Duke University, from 1983 to 1989. At the center of his work as both a scholar and ordained United Methodist elder was his mission to combat the negative attitudes and perspectives that the larger, white society dictated to African Americans. Shockley's numerous published articles as well as his work as President of The Interdenominational Theological Center (1975–1979) and President of Smith College in Little Rock, Arkansas (1979–1983), provide a legacy of intellectual courage. In his academic work and ministry, Shockley embodied a particular perspective in Black theology that provided powerful and lasting images of hope, resilience, and love.[30]

Olivia Pearl Stokes (1916–2002)

Dr. Olivia Pearl Stokes was the first African American woman to receive a doctorate in religious education. She earned the doctorate from Columbia University where she studied in the joint program with Union

Theological Seminary. An ordained Baptist minister, educator, author, ecumenical leader, and administrator, the focus of her academic work as ministry involved interests in leadership training and development, education in the African American church, Black women and children, African culture, and the educational implications of Black Liberation theology in the African American Church. Dr. Stokes developed a holistic approach to religious education that challenged religious educators to consider the relationships between methodology, theology, and real life concerns. She distinguished herself as a pioneer in cultural, cross-cultural, and intercultural education, making many trips to teach in Africa.[31]

STUDY QUESTIONS

1. What does it mean for the Black Church to renew the passing-on of tradition?
2. What most renews the experience of Black Church and Black Christians?
3. What is distinctive about Black Church teaching and learning?
4. What does it mean for the Black Church as a problem-solving institution to educate its people for the myriad of social ills that threaten survival?
5. If Christian education is a tool of liberation, what are the structures and practices of Christian education in the Black Church that keep the church resilient?

ESSENTIAL TEXTS

- *Consciousness and the Work of Grant Shockley* by Charles R. Foster and Fred Smith
- *Dear Sisters: A Womanist Practice of Hospitality* by Nancy Lynne Westfield
- *Soul Stories: African American Christian Education*, rev. ed., by Anne E. Streaty Wimberly
- *Trouble Don't Last Always: Emancipatory Hope among Adolescents* by Evelyn L. Parker

Worship is neither an exercise
in divine data distribution
nor a rehearsal of celestial rules.
Rather, public worship is a
significant even indispensable way
for believers to exercise
and acquire faith.
—Herbert Anderson
and Edward Foley

BLACK CHRISTIAN WORSHIP AS NURTURE

INTRODUCTION

Historically and currently, Christian worship in the Black Church manifests as distinctive and vital communal connections with and responses to God's concern, hope, and activity on behalf of Black people's wholeness in a hostile world. As in the past, this corporate experience continues as nurturing activity that responds to the need for affirmation, sustenance, and direction in the midst of trials and triumphs. Indeed, in this way, worship exists as an essential part of the historical role of Black Christian communities in promoting the well-being of Black people.[1] This chapter provides an overview of the nature, necessity and **functions of nurture** in Black worship, and then explores in fuller detail the content and approaches to nurture found in key activities and liturgical events.

Black people look to worship in the Black Church as vital, relational, and event-full nurturing experience. They continue to need what Staples and Johnson call "a refuge in times of severe trouble . . . [and] reinforcement in resisting personal and social stressors."[2] The need is for what Immanuel Lartey identifies as a **communal-contextual model** of pastoral care in which the "relational and corporate community is both the base and the agent of care," where the wider social realities of people's lives receive attention.[3] On these bases, the worshiping community engages in key nurturing practices. These practices include laying before God the tough burdens of life, concerns, and desires for the present and future; expressing deep emotion and lament connected with personal and communal plight and possibility; and re-framing and affirming a positive Black identity that counters the negative one found in larger society. Or, to use Homer Ashby's words, "they affirm one another in the belief that they are indeed a part of God's good creation. Whatever the world may say Monday through Saturday, the church delivers God's good news that blacks are a people of worth and value."[4] The worshiping community also connects with the promises of God, a vision for a future of hope, and a sense of agency to act on that vision communicated in Scripture, preaching, praying, singing, and testimony. In short, worship functions as nurture as it engages people in these activities and enables them to envision the changes needed in their individual, family, and community life as well as requisite life-changing behaviors.

A VIEW OF NURTURE

The term "nurture" actually derives from the Latin verb *nutrire*, which means to "suckle, nourish, or cultivate." Richard Osmer defines it "as the provision of nourishment to a living organism in order to help it to develop and flourish."[5] It refers to fostering, providing, building up, and maintaining basics for the vitality of life or existence itself. Indeed, it is understood that, without these basics, life would diminish. In Black Christian worship, this expands to an understanding of nurture that is couched in the image of the "nursing mother" who, with love and care, gives nourishment or *food* that a loved one needs and receives in order to live and grow. It is *food* given to enrich the life of the receiver and the receiver's ability to contribute to and give shape to the ongoing life of self, others, and the community.[6] From an incarnational theological perspective, the nourishment, or *food*, is provided through the caring presence and activity of God in Jesus Christ often mysteriously in the sacramental activity of worship and concretely in the care shown by the pastor and others. In this sense, care is linked with nurture and takes the form of concern for or attention given to people's well-being.[7]

Nurture is also evocative and, therefore, is not received passively. More specifically, as shown by Anne Streaty Wimberly in her book *Nurturing Faith and Hope*, nurture prompts people to deal with the nourishment given to them. To make a difference in people's lives, nurture must arouse in them "the 'more' that brings an awareness, a discernment, and even a struggling with what they are to do on behalf of their own and others' life direction and healing." The ability for "people discerning their own sense of direction and the spiritual values and resources needed for decision making"[8] is an extension of worship as nurture. Undergirding this understanding is the view that "worshipers desire and are ready for nurture and have the wherewithal to receive nurture and discern its meaning for their lives." They come together as a community of faith and belief seeking that which they need to be fulfilled and the ability to wrest, welcome, and embrace the blessings that are inherent to their lives as Christians. Toward this end, Black Christians realize that through the shared worship experience they are capable of making sense of and incorporating the nurture of worship "in light of what Augustine calls 'interior truth' . . . what already resides in a person that must be balanced with what the person hears from another."[9] This kind of nurturing activity is, in fact, a necessity in the midst of the ambiguities of Black life—deep trials and tribulations on one hand and triumphs on the other.

Contemporary Circumstances of Black People Calling for Nurture

There is an imperative need for nurture for Black people faced with marginalization, oppression, and a widening range of concerns. Indeed, today, a pervasive situation of crisis seems to exist: an environmental crisis, a drug crisis, a crisis in education, an incarceration crisis, a joblessness crisis, a homelessness crisis, crises in love and the family.[10] The current situation has resulted in what Edward Wimberly calls "relational refugees," or people who are not grounded in nurturing and liberating relationships, but who are desperately seeking this grounding.[11] The current situation of Black people is also marked by diminishing resources such as the stories through which past generations found meaning and convincing reason to continue on in the midst of life's absurdities. In the place of these resources, there is instead a disturbing difficulty for many in imagining the wherewithal to sustain meaningful life; and this difficulty is accompanied by an anguished search by some for the answer to the Nietzschean question, "Is God dead?"

People in our churches and communities are searching for a wise life perspective or worldview that centers on the integrity, courage, and faith in God needed to conduct their lives in turbulent times and to shape our world toward more hopeful ends.[12] There is yearning, indeed, urgency, for nurture that can assist them in arriving at what Stephen Carter calls "the serenity of a person who is confident in the knowledge that he or she is living rightly."[13] This yearning is encapsulated in numerous and varied stories. In one instance, a young army reservist and mother of a six-month-old child struggles with how to reconcile her summons to the dangers of military duty, her love for and obligations to her child, and her deep concern for the adequate care of family in her absence. In another situation, one more youth adds to the steady stream of Black youth into the prison system. And, many agonize over a seemingly bleak future wrought by joblessness due to company downsizing.

A family member tells of the bitterness of divorce and the challenge of single parenthood. One teen attempts to cope with the trauma of parental abuse while another faces the reality of pregnancy and premature parental responsibility, and still another recalls the trauma of racial profiling. A grandparent simply says, "How?" when suddenly thrust into the role of raising grandchildren because of the drug addiction of one of the children's parents and the incarceration of the other. The meaning of life and death loom forth for a young adult diagnosed with AIDS, a retiree diagnosed with cancer, and a family struggling with the decision about nursing home care for an aging and ailing parent. Bombarded by the busyness of our times even amidst the plethora of time saving devices, the mantra of numerous family members is the loss of face-to-face connectedness with one another.

Yet, at the same time, there are heartening stories of weddings, anniversaries, births, graduations, renewed health, and miraculous survival; and, within these stories, hope abides amid wonderment about the future. In the throes of peril and promise, the questions inevitably come forth: Why are things the way they are? Who and Whose am I? What does tomorrow hold and how may we best move toward and into an unknown future? The varied stories of trials on the one hand and triumphs on the other are ones that people bring into the worshiping congregation and for which they seek insight and guidance.[14]

Worship as Nurturing Response

Key ritual activities of worship serve as creative **nurturing pathways** to help people see constructive and self-destructive patterns of living, believe in the redemptive activity of God, and grasp wisdom to move forward in faith and hope. These activities, or pathways of nurture, include music making, proclamation through the preached word, and prayer. These activities are often referred to as the three essential pathways through which nurture occurs in Black worship.[15] Through these pathways, worship enables people to continue on in the midst of a hostile world and the crises of life and to imagine ways of enacting a story of promise for self, family, and community undergirded by a faith that "sees a star of hope." The pathways of nurture raise hope in the face of adversity.[16]

The pathways of nurture do not stand alone as means of nurture in the Black, worshiping congregation. The two primary liturgical events of baptism and Holy Communion (the Eucharist) are powerful nurturing resources. In Black worship, the ritual of baptism is a crucial means of nurturing an embodied awareness of a self-identity that God values and affirms. Holy Communion, or the Eucharist, functions as the Welcome Table for Black people in contrast to their experience of an unwelcoming world. Nurture happens through "the enactment of God's welcome"[17] revealed in Jesus and articulated through Christ's brokenness. Moreover, Holy Communion prompts the experience in worshipers of re-humanizing themselves despite living in a world intent on stripping them of their humanity. They become drawn together by Holy Communion to stand together as "a community of solidarity and a caring people in the world."[18]

Functions of Nurture

Several specific functions of nurture are carried out in the process of Black people's involvement in the pathways of nurture and key liturgical events. In particular, Black Christian worship as a whole and these aspects of worship in particular have healing, guiding, sustaining, and reconciling functions. The first three functions were first presented in the pastoral theological writing of Seward Hiltner.[19] William A. Clebsch and Charles R. Jaekle added the final one.[20] *Healing* pertains to binding up wounds or restoring bodily wholeness and mental functioning caused by disease, impairment, or loss. *Sustaining* consists of the provision of comfort and strength needed by people to endure difficult circumstances. *Guiding* refers to helping people through the provision of principles or educing within people choices, courses of actions, and resources in times of trouble. *Reconciling* seeks to reestablish broken relationships or to bring people in positive relationship with others and God. All four typify key historical functions used by pastoral caregivers in the care of people. Because of the key role of the pastoral caregiver in carrying out these functions, the responsibility for their use in worship lay with the pastor.

In his seminal work, *Pastoral Care in the Black Church*, Edward P. Wimberly describes the relevance of the four functions—healing, sustaining, guiding, and reconciling—to the historical caring role of the Black Church, including worship. He emphasizes that, when carried out within the context of worship, these functions are essential resources and enabling tools that provide the means for people to discern their capacity to envision and enact or continue a personal and communal story of faith and hope. Wimberly deviates from the historical emphasis by pastoral theologians on the pastor's solitary role in carrying out the four functions and, instead, accentuates the caring resources of both the pastor and the entire congregation. He also gives prominent attention to sustaining and guiding functions. This prominence stems from the negative racial climate in America and the necessity of the Black Church's role in affirming the love and care of God for Black people in tandem with providing resources needed to reduce the impact of racism on Black people's sense of self and self-efficacy.[21] Through music, preaching, and prayer, these functions combine consolation and admonition, and present an eschatological or future hope. In an important way, Black worship becomes an activity of nurture that bears witness to the activity of God, shows awareness and concern for life's realities, and provides nourishment in the form of communal solidarity and pastoral awareness and response.

Wimberly later reaffirms the four functions in the book entitled *African American Pastoral Care*. He states: "Caring within a local Black congregation is a response pattern to God's unfolding story in its midst. This unfolding story is one of liberation as well as healing, sustaining, guiding, and reconciling." He also makes the point that "when ritual and worship draw persons into the major story of the faith community, worship and communal resources are brought to bear on personal needs; and when the emotional, interpersonal, and psychological needs of persons are met in the context of ritual and worship, pastoral care takes place."[22]

The centrality of interactivity taking place in Black worship cannot be overemphasized. That is, care is not done *to* a passive congregation; and how it is done passes beyond care to nurture. The pastor, liturgists, musicians, and worshipers engage in interactive communication, or a "call and response" conversation, wherein people are not simply cared for or shown concern for their well-being, but receive nurture. Indeed, the activity of worship in the Black Church may be called evocative worship. The intent of worship as nurture is to trigger or evoke new or renewed life meaning as well as concrete and wise action on the part of Black people in the throes of the pain and promise of life.[23] To this degree, nurture as a key practice in Black worship is a specific kind of care.

CONTENT IN THE NURTURING PROCESS OF BLACK WORSHIP

An emphasis on content in the nurturing process of Black worship centers on the reality that people do not enter worship as *tabula rasa* or devoid of their personal stories. See the earlier point that these stories highlight the necessity of nurture in worship. It is important to add here that the stories and the necessity of nurture they prompt typically reflect several interrelated components:[24]

- *Self-Identity Issues.* People enter worship with quandaries about and problematic perceptions of their self-identities and self-worth. They seek answers to the question: Who and Whose am I in the midst of society's and others' assaults to my dignity?
- *Social Contextual Issues.* People bring into worship concerns about the social milieu in which they carry out their daily lives. They come with thoughts about difficulties related to where they live, work, and attend school and about the availability or non-availability of needed resources and opportunities.
- *Interpersonal Relationship Issues.* People enter worship with confusion, hardship, disappointment, and other deep feelings connected to their relationships with family members, extended family, friends, neighbors, and colleagues. This may also extend to their relationship with God.
- *Life Events Issues.* People enter worship with joy and gratifying memories associated with events in their lives such as life-changing religious experiences, promotions, honors, mended relationships, and reunions. But they also come with thoughts and feelings connected with personal and family crises such as illness, hospitalization, disabling conditions, death, unfair treatment, broken relationships, job loss, homelessness, and incarceration. Moreover, they bring thoughts and concerns about incidents that mark the

ages/stages of their lives, such as marriage, childbirth, school graduations, separation, divorce, becoming orphaned or widowed, and
entering or exiting a chosen lifestyle or occupation.

- *Life Meaning Issues.* Persons attending worship grapple with positive and negative thoughts and feelings about life in general, about
the meaning and purpose of their lives. They come with a sense of
perplexity and judgment about all that makes up their lives and
how to bring order to it. They want to know: What meaning does
my life have? Is there any worth to my life and my place in it?

- *Story Plot Issues.* Entry into worship does not necessarily mean
that people hold an optimistic life perspective or that they
approach it in positive and constructive ways. While numbers of
worshipers may embrace and come into worship with an optimistic
undergirding theme or unfolding story plot, others may enter with
deep struggles, a negative perception of life, and a destructive
approach to life. It is also the case that people's embrace of a story
plot may move from a positive to negative one depending on the
changing realities of their lives.

The strength of nurture in the worshiping congregation lies in the
awareness of those responsible for it that these aspects of people's lives
must be considered pivotal content or *subject matter* to which nurture
must respond.

As indicated earlier, nurture takes place in Black worship principally
through specific pathways and key events occurring as part of the ritual
life of worship. The pathways include music making, proclamation
through the preached word, testimony, and prayer. The key events
include baptism and Holy Communion. Nurture happens through these
experiences insofar as they connect with and respond to the very real
lives of people and because these experiences are recurring and expected
parts of the ritual life of Black congregational worship. Nurture happens
by the repetitive or ritualized honor that is the given content of human
stories. At the same time, Christian nurture in the Black Church means
that the human story is necessarily linked to the Story of God shown in
Jesus Christ contained in Scripture as well as the story of post-biblical
exemplars of the Christian faith. These two stories—God's Story and the
faith stories of exemplars—serve as central content in the nurturing
process. Key points about this content are as follows:

- *God's Story as a Resource.* When worshipers link with God's Story, they find resources of nurture and love, and they are enabled to commit themselves to be part of God's ongoing story of liberation and healing. Nurture that evokes this commitment means that people see the working out of God's Story through their own actions on their own and others' behalf. They see the biblical story and witness as revelatory of God's concern for justice and righteousness and of Jesus' solidarity with marginal and struggling people. God becomes revealed as the God of history, concerned about and involved in history.[25] And the pastor and congregation serve as enablers or nurturing agents of this story and commitment to it in worship.[26]

- *God's Story as Central to a Theology of Worship and Nurture.* For worship to be authentic, it must acknowledge and form human beings in relation to the Divine. To use Valerie Bridgeman Davis's words, "Worship recognizes that God is present, or at least recognizes that God might, in the vernacular of some African American church people, 'show up and show out.' . . . This phrase 'show up and show out' presumes an active God who wants to be in companionship and communication with God's people."[27] A theology of worship and nurture centers on the storied understanding that God cares for people and that God's story is a story of presence in the *wildernesses* of life and action to "defeat the powers of evil, oppression, and suffering."[28]

- *The Impact of God's Story.* Worship as nurturing activity draws the people of God into the unfolding Story of God in order that they might be shaped by this Story. This activity is to result in the transformation of human vision and character. It is to shape people's attitudes, behaviors, intentions, and dispositions to the extent that they have increased ability to act on God's desire for their well-being and the well-being of others.[29] The important point made by Homer Ashby is that recounting the stories of God's deliverance serves the purpose of presenting God, remembering God, and relying on God as "the promise keeper." This becomes the means of restoring hope and of being stewards of the divine promise.[30]

- *Post-biblical Christian Faith Heritage Stories as Resources.* Connecting with post-biblical Christian faith heritage stories in worship, particularly those from the Black community, exposes worshipers to the difficult journeys that forebears traversed with a tenacity of faith and hope. This content includes stories not simply of Black heroes and heroines well known to most Black worshipers but also stories of local family and church exemplars of the faith. Use of these stories in worship conveys that it is possible to continue on with faith and, in fact, to lead others in a hope-filled direction.[31]

- *Impact of the Christian Faith Heritage Story*. Worship as nurturing activity links people to faith-filled and hope-filled stories of well-known forebears and others in order that people may glean from them "an ethical stance on which hope-filled decisions and actions were made and could still be made even when people experience their backs against the wall."[32] Worshipers receive from these stories wise ways of thinking and acting used in the past and useful for the present.

The important point here is that, when the worshiping congregation participates in song, sermon, prayer, baptism and Holy Communion, there must be something in the content with which people can connect and that renews or gives new life. And the kind of content that is pivotal to nurture in the Black worshiping congregation includes stories focused on identity, contexts of daily living, life events, relationships, the meaning of life, and story plot in tandem with the Story of God and Christian faith heritage stories. Moreover, because of the centrality of story to the nurturing process, stories must be integral and ongoing ritual elements in worship.

In fact, according to Herbert Anderson and Edward Foley, "Ritualization is indispensable for entering the story, exercising co-authorship, and realizing a narrative's full potential. Thus, . . . ritual and narrative are symbiotically related."[33] Ritual takes seriously the need of people and congregations "to fashion narratives that weave together divine and human stories into a single fabric."[34]

It is also important to state that when ritual attends to the very real stories of people and the community, it takes on therapeutic value. Repetition contributes to a sense of continuity in the lives of people and the community by linking past, present, and future. Moreover, repetition provides a dependable source of security and comfort, confirmation of identity, a reliable process for shaping what people believe, or a worldview through which meaning derives.[35]

METHODS OF NURTURING PATHWAYS

Music making, preaching, and **praying** serve as powerful nurturing pathways to the degree that they are repetitive acts in the ritual life of Black worship and take seriously the lived stories of Black individuals and the larger Black community. They are pathways to nurture as they contribute to *healing* in the form of people's bodily, emotional, relational, and spiritual restoration. As part of the healing dimension, these pathways evoke in people recognition and acceptance of a present and acting God in their unfolding life story and their imagining a way forward with God. As pathways of nurture, they *guide* people by weaving the stories of their lives with God's Story, assisting their reflection on and learning from experience, and evoking in them ways to reframe or fashion their stories in hopeful ways. They *sustain* people by receiving openly the expression of feelings, tending to these feelings, and evoking in them the resources from God and community that can see them through difficulty. They carry out a *reconciling* function that assists people's sense of harmony with God, self, others, and their life direction.

In an overall sense, the pathways—music making, preaching, and praying—contribute to people's formation of practical wisdom. These pathways make way for healing, guiding, sustaining, and reconciling functions needed for people to see their ability to cope wisely with life's complexities, make sensible judgments, and exhibit responsible behavior based on spiritual values found in the Christian faith. When this happens, Black Christian worship as nurture exhibits "ritual honesty."[36] At the same time, it is clear that each pathway is unique in the manner in which the functions are carried out. The uniqueness is described in the following sections.

Methods of Music Making

The essential nature of worship is praise, adoration, and thanksgiving offered to God. In Black worship, music is typically a primary and highly revered expression of this nature of worship. But it becomes a pathway for healing, guiding, sustaining, and reconciling because the words and musical style or genre of songs convey messages not possible in ordinary language and evoke attitudes, feelings, and responses not otherwise evident. Theo-musicologist Jon Michael Spencer indicates that singing has been known to function as: testimony about the problems and petitions of the saints, laments, means of communal bonding, and as an agent of healing and building courage. It serves as preparation to endure everyday realities.[37] Thomas Hoyt also describes testimony not simply in song but also in sermon and storytelling as a means through which affirmation, encouragement, catharsis, and healing occur.[38] Spencer goes on to describe the "therapeutic" quality of gospel music or the manner in which these songs of faith assist Black people to voice and confront life's circumstances and immediate problems.[39]

As a nurturing pathway in worship, the attempt must be made to select songs that engage people, not simply in the language of praise, adoration, and thanksgiving but also of testimonies of challenge, lament, and overcoming adversity. The selection of a broad spectrum of styles from spirituals, anthems, and hymns (including lining hymns) to the range of gospel music and rap is meant to engage worshipers across the ages/stages in telling their everyday stories not simply of celebration and triumph but also of struggle and pain.

Music as nurture is intended as a means of *externalization*, or of people expressing openly the *stuff* of life and the plea for healing. It is also intended as a means of *internalization*, or people's new discovery and affirmation within themselves of the impact of the music on how they see and may respond to life's realities and God's activity. Moreover, internalization happens as songs remind worshipers about the nature and beliefs of a community of faith and hope they have already grasped and claim anew as important.

Music that assists externalization and internalization draws people into both cognitive and affective experience. This view of music as cognitive-oriented nurture builds on the cognitive psychological and therapeutic emphasis on changing people's cognition or how they think and how they construe reality.[40] Nurture through music accomplishes this by placing people in a position of unparalleled opportunity to imagine meanings of faith by *being* the community of faith and hope and by sharing the *experience* of its message through music.[41] But it also draws worshipers into considering, imagining, and wondering about life as it is and the promise it holds. Indeed, music that nurtures people engages them in evocative experience that summons their thinking, reflecting, and feeling selves on the promise that is theirs as valued creations of God; and it creates a foundation for faith-filled and hope-filled actions.[42]

The method by which music nurtures people in Black worship includes emotion-laden, expressive, and art-full involvement. Bodily responses of clapping, swaying, dancing, and miming, and uses of drama are powerful ways of arousing kinesthetic meanings of faith in God. This approach to music in worship engages and forms people's *emotional* and *kinesthetic* intelligence that opens the way for them to grasp hope and perseverance in the face of an uncertain future with passion and conviction as Christians.[43] From a psychological therapeutic standpoint, this kind of emotional experience has the power to influence perception, cognition, and action.[44] Specifically, bodily responses to music in the Black worshiping congregation tap into and help form a person's ability to act on an indescribable intuitive knowing that affirms the necessity at times in everyday life to move on without clear surety of what to do in advance. People build what may be called an "improvisational movement vocabulary" that contributes to a sense of what is possible moment-by-moment, which leads them to continue to see what the end will be. Indeed, this method, by which music nurtures people, evokes an awareness of a divine space of comfort and direction in which to enter in times of trial. It arouses "listening to both God's heartbeat and the heartbeat of the gathered people."[45] It calls forth an awareness of the activity of the Holy Spirit and response to the Spirit.[46]

Methods of Proclamation through the Sermon

There is no question that, in Black Church worship, the matter of content is extremely important in carrying out the nurturing task in preaching. To be nurturing, Black preaching centers on the Bible while also focusing on life situations. From this perspective, the themes and subjects of sermons focus on the problems and needs of Black people and the Black community. In the *prophetic* sermon, the preacher uses a nurturing method that employs biblical material to challenge people to think about Scripture and its intersection with their lives in new and helpful ways. This usage evokes the worshiper's self-reflection and consideration of what the text portends for change. Included in this sermonic method is the engagement of worshipers in a critique of human behavior and the visualization and anticipation of concrete actions based on a biblical norm or requirement for faithful and hope-filled Christian life.[47]

There is also a *priestly* word in Black Church preaching that nurtures worshipers by calling their attention to coping strategies and life skills that can see them through the challenges of life and assist their formation of stories of promise. This kind of nurture also affirms the value of Black selfhood by redefining and renaming the Black self. The intent is to counter the negative views of self in everyday life, and evoke a sense of the *Imago Dei* that gives rise to a "reflective self-consciousness, alternative interpretations of self-identity, and imagination of life"[48] as a child of God.

Whether through the prophetic or priestly word, the sermon method should serve as an impetus that inspires "Black worshipers to live faithfull and hope-filled lives" in keeping with the life and ministry of Jesus Christ. "The Black preacher is the evocator . . . guided and inspired by the divine Evocator."[49] To carry out the nurturing method in preaching, according to James Harris, "the preacher is compelled to say something that addresses the needs of the people, directing the message to heart and head."[50] Nurture entails the preacher's use of relational, practical, and specific communication that has evocative power. Communication is called for that prompts people's wakefulness to God's Story, a surety of who and Whose they are, and what Olin Moyd calls "the courage to struggle against dehumanizing forces and the power to transcend the human-caused trials and tribulations in countless otherwise hopeless situations."[51] Of central importance, however, is the notion that preaching is nurturing activity insofar as it creates in the worshipers a sense of God's nourishing presence and unconditional care.

Black worshipers are not passive, but active participants in the sermonic experience. Indeed, it may be said that worshipers come with the expectation and intent to enter into the historic "call and response" pattern in the entire conduct of worship, including preaching. This method of involvement calls for an understanding of worshipers as more than simple recipients of nurture. They are, to use Quentin Hand's terms, people who show initiative, intentionality, and movement in their search for wholeness. They are, in a sense, sojourners who are "traveling toward a place of healing and blessing not always clearly known in advance." The sojourner "joins others traveling the same way and welcomes the assistance of a guide." Even though the preacher as guide knows more about exploring new territory than the sojourner, the sojourners do their own walking as they travel together.[52] In the sermonic experience, the worshiper fulfills this special role by engaging in what may be called reflection in action. The worshipers' response of "talking back" to the preacher is action based on the worshipers' listening both to what is said and to the self. This method of involvement of Black worshipers reveals that they are not passive listeners who fail to recognize the flow of language, thought, and the feelings of pastor, self, and others. Rather, they are active participants in the nurturing process who hear the preachers' words in order to engage the preacher in more than a surface level of communicative relationship.[53]

Methods of Praying

Rev. Wyatt Tee Walker highlights prayer as the strength of Black worship.[54] It is worshipers' direct entry into conversation with God; the pathway of expressions of praise to the One who is worthy of praise, and the link to the source of strength. Michael Dash and his colleagues also highlight the importance of prayer because of its all-embracing quality. They indicate, "No area of human life—or of human experience of joy and praise, pain and happiness—is outside of the realm of prayer." Central to prayer as nurture is the view, "Prayer is more than a ritual or a set of specific prayers. It is the belief that God hears all sincere prayers, prayers that tell God 'all about our troubles.'"[55] However, Perry LeFevre's description of prayer is particularly helpful in understanding approaches to conversations with God in the nurturing process occurring in Black worship:

> True prayer involves articulation of that which is deepest in human life, often at an unconscious or nonverbal level . . .
>
> Caught in a situation of fundamental insecurity, aware of the disjunction between what is and what might be, the human being utters a cry of anguish or of joy, a cry of terror or of wonder. This cry is the primal religious act arising out of the search for, or affirmation of, whatever can help in living with the insecurity of human existence. The one who prays seeks what is trustworthy and dependable in the face of the human existence situation. Ultimately, the concern is for the one who is unconditionally trustworthy. Prayer is rooted in this existential question of trust.[56]

As in the case of singing and preaching, prayer in the Black worshiping congregation evolves from and expresses the particular stories of Black people and their perception of an able and trustworthy God. To this degree, the method used by clergy, liturgists, and laity in entering conversations with God is very real, spontaneous, and autobiographical. Whether in prayers of lament, confession, intercession, or commitment, the language spoken by or on behalf of the one seeking nurture is deeply heart-rending, extemporaneous, and replete with deep feeling.

Black worship opens the way for the language of the lament or the moan of the soul that arises from life's struggles and losses. Through this language, people express their complaints and plead to a listening God who can be trusted to respond if not when one wants, then "on time." The method is clearly one of "telling it like it is." Through this method, there is a sense in which nurture derives not simply from the invitation for full disclosure of the self's or others' stories. Rather, prayers are pivotal evocative experiences that help people see themselves and God more fully. Through prayer, people become aware that they can be themselves fully and freely in the presence of God. They discover that prayers actually "open the way for healing."[57] Prayers nurture faith in God and self as well as hope along the sojourn into the unknown future.

Because nurturing does not exclude concerns for life-negating and self-destructive behavior, methods of entering into conversation with God include confessional language. Through this language, people acknowledge their imperfections and sinfulness, seek forgiveness, appeal to God for healing, guidance, sustenance, and reconciliation with God, self, others, and all things, and voice commitment to continue on a faithful and hope-filled journey.

In the Black worshiping congregation, the **altar call** is an accepted and expected experience through which healing is mediated. People experience a connection to the healing presence of God at the altar that is furthered by pastoral prayers and prayers of intercession sometimes offered by laypeople. During prayers at the altar, it is not unusual for physical support in the form of touching to occur as pastoral staff members gently place their hands on the head or shoulder of the praying worshiper. Worshipers may also clasp one another's hands and embrace or hold someone in distress. Actual healing services append this form of physical support by the *laying on of hands* or by pastors praying for God's healing in the people being touched. In whatever form it occurs, touching is deemed a meaningful form of nurture that conveys and is received as love, assurance, and God's promise or hope, especially by people suffering from life's uncertainties, loss, trauma, or physical illness.

The intent is for prayer to be a pathway of nurture that becomes a way of life wherein people's awareness of God, the ultimate source of care and nourishment, overtakes the tendency of humans to be servants of their own minds and will rather than God's.

NURTURING CONTENT AND METHOD IN BAPTISM AND HOLY COMMUNION

The rites of baptism and Holy Communion or Eucharist persist in the Black worshiping congregation as highly meaningful **nurturing events**. The importance of these events lies in the consciousness-raising they evoke about Black personal and communal identity.

Baptism as Nurture

The content and process of baptism focus on three acts: The *naming act*, the *announcing act*, and the *claiming act*.[58] In the *naming act*, people hear their given names called by the pastor and the identification of themselves as God's creations who are baptized in the name of the Creator, the Son, and Holy Spirit. Thus, their named identity becomes linked with the Divine identity; and their identity is affirmed and reaffirmed as valued by God. That is, God gives Black people a valued identity. And, in this way, baptism nurtures awareness that Black people are not invisible and need not claim for themselves the denigrating labels assigned to them.

The *announcing act* includes the pastor's introduction of newly baptized people to the congregation. The announcement goes beyond linking the identities of the baptismal initiates with the Divine identity to linking their identities with that of the community or Christ's family. This act brings the whole community to awareness of the definition of self not simply as a valued creation of God but also as a valued member of Christ's family. Moreover, the whole community is to form images of the meaning of this announcement for the lives of baptized people and the community's life. Nurture takes the form of an invitation to probe the meanings of Black identity.

The *claiming act* extends beyond the pastor's announcement of baptized people as valued creations of God and members of Christ's family to evoking in the whole community an embodied awareness of a Christian communal identity called into being by God and a Christian lifestyle commensurate with this calling. Particular emphasis is placed on the community's care for and guidance of newly baptized people. Importantly, the *claiming act:*

is nurture directed toward the worshipers' embodied awareness of the experience of baptism as a crucial covenantal event in the life of both the baptized person and the congregation. It is the 'act' of enkindling a deep 'in the bones' awareness that what happens to the baptized member makes a difference to every other member to the extent that the congregation can never again be the same.[59]

In this way, the whole congregation is identified as a nurturing agent who takes on the responsibility for the healing, guiding, sustaining, and reconciling functions of nurture.

Communion as Nurture

An earlier section of this chapter alluded to the experience of the Welcome Table as constitutive of the rite of Holy Communion (Eucharist). Two primary acts embody the content and process of this rite as nurture: The *act of remembering* and the *act of re-membering*.[60] These two acts are pivotal to the nurturing process in the Black worshiping congregation because they invite participation in divinely inspired nurture to the end that people experience the presence and love of God through Jesus Christ, anticipate God's love in the wildernesses of life, and show this love to others.

Specifically, the *act of remembering* who God is, how God acts through Jesus Christ in the stories of people, and what it means to respond to God is undertaken by the worshipers as they partake of the Communion elements. Remembering prompts Black people's recognition of Jesus' suffering on their behalf, Jesus' solidarity with suffering people, and Jesus' welcome of all and exclusion of none, including Black people, to the banquet table where God's healing, guidance, sustenance, and reconciliation occur.

The *act of re-membering* during Holy Communion draws the worshiping congregation into a new or renewed experience of being and becoming a community of solidarity. It symbolizes the reconstitution of community based on awareness that God's family is an inclusive one. The content of nurture occurring at the Welcome Table takes the form of the officiating pastor's interpretation of it as the central experience in God's communal *home*. The nurturing process highlights that, in this *home*, people who experience a sense of *homelessness* in their everyday sojourn are welcome. Indeed, as a nurturing event, the experience of the Welcome Table is to prompt "recognition of Jesus Christ as the host who includes homeless sojourners, offering them a shelter in the time of storm and spiritual food for the journey ahead."[61] But more than this, the experience is to evoke formation of a communal ethic and hospitable character that becomes evident in people living rightly and faithfully the Christian story. This is *re-membering* in the clearest sense that surely includes the Christian community's welcome and care of one another and the stranger.

THE ROLES OF PASTOR AND CONGREGATION IN NURTURE

It is important that this chapter closes with some final remarks about the **roles of the pastor and the congregation in nurture** occurring in the Black worshiping congregation. Edward Wimberly summarizes the role of the pastor in the nurturing process. His perspective is that this role includes creating an environment of concern and care, enabling worshipers to sing and pray, keeping the needs of people and the community in mind, and using Scripture and proclamation in ways that contribute to the ability of those in crisis to have courage and strength sufficient to move through emotional and interpersonal challenges.[62] The pastor's task is also to disclose to the worshiping community its role as resources in the healing, guiding, sustaining, and reconciling functions of nurture and to follow through with the pastor's task as pastoral caregiver and counselor outside the worship context when necessary.

The continual challenge for the pastor is what Anderson and Foley call the weaving of "the human story and the divine narrative into a single web."[63] The role of the pastor in integrating the story of God revealed in Jesus Christ with present human stories is essential to nurture in the Black worshiping congregation. Without it, the essential work of nurture diminishes; and there is the risk of the ritual life of worship becoming a dead ritual.

SUMMARY

In many places, this chapter highlights the active role of the congregation in the nurturing process. To review, the worshiping congregation is not passive in the nurturing process. Their task is to become involved in their own and others' nurture. As such, they are participants who actively engage in the "call and response" process of worship, enter into critical reflection in action, openly express feelings, become involved in art-full utterance and demonstration, and act as a caring community. Indeed, in the Black tradition, the total church has the responsibility of being the caring community and demonstrating this care through its welcome, sensitivity, and assistance offered to hurting people during worship. The pastor does not stand alone in carrying out this task. The present and future challenge is to give new priority to worship as a vital context for healing, guiding, sustaining, and reconciling ministry. This priority is crucial given the heightening complexity of issues faced by people in the Black community. The significance of ministry that can assist people in their pursuit of faith-filled and hope-filled living continues to grow in intensity and demands response by pastors and Black congregations.

BIOGRAPHIES

Melva Wilson Costen (1933–   )

Melva Wilson Costen is Helmar Emil Nielsen Professor Emeritus of Worship and Music at Interdenominational Theological Center (ITC). Dr. Costen is considered by liturgists across the world as the preeminent scholar of African American Worship and Liturgy. As an Elder in the Presbyterian Church U.S.A., she is a representative from the South Atlantic Synod and served as moderator of the committee to publish an African American liturgical resource for the PCUSA. Dr. Costen performed as a member of the executive boards of the Presbyterian Association of Musicians (PAM), the African Heritage Presbyterian Association of Musicians, The Hymn Society in the United States and Canada, and the Liturgical Conference. She chaired the Church Ministries Division of the ITC Research Project on African American Christian Worship Traditions and was director of the Mastor of Arts in Church Music Degree program. She is also an active member of the North American Academy of Liturgy and the College Music Society. Her publications include several books on worship on worship and music, including *Worship Music: A Concise Dictionary, African American Christian Worship* and *In Spirit And In Truth: The Music of African American Worship*.[64]

Anne E. Streaty Wimberly (1936–   )
and Edward P. Wimberly (1943–   )

This dynamic couple has brought more than forty years of leadership to the academy as well as to local church ministry. The Wimberlys are currently on faculty at the Interdenominational Theological Seminary in Atlanta, Georgia. Dr. Anne Wimberly is Professor of Christian Education and Church Music as well as Program Director for the Youth Hope-Builders Academy. Dr. Edward Wimberly is Vice President for Academic Affairs/Provost. He is also Professor of Pastoral Care and Counseling. As individuals, each provides a legacy of compassionate service and exemplary scholarship. Each is a prolific scholar having published multiple books and articles in their chosen fields. The Wimberlys are best known for their generosity of spirit and their abilities to connect their scholarly insights with the needs of God's people in the United States as well as in Africa. They both are exemplars of praxis ministry having dedicated their lives to the transformation and healing of African American peoples. As scholars who have dedicated their life's works to pastoral care and Christian education, they are examples of the power and possible pastoral theology as ministry to heal and transform lives.

STUDY QUESTIONS

1. A case is made for a communal-contextual orientation to pastoral care in worship that takes the form of nurture. What is involved in this orientation and what is meant by nurture?
2. Nurturing functions are identified as healing, guiding, sustaining, and reconciling. How do you understand each of these functions?
3. How would you describe the pathways of nurture, nurturing events, and the importance of each of them?
4. How would you characterize the need for nurture in the worshiping congregation? Be specific about the realities of everyday life in your community that call for nurture.
5. Use the description of nurture contained in the chapter to examine the manner(s) in which nurture occurs in worship in your congregation. What similarities occur? What differences?
6. How important are the four functions to the nurturing process in the worshiping congregation? Would you place greater emphasis on any

one of them over the others? Why? What substitutions or additions would you make?

7. What would you hope the outcomes might be for individuals and the community as a whole as the result of an intentional focus on nurture in the worshiping congregation of which you are a part?

8. Identify a specific community concern that requires nurture either in the form of healing, guiding, sustaining, or reconciling. What scriptural reference, sermon topic, music, and corporate prayer would you select as means of carrying out the nurturing function?

9. Examine your role in making nurture come alive in the worshiping congregation.

ESSENTIAL TEXTS

- *African American Christian Worship* by Melva Wilson Costen
- *African American Pastoral Care* by Edward P. Wimberly
- *Nurturing Faith & Hope: Black Worship as a Model for Christian Education* by Anne E. Streaty Wimberly

When called of God, on a
particular occasion, to a
definite work, I said, "No, Lord,
not me." Day by day I was more
impressed that God would have me
work in [God's] vineyard. I thought
it could not be that I was called to
preach—I, so weak and ignorant.
Still, I knew all things were possible
with God, even to confounding the
wise by the foolish things
of this earth.
—Rev. Julia A. J. Foote

The author of chapter 8
"Black Preaching Praxis" is
Dale P. Andrews. Citations from this
chapter should be attributed to
Dale P. Andrews.

BLACK PREACHING PRAXIS

INTRODUCTION

In the academy of homiletics, Black preaching traditions are esteemed practices, performance styles usually thought to be culturally shaped by communal participation in the worship service with the preaching event at its core. Mastery of delivery and engagement of the hearers are central in the admiration of Black preaching. But Black **preaching praxis** also involves the rich cultural history of an enslaved and oppressed people's engagement with Western Christianity. That engagement entailed a transformation of Christianity as Africans and African Americans sought to translate their theological worldviews when confronted with distortion of human life and spiritual values. That translation of worldview involved the interpretation of biblical faith and the cultivation of the Black Church, both of which continue today as the church faces the mutations of oppression. Preaching praxis is the reflexive activity of interpretation and experience that goes into discerning a Word of revelation from biblical texts and the living theologies of the community of faith. **Black practical theology** demands this reflexive understanding of preaching praxis. The transformation of Western Christianity in the evolution of the Black Church is best described through Black homiletics, hermeneutics, and communal care held together in Black preaching praxis.

The development of Black homiletics reflects the development of Black Church dynamics in wrestling specifically with the dialectic between pastoral and prophetic ministries. Biblical and cultural hermeneutics seek to address the demands of historical or social experiences and the challenges of faith that arise therein. The assaults of racism, slavery, Jim and Jane Crow, and "un-civil rights" raise a false split between the challenges of pastoral care as nurturing wholeness and prophetic care as seeking justice. Here, we must avoid the unfortunate bifurcation of the soul and body between the pastoral and prophetic, respectively. Spiritual wholeness and historical liberation are at stake in both pastoral and prophetic ministries. The struggles of the historical Black Church, and therefore African American preaching traditions, are found in the distortions of this vital dialectic. The pastoral–prophetic dialectic represents the development of African American preaching praxis and the evolution of the Black Church, as well as defining the apprenticeship traditions in teaching/learning Black preaching, although the dialectic was not always sustained. Apprenticeship methods developed within cultural and theological contexts as the kaleidoscope of historical conditions helped determine narrative preaching practices, biblical interpretations, and complex rhetorical strategies. This chapter tries to identify and address these developments in the apprenticeship traditions of Black preaching praxis.

PRACTICAL THEOLOGY AND BLACK PREACHING

When we speak of practical theology and Black preaching, we enter into a theology of preaching itself. Olin Moyd points out that for African American traditions, a theology of preaching insists upon the interpretation of God's self-revelation in Scripture, in Christ, and in the context of a church engaging the world. It has never been an abstract philosophical, religious enterprise about the human condition. Black preaching certainly wrestles with philosophical theology about such matters as existence, but it holds that exercise is neither its goal nor its source of revelation or relevance. Black practical theology for preaching interprets the faith and cultivates the church in the tasks and strategies of ministry, understanding that our encounters with God and revelation are always contextual and historical. The universal God is revealed in the unfolding story of Black humanity in redemptive history.[1]

A Black practical theology of preaching praxis has developed in the context of African American **living faith** in meaning-making and social justice, both in the context of ministry. Living faith is the interpretation of faith that emerges from the questions or struggles of living situations.

Black preaching praxis empowers us to engage the faith even in crisis. This reflexive enterprise entails both wholeness and justice as we wrestle with what is held as orthodox theology in the prospect of what is **ortho- praxis** (the questions of what would constitute "right actions").[2] For African Americans, living faith contends with the experiences of racial assault on Black wholeness and Black flourishing. The contexts are historical, psychosocial, and theological. Black preaching praxis must contend not only with the struggles of life or faith seeking self-understanding but also with the struggles of the oppressed seeking liberation. In the tasks of interpreting the faith and transforming a church of liberation, Black preaching praxis, therefore, participates in both pastoral and prophetic offices.

Black preaching has done more than participate, however. It has been integral to the very formation of African American Christianity and the Black Church. The tasks of interpreting the faith and transforming the church did more than create an isolated, *cultural* faith and *cultural* church. Black preaching took on the mantle of pastoral care and prophetic reform. Black preaching praxis became a primary force in confronting and transforming Christianity, challenging American Christianity to live into its faith claims. Somewhere between the *Imago Dei* (image of God) and the *Missio Dei* (mission of God), Black preaching praxis picks up the mantle of God to interpret the faith for personal wholeness and cultivate the church for communal witness or action. When held together, the relationship between personal wholeness and communal witness creates a dialectic between personhood and *peoplehood* in the faith. Black preaching sustains this dialectic in both the pastoral and prophetic functions of Christian ministry.[3]

How we define the pastoral and prophetic functions of preaching helps to clarify the role of preaching in the development and mission of the Black Church. **Pastoral preaching** is the ministry of care that has developed within the larger context of corporate care with its traditions of spiritual and communal values. Spiritual values place pastoral preaching in the context of mutual care. The preacher becomes an agent of God's concern for the person and the community in physical, emotional, and spiritual well-being in either ongoing development or crisis. The communal ethos is an important resource for pastoral preaching; clergy, church leaders, and the faith community-at-large function as critical care providers in theological reflection. Alternatively, **prophetic preaching** is the ministry, or faith consciousness, that insists uncompromisingly upon social justice, whether it is interpersonal, cultural, political, or economic. It is focused upon the relationship between historical values of liberation and the liberation of spiritual values otherwise content with personal thriving. It is an intentional, purposeful consciousness that addresses the needs and concerns of persons living under oppressing conditions. Prophetic preaching is distinguished by distinctive religious meaning in liberation ethics that informs social relationships in both public and private living. Black preaching praxis struggles to hold pastoral and prophetic preaching together, forming the personhood of living faith and the peoplehood of the Black Church. The problems that have emerged through different ages stem largely from a neglect of this dialectic in our preaching. The neglect of liberation ethics and action in the public arena compromises the prophetic aspect, while, at the same time, uncritical focus upon the spiritual, so that it becomes a debilitating refuge, compromises the pastoral.

AFRICAN SPIRITUALITY AND PREACHING

Anthropologists and church historians alike have debated the extent to which we can argue for African retentions in the development of African American Christian traditions. The historical realities that contextualize the African encounter with American racism, slavery, and Christianity are not at stake in the debate. Even the ruthless effort to obliterate African languages, folk wisdom, customs, and spiritual practices could not escape interpretation among enslaved Blacks. That interpretation began with the devastating disruption of their lives and African theological worldview. Peter Paris argues this interpretation would involve the re-appropriation of religious meaning and moral principles. The criteria of this re-appropriation were the theological beliefs on how creation was ordered and how spiritual values preserve balance.[4] The pivotal tenets within the survival of African spiritual values seek to sustain the balance or harmony of creation with the Supreme Being, to sustain balance within one's own being, and to sustain harmony throughout our human relationships and creation itself.[5] These spiritual values guided and shaped the interpretation of life in the encounter with the horrors of Western racism and slavery. Oddly enough, even though the introduction of Christianity to enslaved Africans was part of the effort to erase African life and values, the connections with African theological worldviews in these spiritual values would become central to the interpretation of faith and the formation of Black Church traditions.

The American slave system and racism could not prevail over the need among slaves to interpret this new human evil. The influence of African spiritual values and the notion of shared suffering in the face of horror provided the social cohesion that formed the roots of the transformation of Christianity and the formation of Black Church praxis. The intended destruction of African identity was so thorough and overwhelming in other ways that the transition from African theological worldviews or spiritual values to Christian values and biblical theology slowly provided new forms of social cohesion and spiritual practices. The social cohesion emerging through the transformation of Christianity would transcend lost familial bonds and ancestry.

Arguably among the integral facets of these spiritual values was the function of African oral culture and rhetoric. When considering the destruction of African oral culture, we must be cautious to point out that the destruction did not lead to a simple exchange of one oral culture for another. We must understand that enslaved peoples encountered Christianity within a literary biblical tradition. Still, we know through the early history of the Black Church that despite the efforts to prevent reading skill among the enslaved, literacy quickly became a growing skill set. Enslaved Africans and early free African Americans employed their oral culture in learning English and biblical narratives. Oral cultural skills served to shape the adoption of biblical stories and themes, most commonly through preaching and the birth of Negro spirituals.

Molefi Kete Asante sees the retention of African spiritual values within the formation of an Afrocentric, African American oral culture. Together, the themes of human wholeness, human relations, and our relation to God or the supernatural form public discourse traditions, or practices, that seek to overcome destructive disharmony introduced by evil and sin and to transform Black life. The means of spiritual and historical transformation resided primarily in the force of oral communication. For Asante, the African term **nommo** captures the spiritual force or power of oral communication. *Nommo* is communal in that it is the force of life communicated through the power of the word. It is a collective experience between speaker and hearer. Whether in speech or music, *nommo* blends the content of spiritual values with the experience of the same spiritual values. Therefore, the form and expression in rhythms, physical presence, and participation work together with the content of worldview, folklore, or moral and theological themes. Speakers and hearers generate a collective experience of communication, or public discourse. The formation of speech and musical content relates to the spiritual force of *nommo*. The way in which the stories African Americans shape and pass on actually contribute to the restoration or creation of harmony is vital to Afrocentric orality.[6]

The critical point here is the translation of Afrocentric concepts of communication and spiritual life in the transformation of Christianity through preaching and communal formation of the worship experience. The role of the preacher is multifarious. Preachers are interpreters, heralds, conveyors of truth, witnesses, translators, artists, and performers, all within the experience, relations, and interaction of the community of hearers. The desired nature of speech is the expression or pursuit of harmony that can only be experienced with the restoration of the self, and that cannot be separated from community. Black preaching, therefore, employs forms of speech that draw both from the biblical traditions revealing God's activity to restore harmony and from concrete images of human experience. In *nommo*, expression and content are held together. When fashioned as art and artistic expression, the content of discourse attains the power of *nommo*. But speech must function in the context of the preacher and the community of hearers. For preaching to attain the power of *nommo*, participation of the community is essential. "Call and response" in the Black preaching event captures this dynamic of participation in the power of the word and its experience. The harmony of the self is entwined in the harmony with God and harmony in the context of our human relationships. These spiritual values upend the goal of Western fulfillment. Instead of the proverbial wisdom of Western individualism signified by "I think, therefore I am," African wisdom seeks harmony in relatedness: "I am because we are, and since we are, therefore I am."[7]

It should not be a leap to perceive, then, how African spiritual values and oral culture engaged American Christianity in the racist assault on Black wholeness and relatedness to God and humanity. The preaching event itself, centered in the worship experience—along with other forms of participation that included the Negro spirituals, testimonies, and poetic prayer—thrived in the communal response emerging from shared suffering and the pursuit of restoration and liberation. It is rather ironic that the actual racist system of destruction would provide the backdrop for the development of community among disparate African tribal peoples. Shared suffering and shared spiritual values that broadly defined African theological worldviews converged into religious or spiritual practices in preaching and worship. Additionally, the revivalism of the First and Second Great Awakenings provided fertile soil for the appeal of Christianity because of the intense emphasis on the fervor of spiritual experience in the preaching event and in communal participation. In as much as revivalism led to the evangelization of enslaved and free African Americans, it strengthened the transformation of Christianity and biblical traditions through the centrality of experience and participation with God's activity in restoration and liberation.[8]

INTERPRETATION AND TRANSFORMATION

In one of the early texts dealing exclusively with Black homiletics, William Pipes strongly emphasized the appeal of the Great Awakenings, which for enslaved and free African Americans mixed African and American heritage. Pipes stressed the significant influence that the "religious temperament" of the revivals had in the transformation of Christianity. Emotional appeal and active participation birthed the allure. The manner and purposes of preaching, however, rested in religious instruction or the address of biblical ideas and truth that accentuated moral instruction and social obligations.[9] Pipes underscored the emotional appeal of revivalism and the moral implication of personal salvation, which in his view grew under the stark frustrations of bondage, the failed efforts, or means, to escape slavery, and unrelenting persecution of free African Americans.[10]

It was in the midst of these frustrations that early Black preachers sought to transform the message of Christianity as racist American Christians, particularly slaveholders, gave it to them. Early Black preachers used biblical traditions and stories to defy the growing restrictions on plantation preaching. The focus on freedom was, of course, rather high in early Black preaching. The formation of Black churches in the late eighteenth century stemmed from racist practices impinging upon worship and religious communities. Black freedom and wholeness comprised the central interests in preaching. With the slave insurrections of the early nineteenth century, restrictions dramatically increased on Black preaching and even the availability of Christian worship. In turn, Black worship practices and preaching turned more and more to the already foundational and growing coded speech that not only pervaded the spirituals as religious expressions of faith but also provided a form of communication for the community to function. Clandestine meetings would develop into the invisible institution that would eventuate in the formation of faith communities. Hence, the message of freedom would endure in preaching, though often maneuvering through contexts of oppression and needs for survival. Eugene Genovese notes that, in these developments, the idea of real historical, social freedom is not lost in turning to God as sustainer and deliverer. But like Pipes, Genovese observes a loss of the dialectic in a surrender of sociopolitical preaching under the hostile threat upon life and limb.[11]

Early on, the dialectic of pastoral and prophetic preaching became difficult to sustain. The dialectic revolves around the central theme of freedom. However, as we can see from Pipes and Genovese, a fragile balance has always been at risk between the pursuits of wholeness and historical liberation. The predominance of one pole in the continuum would mark the neglect or disparagement of the other as a viable means toward freedom or even God's manner. It was much easier to distinguish the gospel message of God to Black humanity as quite distinct from white preachers and white society.[12] A Black hermeneutic developed over time that directly reflected the rhetorical strategies of Black preaching. The hermeneutic is the pastoral–prophetic dialectic within the context of oppression and the quest for freedom and equality. Others have portrayed the dialectic between assimilation and revolution, or between persuasion and coercion.[13] Notwithstanding, what remains at stake is how Black preaching participates in the quest for freedom and equality. The risk is losing the dialectic, wherein the predominant rhetoric of equality or assimilation loses sight of the quest for freedom and the social obligations that the work for freedom carries. Conversely, when the pursuit of historical liberation is gained only through revolution and uninformed by the gospel of spiritual values, preaching loses sight of the liberation of the soul from the ravages of oppression in the demonstration of Black moral equality.

Gayraud Wilmore helps us to understand how the historical movements of Black religion have wrestled with questions of survival, Black self-help (elevation), and liberation. Each of these strategies contends with the pastoral–prophetic dialectic between the quests for equality and freedom. Wilmore describes the survival strategies as something more than assimilation for the sake of physical survival. They are also "dissimulation" that seeks to undermine or subvert dehumanizing oppression and the debasement of Black humanity. Preaching participates in the formation of Black wholeness in nothing short of re-humanizing Black personality. Survival strategies in preaching seek to seize upon biblical traditions that will reestablish the harmony of spiritual values in relation to God and creation. These strategies of redefinition and subterfuge serve as coping mechanisms for procurement of Black wholeness and, therefore, survival. Wilmore's turn to elevation and liberation strategies sustains the dialectic. Black uplift or elevation should be understood in the pursuit of freedom in the form of equality. Black humanity would develop strategies to demonstrate moral equality. Moreover, Black humanity would not wait for white society to repent and to refrain from oppressing Black humanity. Freedom from oppression would begin with Black uplift or self-help. Wilmore points to Booker T. Washington as an example of someone who moved from survivalist strategies into elevationist ones. Still, Wilmore sees a stronger relationship between the elevationist and the liberationist. Liberation strategists, like Henry McNeal Turner, understood liberation in concretized social, economic, and political freedom.[14]

What must be clear in each of these strategies is that a Black hermeneutic developed for preaching and adapting American Christianity. That hermeneutic is best described in the pastoral–prophetic dialectic. Assimilation and dissimulation, persuasion and coercion, survival and liberation—the poles of the dialectic are variously depicted. The transformation of American Christianity has been wrought through strategies of pastoral care for Black wholeness and prophetic consciousness for social justice. Freedom and equality have been at the core of the dialectic. Surely, this dialectic has been ravaged at various times in the history of the Black Church. Debates over distortions of the dialectic often emerge between the refuge paradigm of Black ecclesiology and the revolution paradigm of liberation ethics. The distortions are very real and problematic in each generation. However, those debates are beyond the parameters of this chapter. Here we must understand that the transformation of Christianity by enslaved Africans and African Americans in the formation of Black faith communities and Black preaching traditions is grounded in the development of Black hermeneutics in the pastoral–prophetic dialectic.

Black preaching hermeneutics would build upon at least four functional cornerstones. These foundational elements serve as the methodological context for the pastoral–prophetic dialectic in Black preaching. In short, these cornerstones are: the preaching event in faith community, the Word of God, preaching as telling the story, and the manner of interpretation.

The Preaching Event in Faith Community

The context for Black preaching praxis is perhaps best described as an event in community. More specifically, the sermon is the *text* within the *experience* of the preaching event in the faith community. In this chapter, much has already been made of African cultural influences in Black religious experiences of the worship context for preaching. Spiritual values, rhetorical dynamics of oral culture, and expressive participation came together to shape the worship experiences of hush harbors of the invisible institution prayer meetings, and early Black Church services. Communal participation defined the worship experience. Testimony, prayer, and song were the dominant forms of participation. However, in the Black preaching event, these forms of participation took on and retained particular forms and character. The African American sermon is designed with the participation of the hearers in mind. The time for preaching is a time of invitation to experience revelation and to experience the Spirit of God. The preaching event is a communal activity wherein the preacher seeks to engage the hearer to elicit participation and experience.[15] The reasoning is that preaching needs to address the concrete realities and culture of Black life. It is through concrete relevance that the preacher creates occasion for dialogue.[16]

Among the most prominent researchers in Black homiletics, Henry Mitchell argues that the preaching event is incomplete if the preacher does not move the sermon into an ultimate expression of celebration. He maintains that the emotional participation of the hearers in the celebration of the sermon helps the hearers incorporate the spiritual message into their daily living. When people participate in the preaching event they are more likely to identify and retain meaning. It becomes a holistic experience. The benefits of celebration extend into religious instruction and the development of core beliefs.[17] Celebration and, therefore, participation make the sermon event a communal activity. Personal identification with the message also results in interpersonal identification among the participants.[18] Black preaching praxis attempts to create an event in worship. The sermon is part of a phenomenon, or a "happening."[19]

The phenomenon of the preaching event occurs in the hearing and response. Amazingly it is a parallel process of two phenomena in one. The preacher encounters or hears God's self-revelation and then responds in the activity of preaching. The goal of that preaching event becomes a recreation of that encounter; in short the preacher seeks a re-encounter. The participants in the worshiping community experience some form of the original phenomenological experience of the preacher, now recreated in the actual sermon event. The happening is a communal experience of revelation and meaning making. The faith community is integral to the fulfillment of the preaching event. Actually, celebration may be too limiting a term for the range of communal participation possible. Lament, which resides in the faithful memory of the community and Scripture, may shape participation. A soothing peace, breaking into the chaos of strife, may mark the sway of a congregation in the mellifluous response of an old-time spiritual. The event is one of revelation and response.

Black preaching praxis in the faith community thrives in a happening, in an experience. The goals of empowerment may serve to nurture Black wholeness or to encourage living differently in the pursuit of liberation. Even the anticipation of God's activity in the preaching event becomes empowering in that the participants seek a transforming encounter. The transformation may occur between the pastoral or prophetic needs of the hearers. Spiritual and historical liberation are held together as are personhood and peoplehood within the faith community and the event.

The Word of God and Black Preaching

It would probably be easier to refer to this cornerstone in Black preaching hermeneutics simply as the Bible. However, multiple theological claims imbue the term "Word of God" more effectively. The Bible is the Word of God because it gives witness to God's activity in human history. It, therefore, evidences the character and faithfulness of God. Far from the literary power of biblical idolatry, the Bible's power in Black preaching praxis is as a living Word. We meet the God of history in the preaching events of our unfolding history. The Word of God is revelation. The Bible has its heritage and its future as the Word of God living among the people of God. The Bible is dynamic and relevant to any given current age because of this heritage and future together.

Faced with the stark loss of African folk religion, enslaved Africans and early African Americans located their own history in God's interests and involvement with humanity. Thus, it should not be difficult to perceive the void of ancestral faith narratives filled by the biblical traditions. With the destruction of African oral folklore by American slavery, which included eradication of ancestral narratives, proverbial wisdom, and religious practices, the ancestral faith narratives and wisdom literature from the Hebrew Bible and the gospel narratives from Christian Scripture held great appeal to a beleaguered oral culture.[20] Black preaching praxis, therefore, involved an integral appropriation of biblical traditions and sacred heritage. Due to its own historical genres and oral culture, the Bible functioned as the living Word of God despite the efforts to impose illiteracy and even to curb evangelism among the enslaved. Black preachers were typically among the first enslaved Blacks to gain enough access to education to be able to read the Bible. Other African Americans, whether enslaved or free, without the benefit of literary education but with the strong asset of oral cultural tradition, would learn biblical narratives and teachings orally/aurally.[21] An intricate process translated central narratives or sacred themes into formulae for preaching and singing spirituals.[22] The Word of God related God's faithfulness to an oppressed people of faith. Black preaching praxis must translate God's faithfulness into God's will and activity among and on behalf of a new people of God in Black humanity.

Along the continuum from nurturing Black personhood in forms of wholeness and self-worth to living into a peoplehood of God in the values of freedom and social justice, Black preaching praxis highlights at least six predominant biblical themes, or tenets, for interpreting the Word of God into faith traditions in Black life[23]: (1) the sovereignty of God, (2) creation, (3) exodus from slavery, (4) conversion, (5) the suffering of Jesus, and (6) the **kin-dom** or **reigndom** of God.

1. ***The sovereignty of God:*** Rather than selecting a single text to focus on God's sovereignty, Black preaching praxis places God in all aspects of life. God's sovereignty is critical to Black life in that the character of God's sovereignty ensures God's power to operate within Black life to overcome oppression or suffering.[24] It is tempting to condition the tenet of God's sovereignty in a philosophical theology of omnipotence. While God is held as omnipotent, the character of this power is not demonstrated in philosophical debate over the existence of evil. Martin Luther King, Jr., charged that the question between omnipotence and evil is not the critical question. The critical question for Black life asks, "Is God able to subdue all

powers of evil, to conquer evil?"[25] The Word of God testifies to God's power to overcome evil and suffering in Black life.

2. **Creation:** The biblical creation stories affirm that Black humanity is created in the image of God. Like other tenets of faith grounded in the Word of God, the affirmation or divine value of Black humanity established God's will for equality and Black freedom.[26] Personhood is served in creation, and it becomes the foundation for the peoplehood of the African American faith community. James Cone explains that creation in the image of God affirms Black wholeness and insists upon Black sociopolitical liberation as divine revelation.[27] Hence, creation sustains the pastoral–prophetic dialectic for Black preaching.

3. **Exodus from slavery:** One of the clearest appropriations of biblical narratives into tenets of faith transpires with the Israelite exodus out of slavery under the hand of God. The sovereignty of God and the value of Black humanity converge here to create a faith identity. The African American faith community becomes the new Israelite community, that is, the new chosen people on whose behalf God promises to reap liberation.[28] A sense of corporate identity, a peoplehood, is rooted in the exodus liberation. It is prophetic in nature, but deeply related to wholeness and divine sanction.

4. **Conversion:** The experience or acknowledgment of salvation also translates into divine sanction. It is in the conversion experience that revivalism may evidence the strongest effects of doctrine. Theological implications arise directly from salvation tenets like justification and sanctification. Notwithstanding, the Word of God in the gospel message of conversion and salvation directly affirms the value of Black humanity to God. The affirmation garnered in conversion in turn directly subverts racial debasement or subjugation.[29] Often preaching praxis has displaced the conversion experience from its dialectic with the prophetic.

5. **The suffering of Jesus:** The passion of Christ is revealed in the suffering servant, Jesus. The suffering of Jesus demonstrates his identification and compassion for the oppressed. Liberation begins when the Spirit frees one's own spirit from ravages of assault and systematic oppression. The goal is to strip the power of evil by transforming suffering into a spiritual victory. Black preaching praxis establishes personal identification with the suffering, which underscores the power of redemptive suffering as moral victory in defining

how to live faithfully.[30] At other times, identification with the suffering of Jesus is an attempt to embrace liberation in surviving! The ultimate goal is more than survival. The goal of redemptive suffering is to participate with God in God's activity to transform suffering.[31]

6. ***The reigndom or kin-dom of God:*** These theological tenets are alternatives to the "kingdom of God" language that permeates Western Christian traditions. They represent important challenges to Black preaching praxis from Womanist and *Mujerista*[32] theologies. The reigndom of God is concerned with the reign of God that God seeks to establish with humanity. The term preserves the sovereignty and defining authority of God in divine will for creation. While kin-dom is often used synonymously, it is intended here to stress God's desire for human relationships within the reign of God. Kin-dom signifies mutual relations of care, mutual thriving, living into divine will for equality, and freedom to be in relationship. From Black Church traditions, the reign or kin-dom of God depicts the eschatological vision of God. It is the promise of God's future that seeks to break into the present always. The future of redemption history is provided to empower us with a living faith and hope.[33]

The eschatological vision of the reign and kin-dom of God strongly reflects the pastoral–prophetic dialectic in Black preaching praxis. Often, the dialectic here is represented in supposedly disparaging terms as "other-worldly" and "this-worldly." Other-worldly preaching is focused upon the future vision that typically emphasizes the spiritual empowerment to rise out of despair. This-worldly preaching accents the historical liberation of Black humanity in social, economic, and political terms for human thriving. The in-breaking of the reign or kin-dom of God intends to create urgency for our responsive agency and empowerment in the "not-yet." Together, they navigate ways of being in faith and history.[34] Black preaching praxis must insist upon the dialectic between the other-worldly and this-worldly, between pastoral empowerment and prophetic agency.

Preaching as Telling the Story

Narrative preaching experienced a renaissance of sorts in the last fifty years of the twentieth century in Western mainline preaching traditions. Many homiletics scholars have referred to this movement as more of an insurgence than resurgence. In fact, it is often called the "new homiletic." Even the term "new homiletic" is problematic and reflects the cultural racism at play in American Christianity. The critical question here is, "New to whom?"

The "new homiletic" refers more broadly to the consideration of inductive preaching, within which narrative preaching is a primary means. Inductive preaching understands the sermon as an event in time or a movement in time. One moves through the particulars of our experiences to arrive at the central idea of the sermon.[35] Of course, that central idea may come midway or toward the end of the sermon. The fundamental principle here is to identify with the experiences of the anticipated hearers. Part of the decision-making process that goes into the sermon development involves the sort of experience the preacher desires in the sermon event, or what experience is intended by the sermon. The experiences of the hearers are vital to the preaching event of God's self-revelation. Perhaps the most strident claim of inductive preaching is that the hearers may then complete the sermon. Preachers do not ultimately control conclusions, if ever we did. The girding principle to inductive preaching is that God's truth or revelation cannot be apprehended apart from the appropriation of human experience.[36] The effectiveness of inductive preaching rests in the *happening* of the preaching event, or the encounter therein. The task is to relate the sermon to the hearers' lives—or to shape what the sermon does in the lives of the hearers.[37]

The reality is that the "new homiletic" is not new to many traditions of oral culture and folk preaching. Whether one refers to induction, narrative preaching, storytelling, phenomenological experience, the preaching event, a happening, an encounter, a movement, hearer participation, hearer response, or the exigency of cultural language and immediate experience, the "new homiletic" mirrors the long-standing Black preaching praxis in "telling the story."

Telling the story in Black preaching involves the story of the ancestors and the story of the hearers together. For the African and African American forebears in North America, the biblical narratives of the Israelite people of God and the early Christian church became the stories of the ancestors for the faith community. With each passing generation, their own stories added to the ancestral fount of God's self-revelation and wisdom. The biblical narratives retain sacred authority, not as a distant treasure, but as the preaching praxis brings the hearers into the story. The development and life of the Black Church become part of the story of

God's self-revelation in human history. The biblical narratives comprise God's story of redemption history along with the anticipation of God's immediate and future activity.[38] The pastoral–prophetic dialectic is preserved in the dual functions of storytelling in forming a sense of wholeness or healing and in demonstrating God's commitment to freedom or justice.

James Earl Massey designs the story of the biblical ancestors into a preaching event that enables the hearers, along with the preacher, to live into retelling the story. The hearers identify with more than the ancestors. They rehearse the meaning of faith in the story and participate in the agency of the story.[39] Massey turns to James Cone's claim upon the power of telling the story in Black theology:

> In Black churches, the one who preaches the Word, is primarily a storyteller. And thus when the Black Church community invites a minister as pastor, their chief question is: "Can the Reverend tell the story?" This question refers both to the theme of Black religion and also to the act of story-telling itself. It refers to a person's ability to recite God's historical dealings with [God's] people from Abraham to Jesus, from St. Paul to John on the island of Patmos, and to the preacher's ability to relate these biblical stories to contemporary Black stories. The past and present are joined dialectically, creating a Black vision of the future.[40]

The faith community locates itself in the faith story of God's love for humanity through the praxis of storied preaching. The preacher tells the story because in the story of redemption history, the faith community encounters God and God empowers another generation.

The Manner of Interpretation

Closely related to the preceding cornerstone, this one carries the task of the translator more deeply into the lives of African American faith. Recreating the sacred story in African American life carries the process of interpretation right into the delivery moments of the preaching event. Here the methods and manner of Black hermeneutics work as cohorts of sorts. Black preaching seeks to interpret biblical stories into the language, images, imagination, and cultural concepts of African American life. It involves forms of expression, embodiment, and rhetorical strategies that seek to persuade. Concrete teachings and even well-rehearsed biblical narratives are applied to everyday Black life. In that application, the preacher attempts to give life to the message.

The dominant styles of Black preaching, therefore, are often described as *performative*. Performance becomes part of the interpretation.[41] Unlike what their critics claim, the terms *performance* and *rhetoric* do help us better understand Black preaching. Performance or performative styles extend across a vast domain of oratory. These skills in Black preaching praxis typically include memorization, storytelling, poetics, aesthetics, argument, artistic structures such as refrain or phrasing, meter, musical or sonorous techniques, exhortation, and demonstration.[42] The manner of interpretation becomes part of the event or happening.

Within the importance of manner lies how the preacher approaches interpretation for the sermon event. Gerald Davis suggests that the preacher constructs the sermon with blueprints to unite message and manner.

> In sermon performance, the African American preacher is principally concerned with the organization and the language of [the] sermon. The notion of meter, in the sense of rhythmic, mnemonic environment for the logical, pragmatic development of ideas, is not subordinate to the language focus. Rather, it is concurrent with it. The generation of structures for language usage and the structuring of rhythmic environments for the preacher's message are complementary, concurrent processes in the performance of African American sermons.[43]

Language, images, and speech structures from contemporary Black life and the performative styles of the preacher will help comprise interpretation for the sermon event. Together with the tasks of relating the biblical tenets of faith and our sacred story, the questions the preacher brings to sermon preparation involve how to relate these tenets to Black life and how to shape proclamation.[44]

The engagement with Scripture can be wrought with presuppositions that the preacher brings to the interpretation and preaching task. We benefit greatly from the science of hermeneutics when we can recognize the presuppositions we bring to the biblical text and the demands intrinsically placed on Black preaching praxis. The demands that have shaped Black preaching praxis through generations have sustained the pastoral–prophetic dialectic. And yet, we discover in interpretation that our language and rhetorical strategies are often inadequate to the tasks of interpretation.

The manner of interpretation must be buttressed by a reflexive manner of exploration. Are we asking the right questions of the text, of Black life? Do our questions wrestle with the pastoral–prophetic dialectic? Do our presumptions or omissions occasion our employ of language and rhetorical strategies? Womanist theologians and preachers such as Katie Cannon have helped us see how African American hermeneutics and Black preaching praxis have not escaped the ravages of exclusionary of hegemonic interpretation.

Womanist hermeneutics challenges Black preaching praxis to be introspective to the practices of wholeness and liberation within Black life and the faith community as well as the larger society. Where do we find Black women in our sermons and in the preaching event? How are they present or omitted in our language, rhetoric, or preaching ministry? Cannon offers the preacher three heuristic questions for interpretation and preaching: "(1) How is meaning constructed? (2) Whose interests are served? (3) What kind of worlds are envisioned in Black sacred rhetoric?"[45] Womanist interpretation challenges preachers to expand the lens of emancipation ethics or hermeneutics of suspicion into our own Black preaching praxis. We learn to read text and interpretations more closely and deeply. We seek to read from the perspective of those omitted or marginalized. And the manner of our interpretation for the preaching event requires the same scrutiny.[46]

APPRENTICESHIP TRADITIONS— LEARNING TO PREACH

One may find good reason to argue that the apprenticeship traditions of learning to preach in Black churches grew out of the restrictions placed on literacy and access to education. Certainly the historical realities of slavery and violent segregation ensured that Black preachers and churches would develop the study and craft of preaching ministry in quite untraditional ways—that is untraditional to white mainline churches. The apprenticeship practices, however, did build upon traditions of oral culture from African heritage even within a process re-designating and re-developing the fount of folk religion. The focus in apprenticeship very much reflects the role of spiritual values and the cornerstones of Black preaching praxis. In one hand, the spiritual values of harmony—with God, among human relationships, and within oneself—help to interpret living faith for every historical context. Early on, a preaching apprentice must learn to locate the demands of the pastoral–prophetic dialectic for the faith community and begin interpreting the faith. Transformation of the actual faith tradition occurs in dynamic exchange between the preacher and community. Embarking on that journey of interpretation and transformation does not begin in a void. It begins with an emergent theological worldview in a cultural and historical context.

On the other hand, apprenticeship seldom, if ever, starts without some familiarity with the preaching event or some semblance of the preaching task. As you the reader are likely acquainted, it would not be uncommon for a small group of novice preachers to gather to rehearse playfully and test out the "whoop" or manner of some acclaimed preaching mentor. Homiletic forms construct the sermon to connect with the living faith of the Black community that is seeking to survive oppression and thrive in liberation. The apprentice enters the process of learning how to operate with rhetorical strategies for creating a hearing. Because participation of the community is so integral to interpreting and transforming the faith, a preacher learns that the anticipation of a community's encounter with revelation is vital to the event. Responding to God's revelation, preachers seek to equip the community to live into freedom from oppression and fragmentation. The four cornerstones of Black preaching praxis create an encounter for the Black congregation. A faith community anticipates and enters the preaching event seeking to participate in an encounter.

The preacher must learn to identify and interpret the faith, which therefore must connect the sacred message with the lives of the oppressed. The apprentice begins to interpret the faith from within his or her own engagement with oppression and fragmentation, even if only indirectly as a member of the community. Hence, when learning to preach, the apprentice works with a mentor to grapple with the Word of God as it has been shaped thus far in the apprentice's apprehension of the central tenets of faith as well as the anticipated congregation. Telling the story requires the same humility in learning to preach. A mentor guides the apprentice in telling a shared story. One of the common mistakes made by the younger apprentice is attempting to preach a story beyond his or her experience in living faith. Great temptation exists in trying to take on the story or even manner of a mentor. We are grateful that the faith community as a body can function as a mentor through the preaching event, and so will often tolerate such a venture with patience and often with intervening guidance.

221

Ultimately, the apprenticeship-mentor relationship is caught up in a multivalent parallel process.[47] The preaching event is created through a process of encounter and re-encounter. The apprentice begins tutelage from the experience as a listener in the preaching event. A mentor helps the novice to identify the elements of encounter. For the preacher, the encounter begins in exegetical study and sermon preparation. In essence, the preaching event becomes a re-encounter for the preacher, while still an encounter for the community. Black preaching praxis attempts to incorporate the process of deepening familiarity with how the cornerstones of Black preaching stand in the community's encounter. The same process can occur with the mentor's preaching. The mentor helps the apprentice to identify the cornerstones of Black preaching praxis and begins to identify what gifts and what weaknesses the apprentice may possess in preaching. Both the mentor and apprentice learn to assess those strategies that are preferable to the particular apprentice and that need correction. An apprentice needs to learn more than the content of preaching tenets or strategic style. Apprentices learn how they may operate in the lives of the anticipated hearers, which is yet another facet of the parallel learning process in Black preaching praxis. In reality the multiple levels of parallel processing become the vocation of the Black preacher. The future challenge for African American homiletics will be to translate apprenticeship methods or praxis into pedagogy for the seminary classroom.

SUMMARY

Black preaching praxis is characteristically understood within the preaching event. As practical theologians in dialogue with the community, Black preachers attempt to sustain a pastoral–prophetic dialectic throughout the preaching process from the preachers' preparation and delivery to the experience and participation of the faith community. The function of the preaching process is to interpret faith-engaging context; the goal is to transform the faith for living into the divine will of freedom and thriving relatedness. Delineating the pastoral and prophetic into personal wholeness and interpersonal justice, respectively, would be a gross simplification. It would also mislead us into a false impression that the pastoral–prophetic dialectic in Black preaching praxis oscillates by need and nature. Certainly, crises arise that demand primarily pastoral or prophetic response. However, the distortion of the dialectic leads to an inadequate interpretation of the faith tradition in the immediate context and therefore neglects transformation of the faith community and world-at-large. Whether in a small rural congregation or in the exigency of public theology, the dialectic succeeds in mutual tension and function.

By example, Rev. Dr. Martin Luther King, Jr., appeared to understand the necessary tension of the dialectic. Tension is a form of accountability. Critical interpretation seeks strategic response/action to transform our context and even our faith. For King, distortions of faith and behavior were woven into oppression, oppressors, and the oppressed. One year before his assassination, to the day, Dr. King called for a revolution of values to end the assault of racism, poverty, and militarism.[48] His appeal was addressed to oppressors and oppressed alike. The pastoral and the prophetic needs for interpretation and transformation were deeply interspersed between personal wholeness and interpersonal justice for Black humanity and white humanity. The pastoral–prophetic dialectic in Black preaching praxis requires that we contend with the faith community, the Word of God, preaching the story of redemption history, and our manner in seeking the mutuality and freedom of humanity. These cornerstones of Black preaching praxis are thoroughly conditioned by the spiritual values of living faith. The greatest insight, however, is that the tasks of interpretation and transformation of the faith are unrelenting. It seems we are still in need of a revolution of values to redress the assault of racism, exponential poverty, and militarism as an article of faith. Wholeness and liberation are at stake for the oppressed and the oppressors. The ministry of Black preaching praxis is relentless, as are the exigencies of the pastoral–prophetic dialectic in the Black preaching event.

BIOGRAPHIES

Julia A. J. Foote (1823–1900)

In 1823, Julia A. J. Foote was born to former slaves living in Schenectady, New York. Because Schenectady's schools were segregated, Julia's parents sent her to work for the Primes, a white couple whose influence gave Julia the opportunity to go to a country school where she learned to read. In her early teens, Julia and her family moved to Albany and joined the African Methodist Church. At a quarterly meeting when she was fifteen years old, Julia experienced personal conversion and began to read the Bible diligently. Around the age of eighteen, Julia married a sailor, George Foote, and the couple moved to Boston. There, Julia began a household ministry to neighbors, friends, and fellow church members. Some months after the move, Julia received a call to preaching, complete with supernatural visitations, visions, and voices. Eventually she accepted the call, but she was excommunicated almost immediately from her church by the minister, Jehiel Beman. After several months of preaching in meetings, Julia received word that her husband had died and she returned to Boston, staying only briefly before resuming her travels and preaching. These took her as far as Michigan and even into Canada. In the early 1850s, Julia traveled to Cleveland, intending only a visit, but she settled there permanently. In 1894, she was the first woman in the AME Zion Church to receive ordination as a deacon; this was followed by her ordination as an elder sometime later. She was only the second woman to receive ordination in the AME Zion Church. Julia Foote died on November 22, 1900.[49]

Henry H. Mitchell (1919–) and Ella Pearson Mitchell (1917–)

The Rev. Drs. Henry and Ella Mitchell have each been preaching for approximately seventy years. They have journeyed together in marriage and ministry now for more than sixty years. They began their theological education at Union Theological Seminary in New York City. He would go on to receive the Doctor of Theology degree and she the Doctor of Ministry degree, both from the Claremont School of Theology. The Mitchells have sojourned through pastoral ministry and the academy. Through the years, their teaching ministries have graced the classrooms or administrations of American Baptist Seminary of the West, Colgate Rochester Divinity School, Spelman College, Virginia Union Seminary, and United Theological Seminary in Ohio. Most recently, they have taught collaboratively at the Interdenominational Theological Center in Atlanta, Georgia. "Drs. Henry and Ella" (as they are fondly called) have long been regarded as the deans of the Black homiletics guild. The larger academy made it official in the year 2000, when the Mitchells served as co-presidents of the Academy of Homiletics. Their publications are plentiful. Ella has published four volumes of *Those Preaching Women*; she has also produced *Women: To Preach or Not to Preach*. Henry has published numerous texts, some of which have become main staples of Black homiletics research and seminary instruction. Dr. Henry's more prominent texts include *Black Preaching, The Recovery of Preaching, Black Belief, Black Preaching: The Recovery of an Art, Celebration & Experience in Preaching*, and *Black Church Beginnings*. Together, they continue in vocation and partnership as teachers and preachers. They have recently coauthored *Together for Good* and *Fire in the Well*. And, in the fervor of ministry and commitment, The Rev. Drs. Henry and Ella Mitchell continue to travel the church, conference, and seminary circuits, preaching dialogically.

STUDY QUESTIONS

1. How is preaching praxis best understood within the discipline of practical theology and the Black Church? What is distinctive about Black preaching praxis?
2. How do African spiritual values and the concept of *nommo* relate to Black preaching and the formation of the Black Church?
3. What is the Black hermeneutic for the dialectic of pastoral and prophetic preaching? What are some distortions or risks that challenge the pastoral–prophetic dialectic?
4. What are the four cornerstones for Black preaching hermeneutics? How do they operate and interrelate?
5. How do the apprenticeship traditions of learning Black preaching function in the Black Church? In what ways do these apprenticeship traditions relate to homiletic methods in print for the teaching of preaching at seminaries today?
6. What are the issues today that Black preaching and the Black Church struggle to effectively address?

ESSENTIAL TEXTS

- *Black Preaching: The Recovery of a Powerful Art* by Henry H. Mitchell
- *God's Trombones: Seven Negro Sermons in Verse* by James Weldon Johnson
- *Say Amen, Brother! Old-Time Negro Preaching, A Study in American Frustration* by William H. Pipes

NOTES

Introduction

1. "Black philosophy," as indicated in Dr. Henry H. Mitchell's early Black Church Studies curriculum would more than likely be discussed in terms of Black ethics within contemporary theological education.

2. As defined and described by Dr. Mitchell, the field of "Black Ministry Studies" has been subdivided more recently in Black practical theology and pastoral care. As stated by Henry H. Mitchell, *"Preparing Prophets and Priests for the Black Church Tradition"* (keynote presented at the 3rd Annual National Black Church Studies Consultation, Vanderbilt Divinity School, Nashville, Tenn., January 31, 2007).

3. *See* "Definition of Interdisciplinary Work" http://extension.unh.edu/AboutUs/ Workdef.pdf#search=%22definition%20interdisciplinary%22.

4. C. Eric Lincoln, foreword to the first edition of Gayraud S. Wilmore, *Black Religion and Black Radicalism: An Interpretation of the Religious History of African Americans* (Garden City, N.Y.: Anchor Press/Doubleday, 1973), vii, as quoted in C. Eric Lincoln and Lawrence H. Mamiya, *The Black Church in the African-American Experience* (Durham: Duke University Press, 1990), 93.

5. Alasdair MacIntyre, *After Virtue: A Study in Moral Theory,* (Notre Dame: University of Notre Dame Press, 1984), 222.

6. Lincoln, *The Black Experience in Religion* (Garden City, N.Y.: Anchor Press, 1974), 1.

1: Black Church History

Epigraph. Martin Luther King, Jr., *Stride Toward Freedom: The Montgomery Story* (San Francisco: HarperCollins, 1986), 63.

1. Gayraud S. Wilmore, *Black Religion and Black Radicalism: An Interpretation of the Religious History of African Americans,* rev. 3rd ed. (Garden City, N.Y.: Anchor Press/Doubleday, 1973; Maryknoll, N.Y.: Orbis Books, 1998), ix. Page references are to the 1998 edition.

2. Charles H. Long, "Passage and Prayer: The Origin of Religion in the Atlantic World," in *The Courage to Hope: From Black Suffering to Human Redemption,* ed. Quinton H. Dixie and Cornel West (Boston: Beacon Press, 1999), 14.

3. *See also* Melville J. Herskovits, *The Myth of the Negro Past* (New York and London: Harper & Brothers, 1941); John W. Blassingame, *The Slave Community: Plantation Life in the Antebellum South* (New York: Oxford University Press, 1972); Henry H. Mitchell, *Black Belief: Folk Beliefs of Blacks in America and West Africa* (New York: Harper & Row, 1975); Orlando Patterson, *Slavery and Social Death: A Comparative Study* (Cambridge: Harvard University Press, 1982); Peter Kolchin, *American Slavery, 1619-1877* (New York: Hill and Wang, 1993); Joseph E. Holloway, ed., *Africanisms in American Culture* (Bloomington: Indiana University Press, 1990); Michael A. Gomez, *Exchanging Our Country Marks: The Transformation of African Identities in the Colonial and Antebellum South* (Chapel Hill: University of North Carolina Press, 1998); David Brion Davis, *In the Image of God: Religion, Moral Values, and Our Heritage of Slavery* (New Haven: Yale University Press, 2001).

4. *See also* Mechal Sobel, *The World They Made Together: Black and White Values in Eighteenth-century Virginia* (Princeton: Princeton University Press, 1987); Margaret Washington Creel, *A Peculiar People: Slave Religion and Community Culture among the Gullahs* (New York: New York University Press, 1988); Peter H. Wood, *Black Majority: Negroes in Colonial South Carolina from 1670 through the Stono Rebellion* (1974; New York: Norton, 1996).

5. *See also* Winthrop D. Jordan, *White over Black: American Attitudes toward the Negro, 1550–1812* (New York: W. W. Norton, 1977), 79; *See also* Edmund S. Morgan, *American Slavery, American Freedom: The Ordeal of Colonial Virginia* (New York: W. W. Norton, 1975); A. Leon Higginbotham, *In the Matter of Color: Race and the American Legal Process*, vol.1, *The Colonial Period* (New York: Oxford University Press, 1980).

6. *See also* Albert J. Raboteau, *Slave Religion: The "Invisible Institution" in the Antebellum South* (New York: Oxford University Press, 1978).

7. Wilmore, *Black Religion and Black Radicalism*, 44–48; Margarite Fernandez Olmos and Lizabeth Paravisini-Gebert, *Creole Religions of the Caribbean: An Introduction from Vodou and Santeria to Obeah and Espiritismo* (New York: New York University Press, 2003).

8. *See also* Milton C. Sernett, *Black Religion and American Evangelicalism: White Protestants, Plantation Missions, and the Flowering of Negro Christianity, 1787–1865* (Metuchen, N. J.: Scarecrow Press, 1975).

9. Carter G. Woodson, *The History of the Negro Church* (1921; Washington, DC: Associated Publishers, 1992), 42.

10. James M. Simms, *The First Colored Baptist Church in North America* (New York: Negro Universities Press, 1969), 71–75.

11. Nathan O. Hatch, *The Democratization of American Christianity* (New Haven: Yale University, 1989), 40.

12. *See also* Richard Allen, *The Life Experience and Gospel Labors of the Rt. Rev. Richard Allen, to which is annexed the rise and progress of the African Methodist Episcopal Church in the United States of America* (New York, Abingdon Press, 1960); Marcia M. Mathews, *Richard Allen* (Baltimore, Md.: Helicon, 1963); Carol V. R. George, *Segregated Sabbaths: Richard Allen and the Emergence of Independent Black Churches 1760–1840* (New York, Oxford University Press, 1973); Albert J. Raboteau, *A Fire in the Bones: Reflections on African-American Religious History* (Boston: Beacon Press, 1995).

13. Quoted in Darlene Clark Hine, William C. Hine, and Stanley Harrold, *The African-American Odyssey* (Upper Saddler River, N.J.: Prentice Hall, 2000), 160.

14. *See also* James W. Hood, *One Hundred Years of the African Methodist Episcopal Zion Church* (New York: AME Zion Book Concern, 1895).

15. *See also* Gary B. Nash, *Forging Freedom: The Formation of Philadelphia's Black Community, 1720–1840* (Cambridge: Harvard University Press, 1991).

16. Quoted in Hine, *The African-American Odyssey*, 161.

17. Stephen R. Haynes, *Noah's Curse: The Biblical Justification of American Slavery* (New York: Oxford University Press, 2002); David M. Goldenberg, *The Curse of Ham: Race and Slavery in Early Judaism, Christianity, and Islam* (Princeton: Princeton University Press, 2003); Elizabeth Fox-Genovese and Eugene D. Genovese, *The Mind of the Master Class: History and Faith in the Southern Slaveholders' Worldview* (New York: Cambridge University Press, 2005).

18. Quoted in Hine, *The African-American Odyssey*, 141.

19. *See also* Herbert Aptheker, *American Negro Slave Revolts* (New York: International Publishers, 1963); Gerald W. Mullin, *Flight and Rebellion: Slave Resistance in Eighteenth-century Virginia* (New York: Oxford University Press, 1972); Eugene D. Genovese, *From Rebellion to Revolution: Afro-American Slave Revolts in the Making of the Modern World* (Baton Rouge: Louisiana State University Press, 1979); Merton L. Dillon, *Slavery Attacked: Southern Slaves and Their Allies, 1619–1865* (Baton Rouge: Louisiana State University Press, 1990); Douglas R. Egerton, *Gabriel's Rebellion: The Virginia Slave Conspiracies of 1800 and 1802* (Chapel Hill: University of North Carolina Press, 1993); Kenneth S. Greenberg, *Nat Turner: A Slave Rebellion in History and Memory* (New York: Oxford University Press, 2003).

20. For enslaved preachers, recognition of their vocation was a twofold concern. They viewed that their call had come from God; yet fulfilling their call in the midst of chattel slavery was an audacious act of volition.

21. *See* Eddie S. Glaude, Jr., *Exodus! Religion, Race, and Nation in Early Nineteenth-Century Black America* (Chicago: University of Chicago Press, 2000).

22. *See* Evelyn Brooks Higginbotham, *Righteous Discontent: The Women's Movement in the Black Baptist Church, 1880–1920* (Cambridge: Harvard University Press, 1993).

23. *See also* David W. Blight, ed., *Passages to Freedom: The Underground Railroad in History and Memory* (Washington, D.C.: Smithsonian Books, 2004); Fergus M. Bordewich, *Bound for Canaan: The Underground Railroad and the War for the Soul of America* (New York: Amistad, 2005).

24. It must be kept in mind that in most traditions, women, regardless of race, were not ordained in the nineteenth century.

25. *See also* P.J. Staudenraus, *The African Colonization Movement, 1816–1865* (New York: Columbia University Press, 1961).

26. *See also* Kenneth M. Stampp, *The Peculiar Institution: Slavery in the Ante-bellum South* (New York: Knopf, 1956).

27. *See also* David M. Potter, *The Impending Crisis, 1848–1861* (New York: Harper & Row, 1976); Vincent Harding, *There Is a River: The Black Struggle for Freedom in America* (New York: Harcourt Brace Jovanovich, 1981); James M. McPherson, *Battle Cry of Freedom: The Civil War Era* (1988; New York: Oxford University Press, 2003).

28. Benjamin Quarles, *The Negro in the Civil War* (Boston: Little, Brown, 1953); James M. McPherson, *The Negro's Civil War: How American Negroes Felt and Acted during the War for the Union* (New York: Pantheon Books, 1965); Dudley Taylor Cornish, *The Sable Arm: Black Troops in the Union Army, 1861–1865* (New York: Norton, 1966); Edwin S.

Redkey, ed., *A Grand Army of Black Men: Letters from African-American Soldiers in the Union Army, 1861–1865* (New York: Cambridge University Press, 1992).

29. William L. Andrews, ed., *The Oxford Frederick Douglass Reader* (New York: Oxford University Press, 1996), 225.

30. Juan Williams and Quinton Dixie, *This Far by Faith: Stories from the African-American Religious Experience* (New York: W. Morrow, 2003), 109.

31. W.E.B. Du Bois, *Black Reconstruction in America: 1860–1880* (New York: Harcout, Brace, 1935; New York: Simon & Schuster, 1998), 122.

32. Ibid., 124.

33. List adapted from C. Eric Lincoln and Lawrence H. Mamiya, *The Black Church in the African-American Experience* (Durham: Duke University Press, 1990).

34. Quoted in Hine, *The African-American Odyssey*, 265.

35. Ibid.

36. Joe M. Richardson, *Christian Reconstruction: The American Missionary Association and Southern Blacks, 1861–1890* (Athens, Ga.: University of Georgia Press, 1986).

37. Albert J. Raboteau, *Canaan Land: A Religious History of African Americans* (New York: Oxford University Press, 2001). *See also* Ronald E. Butchart, *Northern Schools, Southern Blacks, and Reconstruction: Freedmen's Education, 1862–1875* (Westport, Conn.: Greenwood Press, 1980); Robert C. Morris, *Reading, 'Riting, and Reconstruction: The Education of Freedmen in the South, 1861–1870* (Chicago: University of Chicago Press, 1981); James D. Anderson, *The Education of Blacks in the South, 1860–1935* (Chapel Hill: University of North Carolina Press, 1988).

38. Booker T. Washington, *Up from Slavery: An Autobiography* (1901; New York: Gramercy Books, 1993), 24.

39. Andrew Billingsley, *Mighty Like a River: The Black Church and Social Reform* (New York: Oxford University Press, 1999), 68–70.

40. Quoted in Hine, *The African-American Odyssey*, 341.

41. W.E.B. Du Bois, *The Souls of Black Folk* (1903; New York: W. W. Norton, 1999), 149.

42. James M. Washington, *Frustrated Fellowship: The Black Baptist Quest for Social Power* (Macon, Ga.: Mercer University Press, 1986), 13.

43. Cheryl Townsend Gilkes, *"If It Wasn't for the Women . . .": Black Women's Experience and Womanist Culture in Church and Community* (Maryknoll, N.Y.: Orbis Books, 2001); Daphne C. Wiggins, *Righteous Content: Black Women's Perspectives of Church and Faith* (New York: New York University Press, 2005).

44. William L. Andrews, ed., "The Life and Religious Experience of Jarena Lee" in *Sisters of the Spirit: Three Black Women's Autobiographies of the Nineteenth Century* (Bloomington: Indiana University Press, 1986), 36.

45. Andrews, *Sisters of the Spirit*; Bettye Collier-Thomas, ed., *Daughters of Thunder: Black Women Preachers and Their Sermons, 1850–1979* (San Francisco, Calif.: Jossey-Bass, 1998).

46. Evelyn Brooks Higginbotham, *Righteous Discontent*.

47. Benjamin E. Mays, *Born to Rebel* (New York: Scribner's, 1971), 14–15.

48. Richard Wright, *Uncle Tom's Children* (1940; New York: Harper & Row Perennial edition, 1965), 3.

49. Wilmore, *Black Religion and Black Radicalism*, 163–95.

50. Edwin S. Redkey, *Black Exodus: Black Nationalist and Back-to-Africa Movements, 1890–1910* (New Haven: Yale University Press, 1969); Stephen W. Angell, *Bishop Henry McNeal Turner and African-American Religion in the South* (Knoxville: University of Tennessee Press, 1992).

51. Hine, *The African-American Odyssey*, 343.

52. Edwin S. Redkey, *Respect Black: The Writings and Speeches of Henry McNeal Turner* (New York: Arno Press, 1971), 176.

53. Robert Gregg, *Sparks from the Anvil of Oppression: Philadelphia's African Methodists and Southern Migrants, 1890–1940* (Philadelphia: Temple University Press, 1993); Milton C. Sernett, *Bound for the Promised Land: African-American Religion and the Great Migration* (Durham: Duke University Press, 1997); Wallace D. Best, *Passionately Human, No Less Divine: Religion and Culture in Black Chicago, 1915–1952* (Princeton: Princeton University Press, 2005).

54. Michael W. Harris, *The Rise of Gospel Blues: The Music of Thomas Andrew Dorsey in the Urban Church* (New York: Oxford University Press, 1992).

55. *See* Timothy Smith, "John Wesley and the Second Blessing," http://wesley.nnu.edu/wesleyan_theology/theojrnl/21-25/21-09.htm.

56. Elsie W. Mason, "Bishop C. H. Mason, Church of God in Christ" in Milton C. Sernett, ed., *Afro-American Religious History: A Documentary Witness* (Durham: Duke University Press, 1985), 293.

57. Vinson Synan, *The Holiness-Pentecostal Tradition: Charismatic Movements in the Twentieth Century* (1971; Grand Rapids: W.B. Eerdmans, 1997); Ithiel C. Clemmons, *Bishop C.H. Mason and the Roots of the Church of God in Christ* (Bakersfield, Calif.: Pneuma Life Pub., 1996); Cheryl J. Sanders, *Saints in Exile: The Holiness-Pentecostal Experience in African-American Religion and Culture* (New York: Oxford University Press, 1996).

58. C. Vann Woodward, *The Strange Career of Jim Crow* (New York: Oxford University Press, 1955); Jerrold M. Packard, *American Nightmare: The History of Jim Crow* (New York: St. Martin's Press, 2002); Richard Wormser, *The Rise and Fall of Jim Crow* (New York: St. Martin's Press, 2003).

59. Carl T. Rowan, *Dream Makers, Dream Breakers: The World of Justice Thurgood Marshall* (Boston: Little, Brown, 1993); Mark V. Tushnet, *Making Civil Rights Law: Thurgood Marshall and the Supreme Court, 1936–1961* (New York: Oxford University Press, 1994); Juan Williams, *Thurgood Marshall: American Revolutionary* (New York: Times Books, 1998).

60. Richard Kluger, *Simple Justice: The History of Brown v. Board of Education and Black America's Struggle for Equality* (New York: Knopf, 1975); Derrick A. Bell, *Silent Covenants: Brown v. Board of Education and the Unfulfilled Hopes for Racial Reform* (New York: Oxford University Press, 2004); Charles J. Ogletree, Jr., *All Deliberate Speed: Reflections on the First Half Century of Brown v. Board of Education* (New York: Norton, 2004); Michael J. Klarman, *From Jim Crow to Civil Rights: The Supreme Court and the Struggle for Racial Equality* (New York: Oxford University Press, 2004).

61. Andrew Billingsley, *Mighty Like a River: The Black Church and Social Reform* (New York: Oxford University Press, 1999), 11–12.

62. Martin Luther King, Jr., *Stride Toward Freedom*; Taylor Branch, *Parting the Waters: America in the King Years, 1954–1963* (New York: Simon & Schuster, 1988); Harvard Sitkoff, *The Struggle for Black Equality, 1954–1992* (1981; New York: Hill and Wang,

1993); Stewart Burns, *Daybreak of Freedom: The Montgomery Bus Boycott* (Chapel Hill: University of North Carolina Press, 1997); Michael Eric Dyson, *I May Not Get There With You: The True Martin Luther King, Jr.* (New York: Free Press, 2000).

63. David J. Garrow, *Bearing the Cross: Martin Luther King, Jr. and the Southern Christian Leadership Conference* (New York: W. Morrow, 1986).

64. As the leader of the Indian independence movement, Mahatma Gandhi was convinced that nonviolent civil disobedience formed the basis for any protest. The key concept, therefore, of Gandhi's principals, satyagraha—a synthesis of the Sanskrit words *Satya* (truth) and *Agraha* (persuasion)—serves as the underlying premise that the endurance of redemptive suffering is a means to an ultimately positive end. For more details, see Sudarshan Kapur, *Raising Up a Prophet: The African-American Encounter with Gandhi* (Boston: Beacon Press, 1992).

65. Clayborne Carson, *In Struggle: SNCC and the Black Awakening of the 1960s* (Cambridge: Harvard University Press, 1981).

66. Adam Fairclough, *To Redeem the Soul of America: The Southern Christian Leadership Conference and Martin Luther King, Jr.* (Athens, Ga.: University of Georgia Press, 1987).

67. Taylor Branch, *Pillar of Fire: America in the King Years, 1963–65* (New York: Simon & Schuster, 1998).

68. Jervis Anderson, *Bayard Rustin: Troubles I've Seen: A Biography* (New York: HarperCollins, 1997); Daniel Levine, *Bayard Rustin and the Civil Rights Movement* (New Brunswick, N.J.: Rutgers University Press, 2000); John D'Emilio, *Lost Prophet: The Life and Times of Bayard Rustin* (New York: Free Press, 2003); Devon W. Carbado and Donald Weise, eds., *Time on Two Crosses: The Collected Writings of Bayard Rustin* (San Francisco: Cleis Press, 2003).

69. James M. Washington, *A Testament of Hope: The Essential Writings of Martin Luther King, Jr.* (San Francisco: Harper San Francisco, 1991).

70. Thomas R. West and James W. Mooney, eds., *To Redeem a Nation: A History and Anthology of the American Civil Rights Movement* (St. James, N.Y.: Brandywine Press, 1993), 153–54.

71. Martin Luther King, Jr., "Beyond Vietnam" in *Martin Luther King, Jr., Malcolm X, and the Civil Rights Struggle of the 1950s and 1960s: A Brief History with Documents*, ed. David Howard-Pitney (Boston: Bedford/St. Martins, 2004), 144, 146. Reprinted by arrangement with the Heirs to the Estate of Martin Luther King, Jr., c/o Writers House as agent for the proprietor, New York, N.Y. Copyright 1963 Martin Luther King, Jr., copyright renewed 1991 Coretta Scott King.

72. Martin Luther King, Jr., "Domestic Impact of the War" (address delivered November 1967 to the National Labor Leadership Assembly for Peace); http://www.aavw.org/special_features/speeches_speech_king03.html. Reprinted by arrangement with the Heirs to the Estate of Martin Luther King, Jr., c/o Writers House as agent for the proprietor, New York, N.Y. Copyright 1963 Martin Luther King, Jr., copyright renewed 1991 Coretta Scott King.

73. Martin Luther King, Jr., "I See the Promised Land" in *A Testament of Hope: The Essential Writings and Speeches of Martin Luther King, Jr.*, ed., James M. Washington (San Francisco: HarperCollins, 1991), 286. Reprinted by arrangement with the Heirs to the Estate of Martin Luther King, Jr., c/o Writers House as agent for the proprietor, New York, N.Y. Copyright 1963 Martin Luther King, Jr., copyright renewed 1991 Coretta Scott King.

74. Kwame Ture (Stokely Carmichael) and Charles Hamilton, *Black Power: The Politics of Liberation in America* (New York: Vintage Books, 1967); Manning Marable, *Race, Reform and Rebellion: The Second Reconstruction in Black America, 1945–1992*, 2nd ed. (Jackson: University Press of Mississippi, 1991); William L. Van Deburg, *New Day in Babylon: The Black Power Movement and American Culture, 1965–1975* (Chicago: University of Chicago Press, 1992); Peniel E. Joseph, *Waiting 'Til the Midnight Hour: A Narrative History of Black Power in America* (New York: Henry Holt, 2006).

75. Charles Marsh, *The Beloved Community: How Faith Shapes Social Justice, from the Civil Rights Movement to Today* (New York: Basic Books, 2005); Taylor Branch, *At Canaan's Edge: America in the King Years, 1965–68* (New York: Simon & Schuster, 2006).

76. Henry H. Mitchell, *Black Preaching: The Recovery of a Powerful Art* (Nashville: Abingdon Press, 1990).

77. David L. Chappell, *A Stone of Hope: Prophetic Religion and the Death of Jim Crow* (Chapel Hill: University of North Carolina Press, 2004).

78. Clarence Taylor, "African American Religious Leadership and the Civil Rights Movement," *History Now: American History Online*, no. 8 (The Gilder Lehrman Institute of American History, 2006), http://www.historynow.org/06_2006/historian4.html.

79. Belinda Robnett, *How Long? How Long? African-American Women in the Struggle for Civil Rights* (New York: Oxford University Press, 1997); Charles Marsh, *God's Long Summer: Stories of Faith and Civil Rights* (Princeton: Princeton University Press, 1997); Joanne Grant, *Ella Baker: Freedom Bound* (New York: Wiley, 1998); Rosetta E. Ross, *Witnessing and Testifying: Black Women, Religion, and Civil Rights* (Minneapolis: Augsburg Fortress, 2003); Barbara Ransby, *Ella Baker and the Black Freedom Movement: A Radical Democratic Vision* (Chapel Hill: University of North Carolina Press, 2003).

80. Henry Hampton and Steve Fayer, eds., *Voices of Freedom: An Oral History of the Civil Rights Movement from the 1950s through the 1980s* (New York: Bantam Books, 1990); Vicki L. Crawford, Jacqueline Anne Rouse, and Barbara Woods, eds., *Women in the Civil Rights Movement: Trailblazers and Torchbearers, 1941–1965* (Brooklyn: Carlson, 1990); John Dittmer, *Local People: The Struggle for Civil Rights in Mississippi* (Urbana: University of Illinois Press, 1994); Charles M. Payne, *I've Got the Light of Freedom: The Organizing Tradition and the Mississippi Freedom Struggle* (Berkeley: University of California Press, 1995); Belinda Robnett, *How Long? How Long?*; Deborah Gray White, *Too Heavy a Load: Black Women in Defense of Themselves, 1894–1994* (New York: Norton, 1999); Rosetta E. Ross, *Witnessing and Testifying*.

81. Adam Fairclough, *Better Day Coming: Blacks and Equality 1890–2000* (New York: Penguin Books, 2001), 287.

82. Adolph L. Reed, Jr., *The Jesse Jackson Phenomenon: The Crisis of Purpose in Afro-American Politics* (New Haven: Yale University Press, 1986).

83. Raboteau, *Canaan Land. See also* Andrew Billingsley, *Mighty Like a River*; Fredrick C. Harris, *Something Within: Religion in African-American Political Activism* (New York: Oxford University Press, 1999); R. Drew Smith, ed., *New Day Begun: African-American Churches and Civic Culture in Post-Civil Rights America* (Durham: Duke University Press, 2003).

84. Quoted in Hine, *The African-American Odyssey*, 600.

85. W.E.B. Du Bois, *The Philadelphia Negro: A Social Study* (1899; Philadelphia: University of Pennsylvania Press, 1996); W.E.B. Du Bois, *The Negro Church: Report of a Social Study Made Under the Direction of Atlanta University* (Atlanta: Atlanta University, 1903).

86. Paul Tillich, *Dynamics of Faith* (New York: Harper, 1957), 1.

87. In the preparation of this biography, we have relied on many sources, especially Nathan I. Huggins, ed. *W.E.B. Du Bois: Writings* (New York: Library of America, 1986); W.E.B. Du Bois, David W. Blight, and Robert Gooding-Williams, *The Souls of Black Folk, The Bedford Series in History and Culture* (Boston: Bedford Books, 1997); David Levering Lewis, *W.E.B. Du Bois: Biography of a Race, 1868–1919* (New York: Henry Holt, 1993); and David Levering Lewis, *W.E.B. Du Bois: The Fight for Equality and the American Century, 1919–1963* (New York: Henry Holt, 2000).

88. Adapted from Beverly Guy-Sheftall, ed., *Words of Fire: An Anthology of African-American Feminist Thought* (New York: New Press, 1995).

2: Black Biblical Studies

Epigraph. Cain Hope Felder, "Introduction," in *Stony the Road We Trod: African American Biblical Interpretation*, ed. Cain Hope Felder (Minneapolis: Augsburg Fortress, 1991), 1.

1. Thomas Hoyt Jr., "Interpreting Biblical Scholarship for the Black Church Tradition," in *Stony the Road We Trod: African American Biblical Interpretation*, ed. Cain Hope Felder, 29, 30.

2. Delores Williams, "What Does It Mean to Reconcile the Bible with Black Christian Identity?" (Keynote address presented at the Seventh Annual Black Religious Scholars Group Consultation, San Antonio, Texas, November 19, 2004).

3. Robert E. Hood, *Begrimed and Black: Christian Traditions on Blacks and Blackness* (Minneapolis, Minn.: Augsburg Fortress, 1994), 19, 65, 80–83, 91.

4. Charles B. Copher, *Black Biblical Studies: An Anthology of Charles B. Copher; Biblical and Theological Issues on the Black Presence in the Bible* (Chicago, Ill.: Black Light Fellowship, 1993), 13–14, 22.

5. Rodney S. Sadler, Jr., *Can A Cushite Change His Skin? An Examination of Race, Ethnicity, and Othering in the Hebrew Bible* (New York: T & T Clark, 2005), 26–32.

6. David T. Shannon, "'An Ante-bellum Sermon': A Resource for an African American Hermeneutic," in *Stony the Road We Trod: African American Biblical Interpretation*, ed. Cain Hope Felder, 98–123.

7. Vincent L. Wimbush, "The Bible and African Americans: An Outline of an Interpretive History," in *Stony the Road We Trod: African American Biblical Interpretation*, ed. Cain Hope Felder, 81–97.

8. Vincent Wimbush, "Introduction: Reading Darkness, Reading Scriptures," in *African Americans and the Bible: Sacred Texts and Social Structures*, ed. Vincent Wimbush (New York: Continuum, 2000).

9. Cain Hope Felder, *Troubling Biblical Waters: Race, Class, and Family*. Maryknoll, N.Y.: Orbis, 1989), xiv, 14.

10. This is evident in the volume edited by Hebrew Bible scholar Randall C. Bailey, *Yet With a Steady Beat: Contemporary U.S. Afrocentric Biblical Interpretation*. (Atlanta: Society of Biblical Literature Press, 2003), 2–3.

11. Vincent Wimbush, "Introduction . . ." in *African Americans and the Bible*, 2.

12. Ibid., 9.

13. Felder, *Stony the Road We Trod*, 10; Renita Weems, "Reading Her Way through the Struggle: African American Women and the Bible," in *Stony the Road We Trod*, 10–11, 58, 64–70.

3: Black Theologies

Epigraph. James H. Cone, *Black Theology and Black Power* (San Francisco: Harper & Row, 1969; Maryknoll, N.Y.: Orbis Books, 2006), 31.

1. Vincent Harding, *There Is a River: The Black Struggle for Freedom in America* (New York: Harcourt Brace Jovanovich, 1981), i, xix.

2. C. Eric Lincoln and Larry H. Mamiya, "The Black Sacred Cosmos," in *Down By the Riverside: Readings in African-American Religion*, Larry G. Murphy, ed. (New York: New York University Press, 2000), 41–48.

3. Walter F. Pitts Jr., *Old Ship of Zion: The Afro-Baptist Ritual in the African Diaspora* (New York: Oxford University Press, 1993), 8–9.

4. Howard Thurman, *Jesus and the Disinherited* (Boston: Beacon Press, 1976), 7.

5. Stephen R. Haynes, *Noah's Curse: The Biblical Justification of American Slavery* (New York: Oxford University Press, 2002).

6. Fredrick Douglass, *Narrative of the Life of Fredrick Douglass: An American Slave*, ed., Benjamin Quarles (Cambridge: Belknap Press of the Harvard University Press, 1988), 155.

7. Vincent L. Wimbush with Rosamond C. Rodman, *African Americans and the Bible: Sacred Texts and Social Textures* (New York: Continuum, 2000).

8. Examples of work in this genre are Langdon Gilkey, *Naming the Whirlwind: The Renewal of God-Language* (Indianapolis: Bobbs-Merril, 1969); John A. T. Robinson, *Honest to God* (Philadelphia: Westminster Press, 1963).

9. Thomas F. Gossett, *Race: The History of an Idea in America* (New York: Oxford University Press, 1997), 144; Seymour Drescher, "The Ending of the Slave Trade and the Evolution of European Scientific Racism," in *Social Science History* 14, no. 3 (Autumn, 1990): 415–50.

10. David Walker, *David Walker's Appeal To the Coloured Citizens of the World, but in particular, and very expressly, to those of the United States of America* (1830; Black Classics Press, 1993), 23.

11. Peter J. Paris, *The Social Teachings of the Black Churches* (Philadelphia: Fortress Press 1985), 61.

12. Nicholas C. Cooper-Lewter and Henry H. Mitchell, *Soul Theology: The Heart of Black American Culture* (San Francisco: Harper & Row, 1986), 95.

13. Benjamin Mays, *The Negro's God as Reflected in His Literature* (New York: Negro Universities Press 1969), 14–15.

14. Dwight N. Hopkins, ed., *Black Faith and Public Talk: Critical Essays on James H. Cone's Black Theology and Black Power* (Maryknoll, N.Y.: Orbis 1999), 1.

15. W. Fitzhugh Brundage, ed., *Under Sentence of Death: Lynching in the South* (Chapel Hill: University of North Carolina Press, 1997).

16. *See* Booker T. Washington's speech at the Atlanta Cotton States and International Exposition, September 18, 1895, http://teachingamericanhistory.org/library/index.asp?document=69.

17. Gayraud S. Wilmore, *Black Religion and Black Radicalism* (Garden City, N.Y.: Anchor Press/Doubleday, 1973; Maryknoll, N.Y.: Orbis Books, 1998), ch.1.

18. James H. Cone and Gayraud S. Wilmore, *Black Theology: A Documentary History, 1966–1979* (Maryknoll, N.Y.: Orbis Press, 1979).

19. Ibid., 21.

20. James H. Cone, *Black Theology and Black Power* (San Francisco: Harper & Row, 1969; Maryknoll, N.Y.: Orbis Books, 2006); and *A Black Theology of Liberation* (New York: J.B. Lippincott, 1970).

21. Albert B. Cleage, Jr., *Black Christian Nationalism: New Directions for the Black Church* (Detroit: Luxor Publishers of the Pan-African Orthodox Church, 1972).

22. Katie Geneva Cannon, "The Emergence of Black Feminist Consciousness," in Letty Russell, ed., *Feminist Interpretation of the Bible* (Philadelphia: Westminster, 1985), 30, as quoted in Rosetta E. Ross, *Witnessing & Testifying: Black Women, Religion, and Civil Rights* (Minneapolis: Fortress Press, 2003), 7.

23. *See* Alice Walker, *In Search of Our Mother's Gardens: Womanist Prose* (San Diego: Harcourt Brace Jovanovich, 1983).

4: *The Black Church, Culture, and Society*

Epigraph. W.E.B. Du Bois, *The Souls of Black Folk* (1903; New York: W. W. Norton, 1999), 162.

1. C. Eric Lincoln and Lawrence H. Mamiya, *The Black Church in the African American Experience* (Durham: Duke University Press, 1990) 1.

2. Lincoln and Mamiya, *The Black Church*, 16.

3. *See*, for example, Patricia Hill Collins, *Black Feminist Thought: Knowledge, Consciousness, and the Politics of Empowerment* (New York; London: Routledge, 2000); Angela Y. Davis, *Women, Race, and Class* (New York: Vintage Books, 1983); and bell hooks, *Ain't I a Woman?* (Boston: South End Press, 1981).

4. W.E.B. Du Bois, *The Souls of Black Folk.*

5. Ibid., 5.

6. *See* Olaudah Equiano, *The Interesting Narrative of the Life of Olaudah Equiano, or Gustavus Vassa, the African, Written by Himself: Authoritative Text, Contexts, Criticism; Edited Werner Sollors* (ca. 1792; New York: Norton, 2001).

7. *See* Dale Cannon, *Six Ways of Being Religious: A Framework for Comparative Studies of Religion* (Belmont, Calif.: Wadsworth Publishing, 1996).

8. Arthur Huff Fauset, *Black Gods of the Metropolis: Negro Religious Cults of the Urban North* (Philadelphia: University of Pennsylvania Press, 1971).

9. *See* C. Eric Lincoln, *The Black Muslims in America* (Grand Rapids: W.B. Eerdmans; Trenton, N. J.: African World Press, 1994).

10. Lisa Gail Collins, *The Art of History: African-American Woman Artists Engage the Past* (New Brunswick, N. J.: Rutgers University Press, 2002).

11. Cheryl Townsend Gilkes, "The Roles of Church and Community Mothers: Ambivalent American Sexism or Fragmented African Familyhood," in *African-American Religion: Interpretive Essays in History and Culture*, eds., Timothy E. Fulop and Albert J. Raboteau (New York and London: Routledge, 1997), 365–88.

12. Kelly Brown Douglas, *Sexuality and the Black Church: A Womanist Perspective* (Maryknoll, N.Y.: Orbis Books, 1999).

13. Ibid., 5.

14. http://www.ufc-usa.org/history.htm.

15. Paul Gilroy, *The Black Atlantic: Modernity and Double Consciousness* (Cambridge, Mass.: Harvard University Press, 1993).

16. Ibid., 2.

17. Eric C. Wolf, *Europe and the People without History*. With a new preface and cartographic illustrations by Noel L. Diaz (Berkeley: University of California Press, 1997).

18. Sidney W. Mintz and Richard Price, "The Birth of African-American Culture," in *African-American Religion: Interpretive Essays in History and Culture*, eds. Timothy E. Fulop and Albert J. Raboteau (New York and London: Routledge, 1997), 37–53.

19. *See* Jacob K. Olupona and Regina Gemignani, eds., *African Immigrant Religions in America* (New York: University Press, 2007).

20. For recent examples, see Wallace W. Zane, *Journeys to the Spiritual Lands: The Natural History of a West Indian Religion* (New York and Oxford: Oxford University Press, 1999); and Carol B. Duncan, "Spiritual Baptists in Multicultural Canada," in *Whither Multiculturalism? A Politics of Dissensus*, eds. Barbara A.C. Saunders and David Haljan (Leuven: Leuven University Press, 2003), 205–24.

21. Hans A. Baer and Merrill Singer, *African-American Religion in the Twentieth Century: Varieties of Protest and Accommodation* (Knoxville: The University of Tennessee Press, 1992).

22. Ibid., xv.

5: *African American Christian Social Ethics*

Epigraph. Howard Thurman, *Jesus and the Disinherited* (Boston: Beacon Press, 1976), 108.

1. Albert J. Raboteau, *Slave Religion: The "Invisible Institution" in the Antebellum South* (New York: Oxford University Press, 1978), 4.

2. Ibid.

3. For a further examination of the Black Church as the "moral cement" of the Black community see: Albert J. Raboteau, *Fire in the Bones: Reflections on African-American Religious History* (Boston: Beacon, 1996).

4. For a fuller treatment of this concept, see: Garth Baker-Fletcher, *Somebodyness: Martin Luther King, Jr. and the Theory of Dignity* (Minneapolis: Fortress Press, 1993).

5. Peter J. Paris, *The Social Teaching of the Black Churches* (Philadelphia: Fortress Press, 1985), 2.

6. Samuel K. Roberts, *African American Christian Ethics* (Cleveland: Pilgrim, 2001), 6.

7. Cornel West, *Race Matters* (Boston: Beacon Press, 1993), 123.

8. Paris, *The Social Teaching of the Black Churches*, 10.

9. Luke 4:18, Luke 7:22, and the Beatitudes are but a few examples of the liberating teachings that are given significant weight within the Black Church tradition.

10. Preston Williams, "Afro-American Religious Ethics," in *The Westminster Dictionary of Christian Ethics*, eds. James F. Childress and John Macquarrie (Philadelphia: Westminster John Knox, 1986), 12.

11. Joan M. Martin, *More Than Chains and Toil: A Christian Work Ethic of Enslaved Women* (Louisville: Westminster John Knox, 2000), 82.

12. For an extensive definition of morality see Willliam K. Frankena, "Morality and Religion, Relations of" in *The Westminster Dictionary of Christian Ethics*, eds. James F. Childress and John Macquarrie (Philadelphia: Westminster John Knox, 1986), 402.

13. Enoch H. Oglesby, *Ethics and Theology from the Other Side: Sounds of Moral Struggle* (Washington, D.C.: University Press of America, 1979), 3.

14. Samuel K. Roberts, *In the Path of Virtue* (Cleveland: Pilgrim, 1999), 3.

15. Peter J. Paris, *Virtues and Values: The African and African American Experience* (Minneapolis: Fortress Press, 2004), 2.

16. Ibid., 5.

17. West, *Race Matters*, 19.

18. Howard Thurman, *With Head and Heart: Autobiography* (New York: Harcourt Brace Jovanovich, 1979), 165.

19. Paris, *Virtues and Values*, 16.

20. Ibid., 14.

21. For a fuller examination, see Stacey M. Floyd-Thomas, *Mining the Motherlode: Methods in Womanist Ethics* (Cleveland: Pilgrim, 2006), ch.1.

22. Teresa L. Fry Brown, *God Don't Like Ugly: African American Women Handing on Spiritual Values*, (Nashville: Abingdon Press, 2000), 89.

23. Emilie Townes, "Womanist Ethics," in *The Dictionary of Feminist Theologies*, eds. Letty M. Russell and J. Shannon Clarkson (Louisville: Westminster John Knox, 1996), 91.

24. Roberts, *In the Path of Virtue*, 3–4.

25. Ibid., 106.

26. For a full description of these six virtues, see: Peter J. Paris, *Spirituality of African Peoples* (Minneapolis: Fortress Press, 1995).

27. This typology is based on and adapted from Peter J. Paris, *Virtues and Values*.

28. George D. Kelsey, *Racism and the Christian Understanding of Man* (New York: Charles Scribner's Sons, 1965).

29. Oglesby, *Ethics and Theology from the Other Side*.

30. See Cheryl J. Sanders, *Empowerment Ethics for a Liberated People* (Minneapolis: Augsburg Fortress, 1995).

31. Darryl Trimiew, "Ethics—Moral Evolution: From Customary Societies to Atomistic Individuals," in *Handbook of U.S. Liberation Theologies of Liberation*, ed. Miguel De La Torre (St. Louis: Chalice, 2004), 105.

32. James H. Cone, "God is Black," in *Lift Every Voice: Constructing Christian Theologies from the Underside*, edited by Susan Brooks Thistlethwaite and Mary Potter Engel (San Francisco: Harper & Row, 1990), 85.

33. James H. Cone, *God of the Oppressed* (New York: Seabury, 1975), 206. It is understood, however, that there are many Black churches for which divine liberation is not defined as Cone defines it.

34. Oglesby, *Ethics and Theology from the Other Side*, 154–55.

35. This typology has been adapted from Robert Franklin's "Five Forms of Political Ministry" in *Another Day's Journey: Black Churches Confronting the American Crisis* (Minneapolis: Augsburg Fortress, 1997), 51.

36. Howard Thurman, *The Luminous Darkness* (New York: McGraw-Hill, 1964), 22–23.

37. For a fuller definition see Emile Townes, "Womanist Ethics," in *The Dictionary of Feminist Theologies*, 91. *See also* Jacqueline Grant, *White Women's Christ and Black Women's Jesus: Feminist Christology and Womanist Response* (Atlanta: Scholars Press, 1990) as a text that critically examines Black women's theological response to the ethical problems that suffering presents for them.

38. *See* Katie Cannon's *Black Womanist Ethics*, AARC Academy Series 60 (Atlanta: Scholars Press, 1988); Emilie Townes's *Troubling in My Soul: Woman Perspectives on Evil and Suffering* (Maryknoll, N.Y.: Orbis, 1993); Joan Martin's *More than Chains and Toil*; or Stacey Floyd-Thomas's *Deeper Shades of Purple: Womanism in Religion and Society* (New York: New York University Press, 2006).

39. For a fuller description of these four Womanist moral principles described (also referred to as the four tenets of Womanism and Womanist ethics), as defined by Stacey Floyd-Thomas, see her texts: *Mining the Motherlode: Methods in Womanist Ethics*, (Cleveland: Pilgrim, 2006) and *Deeper Shades of Purple: Womanism in Religion and Society*. For a thorough treatment of these four Womanist virtues, as defined by Katie G. Cannon, see *Black Womanist Ethics* (Atlanta: Scholars Press, 1988).

40. This typology has been culled from Stacey Floyd-Thomas's *Mining the Motherlode* and Katie Cannon's *Black Womanist Ethics*.

41. For a fuller description of "unshouted courage," see Katie Cannon's *Black Womanist Ethics*, 143–48.

42. Katie G. Cannon, "Womanist Virtue," in *The Dictionary of Feminist Theologies*, 313.

43. For a full discussion of the work of African American club movements, see Marcia Y. Riggs, *Awake, Arise, and Act: A Womanist Call for Black Liberation* (Cleveland: Pilgrim, 1994).

44. Teresa Fry Brown, *God Don't Like Ugly*, 89.

45. Katie Cannon, *Black Womanist Ethics*, 105.

46. Stacey M. Floyd-Thomas, *Mining the Motherlode*, 130.

47. Cornel West, *Prophesy Deliverance!: An Afro-American Revolutionary Christianity* (Philadelphia: Westminster John Knox, 1982), 22. For an extensive treatment of "human flourishing" as an ethical concept, see Victor Anderson, *Beyond Ontological Blackness: An Essay on African-American Religious and Cultural Criticism* (New York: Continuum, 1995).

6: *Christian Education in the Black Church Tradition*

Epigraph. Grant H. Shockley, "Black Theology and Religious Education," in *Theologies of Religious Education*, ed. Randolph Crump Miller (Birmingham, Ala.: Religious Education Press, 1995), 323. In this quotation, Shockley is referring to reflections on issues of teaching and learning in oppressive contexts from Brazilian educator Paulo Freire, author of the seminal text *Pedagogy of the Oppressed*. Freire is considered by many to be one of the foremost scholars in liberative pedagogy.

1. For a fuller discussion see Edward Farley, *Practicing Gospel: Unconventional Thoughts on the Church's Ministry* (Louisville: Westminster John Knox Press, 2003).

2. Richard Robert Osmer, *The Teaching Ministry of Congregations* (Louisville: Westminster John Knox Press, 2005), xiv.

3. Ibid.

4. Terry A. Veling, *Practical Theology: "On Earth as It Is in Heaven"* (Maryknoll, N.Y.: Orbis Books, 2005), 8.

5. *See* James H. Cone, *God of the Oppressed* (New York: Seabury, 1975).

6. For further discussion on vocation see Anne E. Streaty Wimberly, *Soul Stories: African American Christian Education*, rev. ed. (Nashville: Abingdon Press, 2005).

7. Lawrence W. Levine, *Black Culture and Black Consciousness: Afro-American Folk Thought from Slavery to Freedom* (New York: Oxford University Press, 1977), xi.

8. W.E.B. Du Bois, *Black Reconstruction in America: 1860–1880* (New York: Harcout, Brace, 1935; New York: Simon & Schuster, 1998), 8–9.

9. Carter G. Woodson, *The Mis-Education of the Negro* (Washington, D.C.: Associated Publishers, 1933) 84–85.

10. Patricia O'Connell Killen, "Gracious Play: Discipline, Insight, and the Common Good" in *Teaching Theology & Religion* 4 (February 2001): 1.

11. Robert L. Browning, ed., *The Pastor as Religious Educator* (Birmingham, Ala.: Religious Education Press, 1989), 13.

12. *See* Woodson, *The Mis-Education of the Negro*.

13. For more information see Cheryl Kirk-Duggan, *African-American Special Days* (Nashville: Abingdon Press, 1996).

14. Charles Foster, *Educating Congregations* (Nashville: Abingdon Press, 1994), 42–50.

15. C. Eric Lincoln and Lawrence H. Mamiya, *The Black Church in the African-American Experience* (Durham: Duke University Press, 1990) 52–53.

16. http://www.cheyney.edu/pages/index.asp?p=428.

17. Ibid.

18. Ibid.

19. www.tucc.org/ministries.htm (accessed July 7, 2006, and used by permission of Trinity United Church of Christ, Chicago).

20. For further discussion see Rosetta E. Ross, *Witnessing & Testifying: Black Women, Religion, and Civil Rights* (Minneapolis: Augsburg Fortress, 2003) and Cheryl Townsend Gilkes, *If It Wasn't For the Women* (Maryknoll, N.Y.: Orbis Books, 2001).

21. www.stanford.edu/group/King/about_king/encyclopedia/nash_diane.htm.

22. Evelyn Parker, *Trouble Don't Last Always* (Cleveland: Pilgrim, 2003), 3.

23. Ibid.

24. James H. Cone, "Black Consciousness and the Black Church: A Historical-Theological Interpretation," *Annals of the American Academy of Political and Social Science* 387 (January 1970): 33.

25. bell hooks, *Teaching to Transgress: Education as the Practice of Freedom* (New York: Routledge, 1994).

26. This term coined by W.E. B. Du Bois was originally published in an 1897 *Atlantic Monthly* article, "Strivings of the Negro People." This was later edited slightly and republished under the title "Of Our Spiritual Strivings" in his collection of essays, *The Souls of Black Folk* (1903; New York: W. W. Norton, 1999). Du Bois spoke of "this sense of always looking at one's self through the eyes of others, of measuring one's soul by the tape of a world that looks on in amused contempt and pity." He also wrote of a two-ness, of being "an American, a Negro . . . two warring ideals in one dark body, whose dogged strength alone keeps it from being torn asunder"(11).

27. For more conversation on transgression as an approach to teaching, see bell hook, *Teaching to Transgress*.

28. It is well known that Rev. Dr. Martin Luther King, Jr., always carried a Bible and a copy of Howard Thurman's book *Jesus and the Disinherited*.

29. The wording of God's concern for the flourishing of Black people belongs to our colleague and co-author Dr. Stephen Ray.

30. Biographical information for Grant Shockley was written by Dr. Charles Foster. It is from the "Christian Educators of the 21st Century Project," www.talbot.edu/ce20 (accessed July 7, 2006).

31. Biographical information for Dr. Olivia Pearl Stokes was written by Dr. Yolanda Smith. It is from the "Christian Educators of the 21st Century Project," www.talbot.edu/ce20 (accessed July 8, 2006).

7: Black Christian Worship as Nurture

Epigraph. Herbert Anderson and Edward Foley, *Mighty Stories, Dangerous Rituals: Weaving Together the Human and the Divine* (San Francisco: Jossey-Bass, 1998), 42.

1. See W.E.B. Du Bois, *The Negro Church* (Atlanta: Atlanta University, 1903); Benjamin E. Mays and Joseph W. Nicholson, *The Negro's Church* (New York: Russell and Russell, 1969); E. Franklin Frazier, *The Negro Church in America* (New York: Schocken Books, 1966); C. Eric Lincoln and Lawrence H. Mamiya, *The Black Church in the African American Experience* (Durham: Duke University Press, 1990); and Andrew Billingsley, *Mighty Like A River: The Black Church and Social Reform* (New York: Oxford University Press, 1999).

2. Robert Staples and Leanor Boulin Johnson, *Black Families at the Crossroads: Challenges and Prospects* (San Francisco: Jossey-Bass, 1993), 213–14.

3. Emmanuel Y. Lartey, *Pastoral Theology in an Intercultural World* (Cleveland: Pilgrim, 2006), 123. For a similar view, also see Homer U. Ashby Jr., *Our Home Is Over Jordan: A Black Pastoral Theology* (St. Louis: Chalice Press, 2003), 37; and Carroll A. Watkins Ali, *Survival and Liberation: Pastoral Theology in African American Context* (St. Louis: Chalice Press, 1999), 1.

4. Ashby, *Our Home Is Over Jordan*, 67.

5. Richard R. Osmer, "Education, Nurture, and Care," *Dictionary of Pastoral Care and Counseling*, ed. Rodney J. Hunter (Nashville: Abingdon, 1990), 336.

6. A discussion of meanings of nurture in Black Christian worship appears in Anne E. Streaty Wimberly, *Nurturing Faith & Hope: Black Worship as a Model for Christian Education* (Cleveland: Pilgrim, 2004), xiii–xiv.

7. *See* Osmer, 336.

8. A. Wimberly, *Nurturing Faith & Hope*, xiv.

9. Ibid., xv. The Augustinian view of "interior truth" appears in: James J. Murphy, *Rhetoric in the Middle Ages: A History of Rhetorical Theology from Saint Augustine to the Renaissance* (Berkeley: University of California Press, 1974), 287–89.

10. *See* Charles M. Johnson, "The Wisdom of Limits,"in *In Context: A Quarterly of Humane Sustainable Culture* 32 (Summer 1992): 48, http://context.org/ICLIB/IC32/Johnston.htm.

11. Edward P. Wimberly, *Relational Refugees: Alienation and Reincorporation in African-American Churches and Communities* (Nashville: Abingdon, 2000), 20.

12. *See* Anne E. Streaty Wimberly and Evelyn Parker, *In Search of Wisdom: Faith Formation in the Black Church* (Nashville: Abingdon, 2002), 12.

13. Stephen L. Carter, *Integrity* (New York: Basic Books, 1996), 7.

14. Wimberly and Parker, *In Search of Wisdom*, 12.

15. *See* Wyatt Tee Walker, *The Soul of Black Worship: A Trilogy—Preaching, Praying, Singing* (New York: Martin Luther King Fellows, 1984).

16. Costen makes the point that worship in the Black Church exists as a key opportunity for raising hope in the face of adversity. *See* Melva Wilson Costen, *African American Christian Worship* (Nashville: Abingdon, 1993), 78.

17. Anne Wimberly, *Nurturing Faith and Hope*, xxv.

18. Ibid.

19. *See* Seward Hiltner, *Pastoral Counseling* (Nashville: Abingdon, 1949); and Seward Hiltner, *Preface to Pastoral Theology* (Nashville: Abingdon Press, 1958).

20. William A. Clebsch and Charles R. Jaekle, *Pastoral Care in Historical Perspective* (Englewood Cliffs, N.J.: Prentice-Hall, 1964), 8–10.

21. Edward P. Wimberly, *Pastoral Care in the Black Church* (Nashville: Abingdon, 1979), 17–38.

22. Edward P. Wimberly, *African American Pastoral Care* (Nashville: Abingdon, 1991), 24.

23. A discussion of evocative nurture appears in A. Wimberly, *Nurturing Faith and Hope*, xiii–xv.

24. These interrelated aspects are explored in detail in Anne Wimberly, *Soul Stories: African American Christian Education*, rev. ed. (Nashville: Abingdon, 2005).

25. Grant Shockley highlights the centrality of images of God in the role of biblical integrity in Black Church preaching, worship, music, and teaching. *See* Grant S. Shockley, "Black Pastoral Leadership in Religious Education," *The Pastor as Religious Educator*, ed. Robert L. Browning (Birmingham, Ala.: Religious Education Press, 1989), 202–203.

26. *See* E. Wimberly, *African American Pastoral Care*, 24–25.

27. Valerie Bridgeman Davis, gen. ed., *The Africana Worship Book, Year A* (Nashville: Discipleship Resources, 2006), 17.

28. E. Wimberly, *African American Pastoral Care*, 25.

29. Ibid., 26.

30. Ashby, *Our Home Is Over Jordan*, 47–48.

31. A. Wimberly, *Soul Stories*, 31–32.

32. Ibid., 32.

33. Anderson and Foley, *Mighty Stories, Dangerous Rituals*, 48.

34. Ibid., 53.

35. Ibid., 49.

36. Ibid., 48, 53–54.

37. Spencer describes these attributes of music as testimony most particularly in the Black Holiness-Pentecostal testimony service. *See* Jon Michael Spencer, *Protest and Praise: Sacred Music of Black Religion* (Minneapolis: Augsburg Fortress, 1990), 177, 181–82.

38. *See* Thomas Hoyt Jr., "Testimony," in *Practicing Our Faith: A Way of Life for a Searching People*, ed. Dorothy C. Bass (San Francisco: Jossey-Bass, 1997).

39. Spencer, *Protest and Praise*, 199.

40. L. Rebecca Propst, "Cognitive Psychology and Psycho-Therapy," *Dictionary of Pastoral Care and Counseling*, ed. Rodney J. Hunter, 188.

41. A. Wimberly, *Nurturing Faith and Hope*, 147–48.

42. Ibid., 149.

43. *See* Ibid., 150.

44. *See* Carroll E. Izard, "Emotion," *Dictionary of Pastoral Care and Counseling,* ed. Rodney J. Hunter, 352.

45. Davis, *The Africana Worship Book,* 20.

46. Ibid.

47. *See* A. Wimberly, *Nurturing Faith and Hope,* 134–39.

48. Ibid., 71–72.

49. Ibid., 131.

50. James H. Harris, *Pastoral Theology: A Black Church Perspective* (Minneapolis: Augsburg Fortress, 1991), 56.

51. Olin P. Moyd, *The Sacred Art: Preaching and Theology in the African-American Tradition* (Valley Forge: Judson, 1995), 56.

52. Quentin L. Hand, "Counselee/Client/Parishioner," in *Dictionary of Pastoral Care and Counseling,* ed. Rodney J. Hunter, 234.

53. Cedarleaf sets forth a description of the passive and active listening role of the pastoral counselor in terms that are quite useful in describing the Black worshipers' listening role during the sermonic experience. *See* J.L. Cedarleaf, "Listening," in *Dictionary of Pastoral Care and Counseling,* ed. Rodney J. Hunter, 654.

54. Walker, *Soul of Black Worship,* 33.

55. Michael I.N. Dash, Jonathan Jackson, and Stephen C. Rasor, *Hidden Wholeness: An African American Spirituality for Individuals and Communities* (Cleveland: United Church Press, 1997), 34.

56. Perry LeFevre, "Prayer," in *Dictionary of Pastoral Care and Counseling,* ed. Rodney J. Hunter, 937.

57. A. Wimberly, *Nurturing Faith and Hope,* 163.

58. *See* Ibid., part 2, 105–109.

59. Ibid., 108–109.

60. *See:* Ibid., 117–22.

61. Ibid., 121.

62. E. Wimberly, *African American Pastoral Care,* 36–37.

63. Anderson and Foley, *Mighty Stories, Dangerous Rituals,* 157.

64. From http://www.blackatlanta.com/news_detail.php?id=189.

8: Black Preaching Praxis

Epigraph. Julia A. J. Foote, *A Brand Plucked from the Fire: An Autobiographical Sketch by Mrs. Julia A. J. Foote,* in *Sisters of the Spirit: Three Black Women's Autobiographies of the Nineteenth Century,* ed. William L. Andrews (Bloomington: Indiana University Press, 1986), 200.

1. Olin P. Moyd, *The Sacred Art: Preaching and Theology in the African-American Tradition* (Valley Forge: Judson, 1995), 2, 7–11, 34–36.

2. Ibid, 95.

3. Dale P. Andrews, *Practical Theology for Black Churches: Bridging Black Theology and African-American Folk Religion* (Louisville: Westminster John Knox Press, 2002), 40, 91.

4. Peter J. Paris, *The Spirituality of African Peoples: The Search for a Common Moral Discourse* (Minneapolis: Fortress Press, 1995), 35–43.

5. Molefi Kete Asante, *The Afrocentric Idea* (Philadelphia: Temple University Press, 1978), 168-172. For a fuller argument of how these spiritual values relate to the development of church praxis and Black ecclesiology, see also Dale Andrews, *Practical Theology for Black Churches*, 12–49.

6. Ibid.

7. John S. Mbiti, *African Religions and Philosophies* (New York: Doubleday, 1969).

8. Emmanuel L. McCall, *Black Church Lifestyles* (Nashville: Broadman Press, 1986), 27, 148–50. *See also* C. Eric Lincoln and Lawrence H. Mamiya, *The Black Church in the African-American Experience* (Durham: Duke University Press, 1990).

9. William H. Pipes, *Say Amen, Brother! Old-Time Negro Preaching: A Study in American Frustration* (1951; Detroit: Wayne State University Press, 1992), 58, 72.

10. Ibid, 69–70.

11. Eugene D. Genovese, *Roll Jordan Roll: The World the Slaves Made* (New York: Pantheon Books, 1974), 255–79.

12. Lawrence W. Levine, *Black Culture and Black Consciousness: Afro-American Folk Thought from Slavery to Freedom* (New York: Oxford University Press, 1977), 45–48.

13. James L. Golden and Richard D. Rieke, *The Rhetoric of Black Americans* (Columbus, Ohio: Charles E. Merrill Publishing, 1971).

14. Gayraud S. Wilmore, *Black Religion and Black Radicalism: An Interpretation of the Religious History of African-Americans* (Garden City, N.Y.: Anchor Press/Doubleday, 1973; Maryknoll, N.Y.: Orbis Books, 1998), 254–75.

15. Henry H. Mitchell, *Black Preaching: The Recovery of a Powerful Art* (Nashville: Abingdon Press, 1990), 106–107.

16. Ibid, 104–105.

17. Ibid, 30–35, 51–55.

18. Frank A. Thomas, *They Like to Never Quit Praisin' God: The Role of Celebration in Preaching* (Cleveland: United Church Press, 1997), 84–90.

19. James Earl Massey, *Designing the Sermon: Order and Movement in Preaching* (Nashville: Abingdon Press, 1980), 20.

20. Mitchell, *Black Preaching*, 57.

21. Pipes, 62–67.

22. Albert J. Raboteau, *Slave Religion: Folk Beliefs of Blacks in America and West Africa* (New York: Oxford University Press, 1978), 241–43.

23. For a more nuanced explication of how many of these tenets comprised the early formation of Black ecclesiology, see Andrews, *Practical Theology for Black Churches*, 40–49.

24. Cleophus J. LaRue, *The Heart of Black Preaching* (Louisville: Westminster John Knox Press, 2000), 114–15.

25. Martin Luther King, Jr., *Strength to Love* (New York: Harper & Row, 1963), chap. 13.

26. Henry H. Mitchell, *Black Belief: Folk Beliefs of Blacks in America and West Africa* (New York: Harper & Row, 1975), 120.

27. James H. Cone, *God of the Oppressed* (New York: Seabury, 1975), 145.

28. Raboteau, *Slave Religion*, 311.

29. Ibid., 267.

30. James Deotis Roberts, "Black Consciousness in Theological Perspective," in *The Black Experience in Religion*, ed. C. Eric Lincoln (Garden City, N.Y.: Anchor Books, 1974), 107.

31. Ibid., 107. For a Womanist perspective on redemptive suffering, see Joanne Marie Terrell, *Power in the Blood? The Cross in the African-American Experience* (Maryknoll, N.Y.: Orbis Books, 1998).

32. *Mujerista* theology, founded by theologian and ethicist Ada María Isasi-Díaz is the theological movement of Latina scholars who in their quest for liberation make a preferential option for Latina culture and struggle to liberate themselves not as individuals but as members of a Latino community. Herein, the notion of "kin-dom" (often attributed to *Mujerista* theology) celebrates a notion of realized eschatology as that which is experienced in community rather than hierarchically (i.e., kingdom).

33. George C. L. Cummings, "The Slave Narratives as a Source of Black Theological Discourse: The Spirit and Eschatology," *Cut Loose Your Stammering Tongue: Black Theology in the Slave Narratives*, eds. Dwight N. Hopkins and George Cummings (Maryknoll, N.Y.: Orbis Books, 1991), 54–56.

34. Ibid., 58.

35. H. Grady Davis, *Design for Preaching* (Philadelphia: Muhlenberg Press, 1958), 163.

36. Fred B. Craddock, *As One Without Authority* (Nashville: Abingdon, 1979), 59, 70.

37. David Randolph, *The Renewal of Preaching* (Philadelphia: Fortress Press, 1969), 5–6, 16.

38. Mitchell, *Black Preaching*, 63–75.

39. Massey, *Designing the Sermon*, chap. 2.

40. James H. Cone, "The Story Context of Black Theology," *Theology Today* 32, no. 2 (July 1975): 147.

41. James H. Harris, *Preaching Liberation* (Minneapolis: Fortress Press, 1995), 58.

42. John W. Blassingame, *The Slave Community: Plantation Life in the Antebellum South* (New York: Oxford University Press, 1972), 131, 137. *See also* Evans E. Crawford and Thomas H. Troeger, *The Hum: Call and Response in African American Preaching* (Nashville: Abingdon Press, 1990).

43. Gerald L. Davis, *I Got the Word in Me and I Can Sing It, You Know: A Study of the Performed African-American Sermon* (Philadelphia: University of Pennsylvania Press, 1985), 51.

44. LaRue, *The Heart of Black Preaching*, 19.

45. Katie G. Cannon, "Womanist Interpretation and Preaching in the Black Church," *Searching the Scriptures*, eds. Elizabeth Schüssler Fiorenza, Shelly Matthews, and Ann Graham Brock (New York: Crossroad, 1993), 334–35.

46. Teresa L. Fry Brown, *Weary Throats and New Songs: Black Women Proclaiming God's Word* (Nashville: Abingdon Press, 2003), 91.

47. For a much fuller and nuanced treatment of this apprentice-mentor parallel process in homiletic instruction, please see the two-part article series: Dale P. Andrews, "Teaching Black Preaching: Encounter and Re-encounter," in *The African-American Pulpit* 9, no. 4 (Fall 2006): 8–12; and idem, "Teaching Black Preaching: Homiletic Instruction as 'Pre-encounter,'" *The African-American Pulpit* 10, no. 1 (Winter 2006–2007): 22–26.

48. Martin Luther King, Jr., "A Time to Break Silence," in *Testament of Hope: The Essential Writings of Martin Luther King, Jr.*, ed. James M. Washington (San Francisco: Harper & Row, 1986), 242.

49. William L. Andrews, *Sisters of the Spirit: Three Black Women's Autobiographies of the Nineteenth Century* (Bloomington: Indiana University Press, 1986), 9–10.

GLOSSARY

African Carryovers: Cultural practices, idiomatic language, and worldviews existing within African diasporan communities that have either explicit or implicit origins in the practices and traditions of African tribal or regional cultures.

African Traditional Religions (also known as African Indigenous Religion): Refers to a wide range of spiritual and cosmological beliefs and sacred ritual practices shared by most pre-colonial African societies.

Afrocentric (or Africentric): A term describing the methodology that de-emphasizes Europe as the ideological "center" of meaning, and focuses on the cultures, rhetoric, spirituality, and philosophy of Africa and African peoples and the roles they play in defining the world.

Altar Call: An accepted, and expected, time during worship when members of the congregation experience a connection to the healing presence of God at the altar. The experience is mediated by pastoral prayer or prayers of intercession offered by laypeople.

Apocryphal: A description pertaining to biblical books included in the Vulgate and accepted in the Roman Catholic and Orthodox canon but considered noncanonical by most Protestant denominations. Also applies to various early Christian writings proposed but rejected as additions to the New Testament canon.

Apprenticeship: Traditions of learning to preach in Black churches. Historical realities of slavery and violent segregation ensured that Black preachers and churches would develop the study and craft of preaching ministry through mentoring and folk systems of instruction. Apprenticeship practices build upon traditions of oral culture from African heritage and African American history within a process of redesignating and redeveloping the fount of folk religion via rites of passage and initiation.

Azusa Street Revivals: A series of Christian revival meetings that took place in Los Angeles, California, beginning in 1906 and lasting for several years. Characterized by Wesleyan theological doctrines, manifestation of spiritual gifts, dramatic worship services, and interracial fellowship, these revivals are considered a primary cause of the rise of Holiness-Pentecostal denominations in the last century.

Banking System: An educational term that connotes the practice of a pedagogy of dominance that treats students as if they are passive recipients of information, like a bank account is to be filled with cash. Learning, in the banking system, is assessed by the amount of material a student can memorize, then regurgitate. The teacher is seen as the sole and unquestionable expert in the classroom.

Beloved Community: A term popularized by Dr. Martin Luther King, Jr., and invested with a deeper significance—not a lofty utopian ideal but a realizable goal that could be achieved by people of good will and conscience who see all people as part of God's Peaceable Kingdom.

Beneficence: The first African/African American virtue that represents Black people's willingness to perform acts of kindness and to practice hospitality in all facets of life. This includes fulfilling moral obligations to both friend and foe alike.

Black Atlantic: A term introduced by sociologist Paul Gilroy in his book of the same name, *The Black Atlantic: Modernity and Double Consciousness*. The Black Atlantic refers to the African Diaspora created by the trans-Atlantic slave trade and the economic and cultural exchange among Europe, Africa, and the Americas. Gilroy suggests that the Black Atlantic, encompassing economic and cultural linkages among Europe, Africa, and the Americas be considered as a unit of analysis. Gilroy asserts that even under conditions of great social inequality such as slavery and colonialism, people from different ethnic, racial, cultural, linguistic and religious groups, among other markers of social difference, still influence each other. The concept of the Black Atlantic challenges the stereotypical categorization of blackness as a monolithic experience. Thus, the Black Atlantic suggests that African diasporan experiences are dynamic and subject to constant change, characterized by movement and adaptation.

Black Christian Worship: Distinctive and vital communal connections with and responses to God's concern, hope, and activity on behalf of Black people's wholeness in a hostile world.

Black Liberation Theology: Asserts the importance of conjoining religious practice and faith with political activism and social change for the betterment of the Black community. The primary affirmations include: (1) God as revealed in Scripture and in Jesus Christ (the Oppressed One) works primarily for the liberation of oppressed people, (2) God takes on the identity of those on whose behalf God is bringing about liberation, (3) In the context of racial oppression in America this means God is Black, and (4) The authentic expression of Christian faith is one that works with the purposes of God, which in the American context is the liberation of Black people.

Black Power: The ideology of the social, political, and cultural movement emerging in the 1960s that sought to replace the integrationist vision of the civil rights movement with the ideas of Black identity and self-determination.

Black Practical Theology: Demands a reflexive understanding of preaching practices in the contexts of the Black faith community and Black life in dialogue with theological studies and the human sciences. The transformation of Western Christianity in the evolution of the Black Church is best described as the transformation of Christianity through Black homiletics, hermeneutics, and communal care held together in Black preaching praxis.

Canon: The collection of texts deemed authoritative for a particular community. The notion of a canon within a canon implies individual choice in determining those texts deemed authoritative for the individual.

Civil Rights Movement: The legal, political, and social movement that began in the 1930s with the goal of dismantling the Jim and Jane Crow system and enabling the full participation of African Americans in the social, political, and economic life of the United States. The most active period of the movement was from 1954 to 1968, marked by protest events and a variety of reform efforts aimed at abolishing public and private acts of racial discrimination against African Americans.

Communal-Contextual Model: A form of pastoral care that emphasizes the relational and corporate community as both the base and the agent of care, and that gives fullest attention to the realities of Black life.

Contemplative Communitarianist: A moral approach that prioritizes community and reconciliation above all else. Social reform begins with personal transformation in order to work for common unity and peace while combating social ills.

Critical Engagement: The fourth Womanist moral principle based on the assumption that Black women possess the unique capability to transform society by imparting a liberating vision of a just and inclusive world. A Black woman's analysis of the status quo that exposes its patriarchal, classist, racist, and heterosexist practices.

Diaspora: From a Greek term that means "dispersal." The term has been used, historically, in reference to the Jewish Diaspora (dispersal) from what is now Israel/Palestine to other areas of the Mediterranean and Europe. Diaspora has also been used to refer to the modern migration of peoples, both voluntary and forced, as in the slave trade, from their homelands to other areas of the world. The African Diaspora emerged as a result of the trans-Atlantic slave trade from the fifteenth through nineteenth centuries that saw an estimated eleven million Africans shipped from the west coast of Africa to western Europe, the Caribbean and North, Central, and South America. While there are significant differences among diasporic experiences, commonalities include a long-term or permanent (over an individual's lifetime) separation from a homeland and distinct cultural characteristics, such as language and religion, around which diasporan identities form.

Disciple: A baptized believer in Jesus Christ; a follower of Jesus; a church member who takes seriously the Scripture passage Luke 9:23 in which Jesus is recorded as saying, "If any want to become my followers, let them deny themselves and take up their cross daily and follow me."

Discipleship: The lifestyle of following Jesus.

Double Consciousness: A term coined by W.E.B. Du Bois to describe the internal conflict of being both African and American incumbent to the Black racial identity formation. It addresses the power that white people have to stereotype and classify Black people as second-class citizens, thereby reflecting the permanence of racism that forever excludes Black people from participating fully within larger American society. Its danger is in the internalization of racism or the attempted assimilation of white ideals by African Americans.

Emancipation Proclamation: An executive order issued by President Abraham Lincoln on January 1, 1863, as the nation approached its third year of bloody civil war. The proclamation declared, "that all persons held as slaves" within the rebellious states "are, and henceforward shall be free." The original document is in the National Archives in Washington, D.C.

Enculturation: The process of adopting norms, values, and behavioral patterns from the surrounding culture as learned through communication in the form of speech, words, and gestures.

Enslaved Africans: People of African descent involuntarily subjected to an inhumane system of forced labor and social oppression in the Americas from the late 1400s to the late 1800s.

Eschatological Vision: An envisioning of a just society that necessitates a continual effort to change oppressive structures in the here and now while being aware that liberation is a process worth investing in, even if it may never be fully realized.

249

Ethics: The study of the actions and decisions people make in order to arrive at general moral standards that aid us in judging good and bad, discerning the right and the just, and reflecting on how to live moral lives. This involves extolling certain virtues or moral habits that we should acquire, the duties that we should carry out, or the consequences of our actions towards self and others.

Ethics, African American Christian Social: The study of the essential virtues, moral approaches, and liberating vision unique to African peoples that aid in preserving and promoting the community by making visible the foundational role that identity (who one is) plays in one's thoughts (what one thinks) and actions (what one does).

Ethics, Dominant/Normative: The system for evaluating right and wrong based on the beliefs, virtues, and values that privilege white dominant culture while excluding groups that do not share the same privilege, cultural privileges, and range of freedom.

Ethics, Liberation: An approach within African American Christian social ethics that employs a system of moral reasoning that looks for ways to develop a just, sustainable, and participatory Black community.

Ethics, Virtue: An approach within African American Christian social ethics that analyzes the essential virtues and moral vision, unique to African peoples, that aid in preserving and promoting the community by making visible the foundational role that identity (who one is) plays in one's thoughts (what one thinks) and actions (what one does). Its main goal is the redefining, and, in some instances, defining of being for the Black community. Virtue ethics develops this moral formation by focusing on the virtues necessary for sustaining the excellence of African Americans in their relation to God, community, family, and their own personhood.

Ethics, Womanist: An approach within African American Christian social ethics that has its origins in the work of Katie G. Cannon's appropriation and canonization of Alice Walker's four-part definition of "Womanist," Womanist ethics is an interstructured analysis of interlocking systems of oppression as they uniquely shape the moral condition and moral agency of Black women. It combines the goals of virtue ethics and liberationist ethics as the means vital for this constructive task.

Exegesis: Analytic investigation of the biblical texts whereby various hermeneutic methodologies are engaged to facilitate a close reading of a particular passage. Exegesis attempts to cross the temporal and social gap that exists between the world of the biblical passage and the contemporary world in order to bring meaning "out of" Scripture.

Forbearance: The second African/African American virtue that represents the patience, tolerance, and open-mindedness of the Black community in spite of the historic experience of racial and economic oppression. As it has fulfilled its role as mediator between the African American community and white society, the Black Church has extolled forbearance as a virtue vital to promoting both racial harmony and Black welfare.

Forgiveness: The fifth African/African American virtue that represents the religious act of showing mercy and mediating tensions in order to bring about reconciliation. The reconciliation of differences allows space for members to transform themselves or their institutions for the purpose of the ongoing life of the community and the common good. Central to this virtue is the emphasis placed on forgiveness as a public act. Whereas private forgiveness is valued within Christian life, public forgiveness is crucial within Black Christianity due to its communal emphasis.

Free African Society: A community organization formed in 1787 that served a combined purpose as a non-denominational church, civil rights group, educational center, and mutual aid association by Richard Allen, Absalom Jones, and many others for the benefit of freed Africans in Philadelphia, Pennsylvania.

Functions of Nurture: Worship embraces healing, sustaining, guiding, and reconciling functions of nurture. *Healing* pertains to binding up wounds or restoring bodily wholeness and mental functioning caused by disease, impairment, or loss. *Sustaining* consists of comfort and strength needed to endure difficult circumstances. *Guiding* refers to helping people by providing principles or educing within persons choices, courses of actions, and resources in times of trouble. *Reconciling* reestablishes broken relationships or brings people into positive relationship with self, God, and others.

Fundamentalist: An adjective for an ideology that focuses on the essential components of Protestantism. Generally used to describe a conservative, evangelical expression of the Christian faith; commonly viewed as biblical literalists.

Glossolalia: More popularly referred to as "speaking in tongues" wherein an ecstatic form of speech comprised of unintelligible words spoken by individuals at the height of spiritual possession by the Holy Spirit. Adherents of the Holiness-Pentecostal movements cite the justification and authority of *glossolalia* as a spiritual gift mentioned in the New Testament's Acts of the Apostles.

Gospel of Prosperity (or Prosperity Gospel): The quasi-religious theological doctrine among certain Christian preachers and televangelists that espouses wealth and material success as obvious evidence of God's favor in the lives of faithful believers; also known by a variety of names: "Word of Faith," "Health and Wealth," and "Name It and Claim It."

Grassroots Revivalist: A moral approach that aims to reach the urban masses through face-to-face spiritual interactions and powerful conversion experiences. This viewpoint emphasizes that individual salvation and personal transformation are the keys to liberation; thus, spiritual needs take precedent over all other social concerns.

Great Migration: The period from the 1890s through the early decades of the twentieth century that saw unprecedented numbers of Black people from Southern states such as Mississippi and the Carolinas migrate to Northern cities—such as New York City, Philadelphia, and Chicago—motivated by the desire to flee legalized racial segregation, popularly known as "Jim Crow," in the South.

Hermeneutics: From a Greek term meaning "to interpret." Frequently used to describe the methodological principles and strategies used when interpreting Scripture.

Human Flourishing: The interdependence of knowledge and virtue used to convey religious meaning that values the fullness of being and liberation of human action to live life as God intended.

Hush Harbors: Secret outdoor gatherings in the antebellum South where enslaved Blacks sang religious songs (known as spirituals), participated in religious worship, celebrated the vestiges of family and community, and shared escape plans and plots of rebellion.

Imago Dei: The human reflection of divinity as indicated in this Latin phrase meaning "God's image." The theological concept and doctrine that asserts that human beings are created in God's image and therefore all humans have an inherent value independent of their moral condition and social circumstance.

Improvisation: The fourth African/African American virtue that represents the capacity to create sustenance out of objects normally not used for this purpose. The sacred reference "making a way out of no way" is used not only as a motivational phrase but also as a moral imperative for evoking this virtue in action, as commonly illustrated in Black sermons and music. The sermonic styles and musical adaptations found within the Black Church display how an art form can simultaneously serve not only as artistic expression of Christian worship but also as political rhetoric or social commentary used to evoke social awareness or political protest.

Interlocking Systems of Oppression: A term coined by Black socialists and used to describe the race-class-gender oppression specifically as they impact women of color in the United States. The theory states that the concurrent, dynamic interaction that occurs between various types of oppression—specifically classism, racism, and sexism—creates a profound experience of oppression that makes it difficult for marginalized groups to form solidarity in overcoming the oppression of all.

Invisible Dignity: The third womanist virtue that exhibits Black women's ability to use their "functional prudence" or "practical wisdom," that is, the ability to discern how and to what extent they can assert moral agency in their effort to overcome any force that threatens their survival.

Invisible Institution: The clandestine worship gatherings of slaves in the antebellum South.

Jim and Jane Crow: The legal and social system of racial segregation established in the United States by the Plessy Decision of 1896 and ending with the Civil Rights Act of 1965. The system was symbolized by signs reading "whites only" in many public facilities and private businesses.

Justice: The sixth and ultimate African/African American virtue that represents the distribution of righteousness in order to maintain social harmony. The tradition of the Black Church to link divine justice to social justice as an ethic of full participation, a covenanted practice to remain in a mutually recognizing community as a living process that not only affirms humanity but is necessary for the will of God.

Liberative/Liberation: Acting to facilitate and alleviate oppression resulting in any form of freedom, from survival to empowerment.

Living Faith: The interpretation(s) of faith that emerges from the questions of or struggles with living situations.

Megachurch: A large, independent, usually nondenominational church that typically has several thousand worshipers at weekly services; these large congregations are a significant development within Protestant Christianity, challenging the dominance of denominationalism as the primary source of ministerial resources and training as well as religious identity and authority.

Middle Passage: The more popular phrase for the Atlantic slave trade in which African people were transported from Africa to slave markets in the Western Hemisphere (North America, South America, and the Caribbean). The term "Middle Passage" derived from the central phase of the "Triangular Trade."

Million Man March: An African American march of protest and unity convened by Nation of Islam leader Louis Farrakhan in Washington, D.C., on October 16, 1995. The actual number of participants is disputed. The event included efforts to register African Americans to vote and to increase African American involvement in volunteerism and community activism.

Mis-Education: A term attributed to Carter G. Woodson, author of *The Mis-Education of the Negro*, who points to the shackled minds and impossible situation oppression has created for African American people. According to Woodson the notion of miseducation espouses that those persons who have not learned to be self-sufficient and who must "depend solely on others never obtain any more rights and privileges in the end than they had in the beginning" (p. 186).

Moral Agency: The human capacity to act or exert power over one's life; a person's capacity for making ethical judgments and acting in such a way that is consistent with and reflective of ethical reflection.

Moral Reasoning: The thinking that informs the ethical choices and actions we make. The logic, explanation, or justification behind our actions or understanding of what is right, wrong, just, or good, often based on our reflection about our ultimate concern.

Moral Wisdom: The accumulated knowledge needed to make sound ethical choices or judgments, or the good sense evident in the consistent practice of applying life-learned lessons to everyday experiences and existential realties.

Mother Wit: The "tried and true" moral wisdom primarily characteristic of Black women.

Mutual Inscription: Thomas Hoyt's term for the Black Church's engagement with the Bible that both reads itself into scriptural narratives and reads the scriptural narratives as describing its own context.

Nommo: An African concept regarding the force of life communicated through the power of the word in community. It is a collective experience between speaker and hearer. Whether in speech or music, *nommo* blends the content of spiritual values with the experience of those same values. Therefore, form and expression in rhythms, physical presence, and participation work together with the content of worldview, folklore, or moral and theological themes. Speakers and hearers generate a collective experience of communication or public discourse. The formation of speech and musical content relates to the spiritual force of *nommo*.

Normative Gaze: A term popularized in critical race theory by Cornel West as the establishment of Eurocentric perspectives and characteristics as the standard of what is considered normal. People of color experience the normative gaze as social discrimination and as an intimidating factor designed to project internalized images of inferiority and self-hatred while white people experience it as a confirmation of white superiority and privileged status.

Nurture: Fostering, providing, building up, and maintaining basics for the vitality of life or existence itself. It is "food" given to enrich the life of the receiver and the receiver's ability to contribute to and give shape to the ongoing life of self and others and the community.

Nurturing Events: Nurture and healing happen through consciousness-raising and through personal and communal identity and solidarity evoked through baptism and Holy Communion or Eucharist.

Nurturing Pathways: Ritual activities in worship including music making, proclamation through the preached word, and prayer that help people see constructive and self-destructive patterns of living, believe in the redemptive activity of God, and grasp wisdom to move forward in faith and hope.

Nurturing Pathway, Music Making as: A communal means of nurture that engages people in the language of praise, adoration, and thanksgiving as well as in testimonies of challenge, lament, and overcoming adversity. Music assists persons in voicing and confronting life's circumstances and immediate problems.

Nurturing Pathway, Prayer as: A means of nurture that helps people see themselves and their relationship with God more fully; evokes awareness that nothing need be hidden from God, that healing evolves from this relationship with God.

Nurturing Pathway, Preaching as: A means of prophetic nurture that employs biblical material to challenge people to reflect on Scripture and its intersection with their lives in new and helpful ways; a means of priestly nurture that calls attention to coping strategies and life skills that can see people through the challenges of life and assist their formation of stories of promise.

Ontological Blackness: A term coined by ethicist Victor Anderson to describe the "blackness that whiteness created" wherein Black identity is limited how it is perceived by white, dominant culture.

Orisha: A traditional African religion of the Yoruba in what is now contemporary Nigeria. The *orisha* is also the collective name of the deities of this tradition. The *orisha* can be conceptualized as divine patterns of energy that manifest themselves in natural phenomena such as thunder, lightning, the ocean, and rivers as well as human emotions and life experiences. Because of the trans-Atlantic slave trade, enslaved Africans brought the *Orisha* religion to the Americas. In the Americas it was syncretized with Roman Catholicism and indigenous beliefs in the development of African-derived traditions such as *Santería* in Cuba and Puerto Rico and *Candomblé* in Brazil. These traditions continue to be practiced in their countries of origin as well as in the United States where migrants have brought them. By the late twentieth century, they had also attracted African American converts who had no recent experience with these traditions thereby contributing to the growing diversity of Black religious experience in the United States.

Orthopraxis: That which would constitute "right actions" in the study and questions of practical theology.

Pastoral Preaching: The ministry of care that has developed within corporate care in the traditions of spiritual and communal values. Spiritual values place pastoral preaching in the context of mutual care. The preacher becomes an agent of God's concern for the person and the community in physical, emotional, and spiritual well-being, in either ongoing development or in crisis.

Patriarchy: Its most literal form means "rule of the father," from two Greek words, *pater* (father) and *arch* (rule). In popular usage, patriarchy refers to the systemic organization of power in which male dominance is institutionalized within a society in all major arenas including social, political, and economic. In addition, these ways of organizing society, that support the rule of men over women and children, are substantiated by ideologies that serve to justify the existence of patriarchy. Patriarchy coexists with other systems of domination based on race and class so that organizationally poor women of color are relegated to the lowest social status.

Performance or Performative Styles: The rhetorical strategies (e.g., poetics, refrain, meter) employed in sermon composition with particular attention to delivery, with the goal of provoking or inspiring response, dialogue, and participation from the congregation.

Positive Thought Materialist: A moral approach that is commonly known as prosperity gospel that focuses on a morality of material prosperity. This theological worldview insists that health, wealth, and success are God's guaranteed provisions given to the "faithful."

Practical Theology: The study of institutional activities of Christianity including Christian education, preaching, church administration, pastoral care, liturgics, and spirituality; also refers to the branch of Christian theology that seeks to construct action-guiding theories of Christian praxis in particular social contexts.

Practical Wisdom: The third African/African American virtue that represents the ability to discern what is necessary in order to survive and thrive. The Black Church conveys practical wisdom to its children and youth through actions more than words. Emphasis is placed on intentionally designed rituals and mentoring programs, such as rites of passage ceremonies and youth religious training programs in order to ensure the "living out" and practice of this knowledge.

Pragmatic Accommodationist: A moral approach that uses assimilation to attain social order. This perspective often insists that Black people should accommodate or measure up to the expectations of prevalent white culture. Survival is viewed as a means of validating a community's presence in society by first assimilating to the mores of the majority culture.

Praxis: The activity of using knowledge through a cyclical process of action and reflection to create a *critical consciousness* that will help to eradicate oppression and transform the world.

Preaching Praxis: The reflexive activity of interpretation and experience that goes into the discernment of a word of revelation from biblical texts and the living theologies in the community of faith.

Prophetic Preaching: The ministry or faith consciousness that insists uncompromisingly upon social justice, whether it is interpersonal, cultural, political, or economic. It is focused upon the relationship between historical values of liberation and the liberation of spiritual values otherwise content with personal thriving. It is an intentional or purposeful consciousness that addresses the needs and concerns of people living under oppressing conditions.

Prophetic Radicalist: The moral approach that represents those within the Black community who believe that by assimilating to the political structures of oppression one contributes to one's own oppression, and that liberation and justice will come only through confronting the systems of oppression. This position promotes a concept of liberation that links divine justice to social justice. Unjust institutions, by necessity, must be confronted and abolished in the name of human freedom and racial equality.

Quiet Grace: The second Womanist virtue that represents Black women's propensity to find their voice and express their human dignity in defiance of dehumanizing and degrading oppression.

Racism: Ideas and beliefs that some races are inherently superior on physical, intellectual, theological, or cultural levels to others and thus have a right to dominate or exterminate them. Racism can be manifested in institutionalized, individual, or internalized modes. Within an American context, racism, particularly by whites against Blacks, has created profound racial divisions and historic conflicts in society.

Radical Subjectivity: The foundational Womanist moral principle that represents Black women's defiant posture and audacious, inquisitive nature to rise above their circumstances and experience that otherwise would be denied. This moral courage is noted early on in the development of Black girls and is cultivated intergenerationally among Black women in order to aid Black women of all ages in cultivating a sense of self-determination that will help them to combat and conquer the patriarchal, racist, and/or classist forces that threaten them in society.

Redemptive Nationalist: A moral approach that seeks to reclaim a separate nation (either on the North American continent or in Africa) in order to achieve total liberation from the dehumanizing conditions of racism and discrimination that plague the American political system. This radical separatist view emphasizes complete autonomy, ethnic purity, and geographic division from an oppressive society.

Redemptive Self-love: The third Womanist principle founded upon Black women's ability to esteem and reclaim the unique aspects of Black femininity that normative society usually disparages—the assertion of the humanity, customs, and aesthetic value of Black women as well as the admiration and celebration of the distinctive and identifiable beauty of Black women.

Reigndom or Kin-dom of God: Theological tenets that offer alternatives to the "kingdom of God" language that permeate Western Christian traditions. They represent important challenges to Black preaching praxis from Womanist and *Mujerista* theologies. The reigndom of God is concerned with the reign of God that God seeks to establish with humanity. The term preserves the sovereignty and defining authority of God in divine will for creation. While kin-dom is often used synonymously, it is intended here to stress God's desire for human relationships within the reign of God. Kin-dom signifies mutual relations of care, mutual thriving, living into divine will for equality, and freedom to be in relationship. From Black Church traditions, the reign or kin-dom of God depicts the eschatological vision of God.

Roles of the Pastor and Congregation in Nurture: The pastor as responsible agent of the healing, guiding, sustaining, and reconciling functions within the worshiping congregation and in follow-through outside the worship context in tandem with the congregation as a caring community that demonstrates caring through its welcome, sensitivity, and assistance to hurting persons.

Sacrality: Ascription of holiness or sacred value to an object, in this case Scripture.

Sacred Worldview: The essential conceptual framework centered on pervasive residual African religious and cultural beliefs that informs ways of knowing, shapes ways of apprehending and perceiving reality, and influences worship options modes of expression for peoples of the African Diaspora.

Sanctification: Commonly understood as a phase of Christian faith development beyond salvation in which the faithful believer is consecrated by God's grace and, having been separated from a state of sinfulness and worldliness, is made receptive to God's will.

Scripture: Literally, "that which is written," but the term has the connotation of "sacred writing" for many religious groups. For Protestant Christians the term *Scripture* represents the sixty-six books that make up the biblical canon. For African Americans, Scripture can also include Bible-derived "folk wisdom" handed down in the community.

Sexism: An ideology that supports the idea of male domination over women as natural and inevitable. There are two main components to this ideology. The first suggests that there are fundamental differences between men and women that are "natural" and biologically determined. The second, emerging from this assumption, stipulates that the identities of men and women, in which men are dominant, are fixed and unchanging, thus deeming unequal relations of power between men and women as inevitable.

Slave Codes: Laws passed in the colonial and early American periods intended to regulate the lives and status of Black women, men, and children trapped in chattel slavery. Slave codes were long criticized by abolitionists for their cruelty and inhumanity and were abolished after the U.S. Civil War with the passage of constitutional amendments and other civil rights legislation.

Somebodyness: An African American colloquialism originally stated by Rev. Dr. Martin Luther King, Jr., and Rev. Jesse Jackson, and subsequently canonized within African American ethics by Garth Baker Fletcher. This term highlights the signification and celebration of Black people's dignity regardless of white, dominant society's social disregard of them.

Syncretism: The process of merging differing systems of philosophical or religious belief; the term can also refer to the combining of divergent languages or esoteric elements into new cultural forms.

Traditional Communalist: The second Womanist moral principle in which the practical wisdom and common sense of Black women support the survival and success of the Black community. Black women's personification of Black culture, Black identity, and the Black experience as the affirmation of the loving connections and relational bonds formed by Black women including familial, maternal, platonic, religious, sexual, and spiritual. Black women's ability to create, re-member, nurture, protect, sustain, and liberate communities are marked and measured not by those outside of one's own community but by the acts of inclusivity, mutuality, reciprocity, and self-care practiced within it.

Unctuousness: The fourth Womanist virtue that conveys Black women's "feistiness about life" as their resilience to survive in the face of adversity.

Underground Railroad: A secret network of escape routes, covert operatives, and safe houses that aided Black fugitives from slavery in the South to reach the free Northern states or Canada during the first half of the 1800s.

Unshouted Courage: The first Womanist virtue that represents Black women's fortitude and unrelenting resolve for self-determination, and their unwillingness to conform to or comply with anything or anyone that threatens their survival and progress.

Virtue: A character trait valued as being good, that leads to or depicts moral excellence.

Visible Institution: The sociological and historic function for Africans and African Americans to openly identify and voluntarily assemble as Christian communities of faith in the antebellum North; gave rise to evident and enduring expressions of the Black Church tradition in the United States.

Womanist: Perspectives for understanding the social and cultural phenomena position of Black women's historical and contemporary experiences as valid bases of critique. Writer Alice Walker introduced the term "Womanist" in her collection of essays *In Search of Our Mothers' Gardens* by noting that it was the opposite of "feminist." Walker's aim in this contrast was to underscore the fact that mainstream feminist approaches tended to be based on white, middle-class women's experiences and perspectives in the United States. "Womanist" drew on the expression "womanish," from the Southern, African American term that indicated a Black girl or woman who acted in ways that challenged stereotypical notions of conformity or docility. Instead, the Womanist perspective as outlined by Walker pointed to capability, social consciousness, and love of self and Black community. Walker's definition was taken up by African American theologians such as Jacquelyn Grant, Delores Williams, and Katie

Geneva Cannon whose works outlined approaches to religious and theological studies rooted unapologetically in African American women's experiences and concerns. Womanism, as the body of thought is collectively termed, has also been taken up outside of the continental United States by women of African descent in the Caribbean, Africa, and Canada. In addition, Womanist thought has also influenced other areas of theological discourse. For example, Womanist theologians have posed a serious critique of Black theology by pointing to its lack of inclusion of Black women's voices and perspectives. Proponents of Black theology, such as James Cone, subsequently have responded to this critique.

BIBLIOGRAPHY

Ali, Carroll A. Watkins. *Survival and Liberation: Pastoral Theology in African American Context*. St. Louis: Chalice Press, 1999.

Allen, Richard. *The Life Experience and Gospel Labors of the Rt. Rev. Richard Allen, to which is annexed the rise and progress of the African Methodist Episcopal Church in the United States of America*. New York, Abingdon Press, 1960.

Anderson, Herbert, and Edward Foley. *Mighty Stories, Dangerous Rituals: Weaving Together the Human and the Divine*. San Francisco: Jossey-Bass, 1998.

Anderson, James D. *The Education of Blacks in the South, 1860–1935*. Chapel Hill: University of North Carolina Press, 1988.

Anderson, Jervis. *Bayard Rustin: Troubles I've Seen: A Biography*. New York: HarperCollins, 1997.

Anderson, Victor. *Beyond Ontological Blackness: An Essay on African-American Religious and Cultural Criticism*. New York: Continuum, 1995.

Andrews, Dale P. *Practical Theology for Black Churches: Bridging Black Theology and African-American Folk Religion*. Louisville: Westminster John Knox Press, 2002.

———. "Teaching Black Preaching: Encounter and Re-encounter." *The African-American Pulpit* 9, no. 4 (Fall 2006): 8–12.

———. "Teaching Black Preaching: Homiletic Instruction as 'Pre-encounter.'" *The African-American Pulpit* 10, no. 1 (Winter 2006–2007): 22–26.

Andrews, Joyce. *Bible Legacy of the Black Race: The Prophecy Fulfilled*. Nashville, Tenn.: Winston-Derek Publishers, 1993.

Andrews, William L. *The Oxford Frederick Douglass Reader*. New York: Oxford University Press, 1996.

Anderews, William L., Jarena Lee, Zilpha Elaw, and Julia A. J. Foote. *Sisters of the Spirit: Three Black Women's Autobiographies of the Nineteenth Century*. Bloomington: Indiana University Press, 1986.

Angell, Stephen W. *Bishop Henry McNeal Turner and African-American Religion in the South*. Knoxville: University of Tennessee Press, 1992.

Aptheker, Herbert. *American Negro Slave Revolts*. New York: International Publishers, 1963.

Asante, Molefi Kete. *The Afrocentric Idea*. Philadelphia: Temple University Press, 1978.

Ashby, Homer U., Jr. *Our Home Is Over Jordan: A Black Pastoral Theology*. St. Louis: Chalice Press, 2003.

Baer, Hans A., and Merrill Singer. *African-American Religion in the Twentieth Century: Varieties of Protest and Accommodation*. Knoxville: The University of Tennessee Press, 1992.

Bailey, Randall C. *Yet With a Steady Beat: Contemporary U.S. Afrocentric Biblical Interpretation. Semeia Studies*. Atlanta: Society of Biblical Literature Press, 2003.

Bailey, Randall C., and Jacquelyn Grant, eds. *The Recovery of Black Presence: an Interdisciplinary Exploration: Essays in Honor of Dr. Charles B. Copher*. Nashville: Abingdon Press, 1995.

Baker-Fletcher, Garth. *Somebodyness: Martin Luther King, Jr. and the Theory of Dignity*. Minneapolis: Fortress Press, 1993.

Bell, Derrick A. *Silent Covenants: Brown v. Board of Education and the Unfulfilled Hopes for Racial Reform*. New York: Oxford University Press, 2004.

Best, Wallace D. *Passionately Human, No Less Divine: Religion and Culture in Black Chicago, 1915–1952*. Princeton: Princeton University Press, 2005.

Billingsley, Andrew. *Mighty Like a River: The Black Church and Social Reform*. New York: Oxford University Press, 1999.

BlackAtlanta.com. http://www.blackatlanta.com/news_detail.php?id=189.

Blassingame, John W. *The Slave Community: Plantation Life in the Antebellum South*. New York: Oxford University Press, 1972.

Blight, David W., ed. *Passages to Freedom: The Underground Railroad in History and Memory*. Washington, D.C.: Smithsonian Books, 2004.

Bordewich, Fergus M. *Bound for Canaan: The Underground Railroad and the War for the Soul of America*. New York: Amistad, 2005.

Branch, Tayor. *At Canaan's Edge: America in the King Years, 1965–68*. New York: Simon & Schuster, 2006.

———. *Parting the Waters: America in the King Years, 1954–1963*. New York: Simon & Schuster, 1988.

———. *Pillar of Fire: America in the King Years, 1963–65*. New York: Simon & Schuster, 1998.

Brown, Michael Joseph. *Blackening the Bible: The Aims of African American Biblical Scholarship*. Harrisburg, Pa.: Trinity Press, 2004.

Brown, Teresa L. Fry. *God Don't Like Ugly: African American Women Handing on Spiritual Values*. Nashville: Abingdon Press, 2000.

———. *Weary Throats and New Songs: Black Women Proclaiming God's Word*. Nashville: Abingdon Press, 2003.

Browning, Robert L., ed. *The Pastor as Religious Educator*. Birmingham, Ala.: Religious Education Press, 1989.

Brundage, W. Fitzhugh, ed. *Under Sentence of Death: Lynching in the South*. Chapel Hill: University of North Carolina Press, 1997.

Burns, Stewart. *Daybreak of Freedom: The Montgomery Bus Boycott*. Chapel Hill: University of North Carolina Press, 1997.

Burtchart, Ronald E. *Northern Schools, Southern Blacks, and Reconstruction: Freedmen's Education, 1862–1875*. Westport, Conn.: Greenwood Press, 1980.

Cannon, Dale. *Six Ways of Being Religious: A Framework for Comparative Studies of Religion*. Belmont, Calif.: Wadsworth Publishing, 1996.

Cannon, Katie Geneva. *Black Womanist Ethics*. Atlanta: Scholars Press, 1988.

———. "The Emergence of Black Feminist Consciousness." In *Feminist Interpretation of the Bible*. Edited by Letty Russell. Philadelphia: Westminster, 1985.

———. *Teaching Preaching: Isaac Rufus Clark and Black Sacred Rhetoric*. New York: Continuum, 2002.

———. "Womanist Interpretation and Preaching in the Black Church." In *Searching the Scriptures*. Edited by Elizabeth Schüssler Fiorenza, Shelly Matthews, and Ann Graham Brock. New York: Crossroad, 1993.

———. "Womanist Virtue." In Russell and Clarkson, *The Dictionary of Feminist Theologies*.

Carbado, Devon W., and Donald Weise, eds. *Time on Two Crosses: The Collected Writings of Bayard Rustin*. San Francisco: Cleis Press, 2003.

Carmichael, Stokely, Kwame Ture, and Charles Hamilton. *Black Power: The Politics of Liberation in America*. New York: Vintage Books, 1967.

Carson, Clayborne. *In Struggle: SNCC and the Black Awakening of the 1960s*. Cambridge: Harvard University Press, 1981.

Carter, Stephen L. *Integrity*. New York: Basic Books, 1996.

Cedarleaf, J. L. "Listening." In Hunter, *Dictionary of Pastoral Care and Counseling*, 654.

Chappell, David L. *A Stone of Hope: Prophetic Religion and the Death of Jim Crow*. Chapel Hill: University of North Carolina Press, 2004.

Cheyney University of Pennsylvania. http://www.cheyney.edu/pages/index.asp?p=428.

Childress, James F., and John Macquarrie, eds. *The Westminster Dictionary of Christian Ethics*. Philadelphia: Westminster John Knox, 1986.

Cleage, Albert B., Jr. *Black Christian Nationalism: New Directions for the Black Church*. Detroit: Luxor Publishers of the Pan-African Orthodox Church, 1972.

———. *The Black Messiah*. Trenton, N. J.: Africa World Press, 1989.

Clebsch, William A., and Charles R. Jaekle. *Pastoral Care in Historical Perspective*. Englewood Cliffs, N.J.: Prentice-Hall, 1964.

Clemmons, Ithiel C. *Bishop C.H. Mason and the Roots of the Church of God in Christ*. Bakersfield, Calif.: Pneuma Life, 1996.

Collier-Thomas, Bettye, ed. *Daughters of Thunder: Black Women Preachers and Their Sermons, 1850–1979*. San Francisco, Calif.: Jossey-Bass, 1998.

Collins, Lisa Gail. *The Art of History: African-American Woman Artists Engage the Past*. New Brunswick, N.J.: Rutgers University Press, 2002.

Collins, Patricia Hill. *Black Feminist Thought: Knowledge, Consciousness, and the Politics of Empowerment*. New York and London: Routledge, 2000.

Cone, James H. "Black Consciousness and the Black Church: A Historical-Theological Interpretation." *Annals of the American Academy of Political and Social Science* 387, (January 1970): 33.

———. *Black Theology and Black Power*. San Francisco: Harper & Row, 1969. Maryknoll, N.Y.: Orbis Books, 2006.

———. *A Black Theology of Liberation*. New York: J.B. Lippincott, 1970.

———. "God Is Black." In *Lift Every Voice: Constructing Christian Theologies from the Underside*. Edited by Susan Brooks Thistlethwaite and Mary Potter Engel. San Francisco: Harper & Row, 1990.

———. *God of the Oppressed*. Maryknoll, N.Y.: Orbis Books, 2003. First published 1975 by Seabury.

————. "The Story Context of Black Theology." *Theology Today* 32, no. 2 (July 1975): 147.

Cone, James H., and Gayraud S. Wilmore. *Black Theology: A Documentary History, 1966–1979*, Vol.1. Maryknoll, N.Y.: Orbis Press, 1979.

Cooper-Lewter, Nicholas C., and Henry H. Mitchell. *Soul Theology: The Heart of Black American Culture*. San Francisco: Harper & Row, 1986.

Copher, Charles B. *Black Biblical Studies: An Anthology of Charles B. Copher; Biblical and Theological Issues on the Black Presence in the Bible*. Chicago, Ill.: Black Light Fellowship, 1993.

Cornish, Dudley Taylor. *The Sable Arm: Black Troops in the Union Army, 1861–1865*. New York: Norton, 1966.

Costen, Melva Wilson. *African American Christian Worship*. Nashville: Abingdon, 1993.

Craddock, Fred B. *As One Without Authority*. Nashville: Abingdon, 1979.

Crawford, Evans E., and Thomas H. Troeger. *The Hum: Call and Response in African American Preaching*. Nashville: Abingdon Press, 1990.

Crawford, Vicki L., Jacqueline Anne Rouse, and Barbara Woods, eds. *Women in the Civil Rights Movement: Trailblazers and Torchbearers, 1941–1965*. Brooklyn: Carlson, 1990.

Creel, Margaret Washington. *A Peculiar People: Slave Religion and Community Culture among the Gullahs*. New York: New York University Press, 1988.

Cummings, George C. L. "The Slave Narratives as a Source of Black Theological Discourse: The Spirit and Eschatology." In *Cut Loose Your Stammering Tongue: Black Theology in the Slave Narratives*. Edited by Dwight N. Hopkins and George Cummings. Maryknoll, N.Y.: Orbis Books, 1991. 54–56.

Dash, Michael I. N., Jonathan Jackson, and Stephen C. Rasor. *Hidden Wholeness: An African American Spirituality for Individuals and Communities*. Cleveland: United Church Press, 1997.

Davis, Angela Y. *Women, Race, and Class*. New York: Vintage Books, 1983.

Davis, David Brion. *In the Image of God: Religion, Moral Values, and Our Heritage of Slavery*. New Haven: Yale University Press, 2001.

Davis, Gerald L. *I Got the Word in Me and I Can Sing It, You Know: A Study of the Performed African-American Sermon*. Philadelphia: University of Pennsylvania Press, 1985.

Davis, H. Grady. *Design for Preaching*. Philadelphia: Muhlenberg Press, 1958.

Davis, Valerie Brdigeman, gen. ed. *The Africana Worship Book, Year A*. Nashville: Discipleship Resources, 2006.

D'Emilio, John. *Lost Prophet: The Life and Times of Bayard Rustin*. New York: Free Press, 2003.

Dillon, Merton L. *Slavery Attacked: Southern Slaves and Their Allies, 1619–1865*. Baton Rouge: Louisiana State University Press, 1990.

Dittmer, John. *Local People: The Struggle for Civil Rights in Mississippi*. Urbana: University of Illinois Press, 1994.

Dixie, Quinton H., and Cornel West, eds. *The Courage to Hope: From Black Suffering to Human Redemption*. Boston: Beacon Press, 1999.

Douglas, Kelly Brown. *Sexuality and the Black Church: A Womanist Perspective*. Maryknoll, N.Y.: Orbis Books, 1999.

Douglass, Fredrick. *Narrative of the Life of Fredrick Douglass: An American Slave*. Edited by Benjamin Quarles. Cambridge: Belknap Press of the Harvard University Press, 1988.

Drescher, Seymour. "The Ending of the Slave Trade and the Evolution of European Scientific Racism." In *Social Science History* 14, no. 3 (Autumn, 1990): 415–50.

Du Bois, William Edward Burghardt. *Black Reconstruction in America: 1860–1880*. New York: Simon & Schuster, 1998. First published 1935 by Harcourt, Brace.

———. *The Negro Church: Report of a Social Study Made under the Direction of Atlanta University*. Atlanta: Atlanta University, 1903.

———. *The Philadelphia Negro: A Social Study. 1899.* Philadelphia: University of Pennsylvania Press, 1996.

———. *The Souls of Black Folk*. New York: W. W. Norton, 1999. First published 1903.

Du Bois, William Edward Burghardt, David W. Blight, and Robert Gooding-Williams. *The Souls of Black Folk*. The Bedford Series in History and Culture. Boston: Bedford Books, 1997.

Duncan, Carol B. "Spiritual Baptists in Multicultural Canada." In *Whither Multiculturalism? A Politics of Dissensus*. Edited by Barbara A.C. Saunders and David Haljan. Leuven: Leuven University Press, 205–24.

Dunston, Alfred. *The Black Man in the Old Testament and Its World*. Trenton, N. J.: Africa World Press, 1993.

Dyson, Michael Eric. *I May Not Get There With You: The True Martin Luther King, Jr*. New York: Free Press, 2000.

Egerton, Douglas R. *Gabriel's Rebellion: The Virginia Slave Conspiracies of 1800 and 1802*. Chapel Hill: University of North Carolina Press, 1993.

Ellis, Catherine, and Stephen Drury Smith. *Say It Plain: A Century of Great African American Speeches* (with CD Included). New York: W. W. Norton. 2005.

Equiano, Olaudah. *The Interesting Narrative of the Life of Olaudah Equiano, or Gustavus Vassa, the African, Written by Himself: Authoritative Text, Contexts, Criticism; Edited Werner Sollors*. New York: Norton, 2001. First published ca.1792.

Fairclough, Adam. *Better Day Coming: Blacks and Equality 1890–2000*. New York: Penguin Books, 2001.

———. *To Redeem the Soul of America: The Southern Christian Leadership Conference and Martin Luther King, Jr*. Athens, Ga.: University of Georgia Press, 1987.

Farley, Edward. *Practicing Gospel: Unconventional Thoughts on the Church's Ministry*. Louisville: Westminster John Knox Press, 2003.

Fauset, Arthur Huff. *Black Gods of the Metropolis: Negro Religious Cults of the Urban North*. Philadelphia: University of Pennsylvania Press, 1971.

Felder, Cain Hope, ed. *Stony the Road We Trod: African American Biblical Interpretation*. Minneapolis: Augsburg Fortress, 1991.

———. *Troubling Biblical Waters: Race, Class, and Family*. Maryknoll, N.Y.: Orbis, 1989.

Floyd-Thomas, Stacey. *Deeper Shades of Purple: Womanism in Religion and Society*. New York: New York University Press, 2006.

———. *Mining the Motherlode: Methods in Womanist Ethics*. Cleveland: Pilgrim, 2006.

Foote, Julia A. J. *A Brand Plucked from the Fire: An Autobiographical Sketch by Mrs. Julia A. J. Foote*. In *Sisters of the Spirit: Three Black Women's Autobiographies of the Nineteenth Century*. Edited by William L. Andrews. Bloomington: Indiana University Press, 1986.

Forbes, James. *The Holy Spirit & Preaching*. Nashville: Abingdon Press, 1989.

Foster, Charles R. "Christian Educators of the 21st Century Project." www.talbot.edu/ce20 (accessed July 7, 2006). Bibiographic information on Grant Shockley.

————. *Educating Congregations*. Nashville: Abingdon Press, 1994.

Foster, Charles R., and Fred Smith. *Black Religious Experience: Conversations on Double Consciousness and the Work of Grant Shockley*. Nashville: Abingdon Press, 2004.

Fox-Genovese, Elizabeth, and Eugene D. Genovese. *The Mind of the Master Class: History and Faith in the Southern Slaveholders' Worldview*. New York: Cambridge University Press, 2005.

Frankena, William K. "Morality and Religion, Relations of." In Childress and Macqurrie, *The Westminster Dictionary of Christian Ethics*, 402.

Franklin, Robert M. *Another Day's Journey: Black Churches Confronting the American Crisis*. Minneapolis: Augsburg Fortress, 1997.

Frazier, E. Franklin. *The Negro Church in America*. New York: Schocken Books, 1966.

Freire, Paulo. *Pedagogy of the Oppressed*. New York: Herder and Herder, 1970. Reprint, New York: Continuum, 1981.

Fulop, Timothy E., and Albert J. Raboteau, eds. *African-American Religion: Interpretive Essays in History and Culture*. New York and London: Routledge, 1997.

Garrow, David J. *Bearing the Cross: Martin Luther King, Jr. and the Southern Christian Leadership Conference*. New York: W. Morrow, 1986.

Genovese, Eugene D. *From Rebellion to Revolution: Afro-American Slave Revolts in the Making of the Modern World*. Baton Rouge: Louisiana State University Press, 1979.

————. *Roll Jordan Roll: The World the Slaves Made*. New York: Pantheon Books, 1974.

George, Carol V. R. *Segregated Sabbaths: Richard Allen and the Emergence of Independent Black Churches 1760–1840*. New York: Oxford University Press, 1973.

Gilkes, Cheryl Townsend. *"If It Wasn't for the Women . . .": Black Women's Experience and Womanist Culture in Church and Community*. Maryknoll, N.Y.: Orbis Books, 2001.

————. "The Roles of Church and Community Mothers: Ambivalent American Sexism or Fragmented African Familyhood." In Fulop and Raboteau, *African-American Religion: Interpretive Essays in History and Culture*, 365–88.

Gilkey, Langdon. *Naming the Whirlwind: The Renewal of God-Language*. Indianapolis: Bobbs-Merril, 1969.

Gilroy, Paul. *The Black Atlantic: Modernity and Double Consciousness*. Cambridge, Mass.: Harvard University Press, 1993.

Glaude, Eddie S., Jr. *Exodus! Religion, Race, and Nation in Early Nineteenth-Century Black America*. Chicago: University of Chicago Press, 2000.

Golden, James L., and Richard D. Rieke. *The Rhetoric of Black Americans*. Columbus, Ohio: Charles E. Merrill Publishing, 1971.

Goldenberg, David M. *The Curse of Ham: Race and Slavery in Early Judaism, Christianity, and Islam*. Princeton: Princeton University Press, 2003.

Gomez, Michael A. *Exchanging Our Country Marks: The Transformation of African Identities in the Colonial and Antebellum South*. Chapel Hill: University of North Carolina Press, 1998.

Gossett, Thomas F. *Race: The History of an Idea in America*. New York: Oxford University Press, 1997.

Grant, Jacqueline. *White Women's Christ and Black Women's Jesus: Feminist Christology and Womanist Response*. Atlanta: Scholars Press, 1990.

Grant, Joanne. *Ella Baker: Freedom Bound*. New York: Wiley, 1998.

Greenberg, Kenneth S. *Nat Turner: A Slave Rebellion in History and Memory*. New York: Oxford University Press, 2003.

Gregg, Robert. *Sparks from the Anvil of Oppression: Philadelphia's African Methodists and Southern Migrants, 1890–1940*. Philadelphia: Temple University Press, 1993.

Guy-Sheftall, Beverly. *Words of Fire: An Anthology of African-American Feminist Thought*. New York: New Press, 1995.

Hampton, Henry, and Steve Fayer, eds. *Voices of Freedom: An Oral History of the Civil Rights Movement from the 1950s through the 1980s*. New York: Bantam Books, 1990.

Hand, Quentin L. "Counselee/Client/Parishioner." In Hunter, *Dictionary of Pastoral Care and Counseling*, 234.

Harding, Vincent. *There Is a River: The Black Struggle for Freedom in America*. New York: Harcourt Brace Jovanovich, 1981.

Harris, Fredrick C. *Something Within: Religion in African-American Political Activism*. New York: Oxford University Press, 1999.

Harris, James H. *Pastoral Theology: A Black Church Perspective*. Minneapolis: Augsburg Fortress, 1991.

———. *Preaching Liberation*. Minneapolis: Fortress Press, 1995.

———. *The Word Made Plain: The Power and Promise of Preaching*. Minneapolis, Minn.: Fortress Press, 2004.

Harris, Michael W. *The Rise of Gospel Blues: The Music of Thomas Andrew Dorsey in the Urban Church*. New York: Oxford University Press, 1992.

Hatch, Nathan O. *The Democratization of American Christianity*. New Haven: Yale University, 1989.

Haynes, Stephen R. *Noah's Curse: The Biblical Justification of American Slavery*. New York: Oxford University Press, 2002.

Herskovits, Melville J. *Black Belief: Folk Beliefs of Blacks in America and West Africa*. New York: Harper & Row, 1975.

———. *The Myth of the Negro Past*. New York and London: Harper & Brothers, 1941.

Higginbotham, A. Leon. *In the Matter of Color: Race and the American Legal Process. Vol. 1, The Colonial Period*. New York: Oxford University Press, 1980.

Higginbotham, Evelyn Brooks. *Righteous Discontent: The Women's Movement in the Black Baptist Church, 1880–1920*. Cambridge: Harvard University Press, 1993.

Hiltner, Seward. *Pastoral Counseling*. Nashville: Abingdon, 1949.

———. *Preface to Pastoral Theology*. Nashville: Abingdon, 1958.

Hine, Darlene Clark, William C. Hine, and Stanley Harrold. *The African-American Odyssey*. Upper Saddler River, N.J.: Prentice Hall, 2000.

Holloway, Joseph E., ed. *Africanisms in American Culture*. Bloomington: Indiana University Press, 1990.

Hood, James W. *One Hundred Years of the African Methodist Episcopal Zion Church*. New York: AME Zion Book Concern, 1895.

Hood, Robert E. *Begrimed and Black: Christian Traditions on Blacks and Blackness*. Minneapolis: Augsburg Fortress, 1994.

hooks, bell. *Ain't I a Woman?* Boston: South End Press, 1981.

———. *Teaching to Transgress: Education as the Practice of Freedom.* New York: Routledge, 1994.

Hopkins, Dwight N., ed. *Black Faith and Public Talk: Critical Essays on James H. Cone's Black Theology and Black Power.* Maryknoll, N.Y.: Orbis 1999.

Hoyt, Thomas, Jr. "Interpreting Biblical Scholarship for the Black Church Tradition." In Felder, *Stony the Road We Trod,* 17–39.

———. "Testimony." In *Practicing Our Faith: A Way of Life for a Searching People.* Edited by Dorothy C. Bass. San Francisco: Jossey-Bass, 1997.

Huggins, Nathan I., ed. *W.E.B. Du Bois: Writings.* New York: Library of America, 1986.

Hunter, Rodney J., ed. *Dictionary of Pastoral Care and Counseling.* Nashville: Abingdon, 1990.

Hurston, Zora Neale. *Dust Tracks on a Road: An Autobiography.* Philadelphia: Lippincott Press, 1971. First published ca. 1942.

———. *Their Eyes Were Watching God.* Urbana: University of Illinois Press, 1991.

Izard, Carroll E. "Emotion." In Hunter, *Dictionary of Pastoral Care and Counseling,* 352.

Johnson, Charles M. "The Wisdom of Limits." In *In Context: A Quarterly of Humane Sustainable Culture* 32 (Summer 1992): 48. http://context.org/ICLIB/IC32/Johnston.htm.

Johnson, James Weldon. *God's Trombones: Seven Negro Sermons in Verse.* New York: Viking, 1927. Reprint, New York: Penguin Books, 1990.

Johnson, John L. *The Black Biblical Heritage: Four Thousand Years of Black Biblical History.* Nashville: Winston-Derek Publishers, 1991.

Jones, Amos. *Paul's Message of Freedom: What Does It Mean to the Black Church?* Valley Forge: Judson, 1984.

Jordan, Winthrop D. *White over Black: American Attitudes toward the Negro, 1550–1812.* New York: W. W. Norton, 1977.

Joseph, Peniel E. *Waiting 'Til the Midnight Hour: A Narrative History of Black Power in America.* New York: Henry Holt, 2006.

Kapur, Sudarshan. *Raising Up a Prophet: The African-American Encounter with Gandhi.* Boston: Beacon Press, 1992.

Kelley, Shawn. *Racializing Jesus: Race, Ideology and the Formation of Modern Biblical Scholarship.* New York and London: Routledge Press, 2002.

Kelsey, George D. *Racism and the Christian Understanding of Man.* New York: Charles Scribner's Sons, 1965.

Killen, Patricia O'Connell. "Gracious Play: Discipline, Insight, and the Common Good." *Teaching Theology & Religion* 4 (February 2001): 1.

King, Martin Luther, Jr. "Beyond Vietnam." In *Martin Luther King Jr., Malcolm X, and the Civil Rights Struggle of the 1950s and 1960s: A Brief History with Documents.* Edited by David Howard-Pitney. Boston: Bedford/St. Martins, 2004.

———. "Domestic Impact of the War." Address delivered November 1967 to the National Labor Leadership Assembly for Peace. http://www.aavw.org/special_features/speeches_speech_king03.html.

———. "I See the Promised Land." In Washington, *A Testament of Hope: The Essential Writings and Speeches of Martin Luther King, Jr.*

———. *Strength to Love.* New York: Harper & Row, 1963.

————. *Stride Toward Freedom: The Montgomery Story*. New York: Harper, 1958. San Francisco: HarperCollins, 1986.

————. "A Time to Break Silence." In Washington, *A Testament of Hope: The Essential Writings of Martin Luther King, Jr.*

————. *Why We Can't Wait*. New York: Signet Classic, 2000.

Kirk-Duggan, Cheryl. *African-American Special Days*. Nashville: Abingdon Press, 1996.

Klarman, Michael J. *From Jim Crow to Civil Rights: The Supreme Court and the Struggle for Racial Equality*. New York: Oxford University Press, 2004.

Kluger, Richard. *Simple Justice: The History of Brown v. Board of Education and Black America's Struggle for Equality*. New York: Knopf, 1975.

Kolchin, Peter. *American Slavery, 1619–1877*. New York: Hill and Wang, 1993.

Lartey, Emmanuel Y. *Pastoral Theology in an Intercultural World*. Cleveland: Pilgrim, 2006.

LaRue, Cleophus J. *The Heart of Black Preaching*. Louisville: Westminster John Knox Press, 2000.

LeFevre, Perry. "Prayer." In Hunter, *Dictionary of Pastoral Care and Counseling*, 937.

Levine, Daniel. *Bayard Rustin and the Civil Rights Movement*. New Brunswick, N.J.: Rutgers University Press, 2000.

Levine, Lawrence W. *Black Culture and Black Consciousness: Afro-American Folk Thought from Slavery to Freedom*. New York: Oxford University Press, 1977.

Lewis, David Levering. *W.E.B. Du Bois: Biography of a Race, 1868–1919*. New York: Henry Holt, 1993.

————. *W.E.B. Du Bois: The Fight for Equality and the American Century, 1919–1963*. New York: Henry Holt, 2000.

Lincoln, C. Eric. *The Black Experience in Religion*. Garden City, N.Y.: Anchor Press, 1974.

————. *The Black Muslims in America*. Grand Rapids: Wm. B. Eerdmans; Trenton, N. J.: African World Press, 1994.

————. "Foreword." In *Black Religion and Black Radicalism*, by Gayraud Wilmore. 1st ed. Garden City, N.Y.: Anchor Press/Doubleday, 1973.

Lincoln, C. Eric, and Lawrence H. Mamiya. *The Black Church in the African-American Experience*. Durham: Duke University Press, 1990.

————. "The Black Sacred Cosmos." In *Down By the Riverside: Readings in African-American Religion*. Edited by Larry G. Murphy. New York: New York University Press 2000, 41–48.

Long, Charles H. "Passage and Prayer: The Origin of Religion in the Atlantic World." In *The Courage to Hope: From Black Suffering to Human Redemption*. Edited by Quinton H. Dixie and Cornel West. Boston: Beacon Press, 1999.

MacIntyre, Aladair. *After Virtue: A Study in Moral Theory*. Notre Dame: University of Notre Dame Press, 1984.

Marable, Manning. *Race, Reform and Rebellion: The Second Reconstruction in Black America, 1945–1992*. 2nd ed. Jackson: University Press of Mississippi, 1991.

Marsh, Charles. *The Beloved Community: How Faith Shapes Social Justice, from the Civil Rights Movement to Today*. New York: Basic Books, 2005.

————. *God's Long Summer: Stories of Faith and Civil Rights*. Princeton: Princeton University Press, 1997.

Martin, Joan M. *More Than Chains and Toil: A Christian Work Ethic of Enslaved Women*. Louisville: Westminster John Knox, 2000.

Mason, Elsie W. "Bishop C. H. Mason, Church of God in Christ." In *Afro-American Religious History: A Documentary Witness*. Edited by Milton C. Sernett. Durham: Duke University Press, 1985.

Massey, James Earl. *Designing the Sermon: Order and Movement in Preaching*. Nashville: Abingdon Press, 1980.

Mathews, Marcia M. *Richard Allen*. Baltimore: Helicon, 1963.

Mays, Benjamin E. *Born to Rebel*. New York: Scribner's, 1971.

———. *The Negro's God as Reflected in His Literature*. New York: Negro Universities Press 1969.

Mays, Benjamin E., and Joseph W. Nicholson. *The Negro's Church*. New York: Russell and Russell, 1969.

Mbiti, John S. *African Religions and Philosophies*. New York: Doubleday, 1969.

McCall, Emmanuel L. *Black Church Lifestyles*. Nashville: Broadman Press, 1986.

McCray, Walter Arthur. *The Black Presence in the Bible: Discovering the Black and African Identity of Biblical Persons and Nations*. Chicago: Black Light Fellowship, 1990.

McPherson, James M. *Battle Cry of Freedom: The Civil War Era*. New York: Oxford University Press, 2003.

———. *The Negro's Civil War: How American Negroes Felt and Acted during the War for the Union*. New York: Pantheon Books, 1965.

Mintz, Sidney W., and Richard Price. "The Birth of African-American Culture." In Fulop and Raboteau, *African-American Religion: Interpretive Essays in History and Culture*, 37–53.

Mitchell, Ella Pearson. *Women: To Preach and Not to Preach: 21 Outstanding Black Preachers Say Yes!* Valley Forge: Judson, 1991.

Mitchell, Henry H. *Black Belief: Folk Beliefs of Blacks in America and West Africa*. New York: Harper & Row, 1975.

———. *Black Preaching: The Recovery of a Powerful Art*. Nashville: Abingdon Press, 1990. Originally published by Harper & Row as *Black Preaching* (1970) and *The Recovery of Preaching* (1977).

———. *Celebration and Experience in Preaching*. Nashville: Abingdon Press, 1990.

———. "Preparing Prophets and Priests for the Black Church Tradition." Keynote presented at the 3rd Annual National Black Church Studies Consultation, Vanderbilt Divinity School, Nashville, January 31, 2007.

Mitchem, Stephanie Y. *Introducing Womanist Theology*. Maryknoll, N. Y.: Orbis Books, 2002.

Morgan, Edmund S. *American Slavery, American Freedom: The Ordeal of Colonial Virginia*. New York: Norton, 1975.

Morris, Robert C. *Reading, 'Riting, and Reconstruction: The Education of Freedmen in the South, 1861–1870*. Chicago: University of Chicago Press, 1981.

Moyd, Olin P. *The Sacred Art: Preaching and Theology in the African-American Tradition*. Valley Forge: Judson, 1995.

Mullin, Gerald W. *Flight and Rebellion: Slave Resistance in Eighteenth-century Virginia*. New York: Oxford University Press, 1972.

Murphy, James J. *Rhetoric in the Middle Ages: A History of Rhetorical Theology from Saint Augustine to the Renaissance*. Berkeley: University of California Press, 1974.

Nash, Gary B. *Forging Freedom: The Formation of Philadelphia's Black Community, 1720–1840*. Cambridge: Harvard University Press, 1991.

Odyssey Productions Ltd. "The Great Preachers," Video-Recording Series. Worcester, Pa.: Gateway Films/Vision Video, 1977–.

Oglesby, Enoch H. *Ethics and Theology from the Other Side: Sounds of Moral Struggle*. Washington, D.C.: University Press of America, 1979.

Ogletree, Charles J., Jr. *All Deliberate Speed: Reflections on the First Half Century of Brown v. Board of Education*. New York: Norton, 2004.

Olmos, Margarite Fernandez, and Lizabeth Paravisini-Gebert. *Creole Religions of the Caribbean: An Introduction from Vodou and Santeria to Obeah and Espiritismo*. New York: New York University Press, 2003.

Olupona, Jacob K., and Regina Gemignani. *African Immigrant Religions in America*. New York: University Press, 2007.

Osmer, Richard Robert. "Education, Nurture, and Care." In Hunter, *Dictionary of Pastoral Care and Counseling*, 336.

———. *The Teaching Ministry of Congregations*. Louisville: Westminster John Knox Press, 2005.

Packard, Jerrold M. *American Nightmare: The History of Jim Crow*. New York: St. Martin's Press, 2002.

Palmer, Parker J. *The Courage to Teach*. San Francisco: Jossey-Bass, 1998.

Paris, Peter J. *The Social Teachings of the Black Churches*. Philadelphia: Fortress Press 1985.

———. *The Spirituality of African Peoples*. Minneapolis: Fortress Press, 1995.

———. *Virtues and Values The African and African American Experience*. Minneapolis: Fortress Press, 2004.

Parker, Evelyn. *Trouble Don't Last Always: Emancipatory Hope among African American Adolescents*. Cleveland: Pilgrim, 2003.

Patterson, Orlando. *Slavery and Social Death: A Comparative Study*. Cambridge: Harvard University Press, 1982.

Payne, Charles M. *I've Got the Light of Freedom: The Organizing Tradition and the Mississippi Freedom Struggle*. Berkeley: University of California Press, 1995.

Perry, Rufus L., and Thomas McCants Stewart. *The Cushite: The Children of Ham (The Negro Race) as Seen by the Ancient Historians and Poets*. New York: African Islamic Mission Publications, 1991.

Pipes, William H. *Say Amen, Brother! Old-Time Negro Preaching: A Study in American Frustration*. New York: The William-Frederick Press, 1951. Detroit: Wayne State University Press, 1992.

Pitts, Walter F., Jr. *Old Ship: The Afro-Baptist Ritual in the African Diaspora*. New York: Oxford University Press 1993.

Potter, David M. *The Impending Crisis, 1848–1861*. New York: Harper & Row, 1976.

Propst, L. Rebecca. "Cognitive Psychology and Psycho-Therapy." In Hunter, *Dictionary of Pastoral Care and Counseling*, 188.

Quarles, Benjamin. *The Negro in the Civil War*. Boston: Little, Brown, 1953.

Raboteau, Albert J. *Canaan Land: A Religious History of African Americans*. New York: Oxford University Press, 2001.

———. *A Fire in the Bones: Reflections on African-American Religious History*. Boston: Beacon Press, 1995.

———. *Slave Religion: The "Invisible Institution" in the Antebellum South*. New York: Oxford University Press, 1978.

Randolph, David. *The Renewal of Preaching*. Philadelphia: Fortress Press, 1969.

Ransby, Barbara. *Ella Baker and the Black Freedom Movement: A Radical Democratic Vision.* Chapel Hill: University of North Carolina Press, 2003.

Redkey, Edwin S., ed. *Black Exodus: Black Nationalist and Back-to-Africa Movements, 1890–1910.* New Haven: Yale University Press, 1969.

———. *A Grand Army of Black Men: Letters from African-American Soldiers in the Union Army, 1861–1865.* New York: Cambridge University Press, 1992.

———. *Respect Black: The Writings and Speeches of Henry McNeal Turner.* New York: Arno Press, 1971.

Reed, Adolph L., Jr. *The Jesse Jackson Phenomenon: The Crisis of Purpose in Afro-American Politics.* New Haven: Yale University Press, 1986.

Rhoades, F. S. *Black Characters and References of the Holy Bible.* New York: Vantage Press, 1980.

Richardson, Joe M. *Christian Reconstruction: The American Missionary Association and Southern Blacks, 1861–1890.* Athens, Ga.: University of Georgia Press, 1986.

Riggs, Marcia Y. *Awake, Arise, and Act: A Womanist Call for Black Liberation.* Cleveland: Pilgrim, 1994.

———. *Plenty Good Room: Women Versus Male Power in the Black Church.* Cleveland: Pilgrim, 2003.

Roberts, James Deotis. "Black Consciousness in Theological Perspective." In *The Black Experience in Religion,* ed. C. Eric Lincoln. Garden City, N.Y.: Anchor Books, 1974.

Roberts, Samuel K. *African American Christian Ethics.* Cleveland: Pilgrim, 2001.

———. *In the Path of Virtue The African American Moral Tradition.* Cleveland: Pilgrim, 1999.

Robinson, John A. T. *Honest to God.* Philadelphia: Westminster Press, 1963.

Robnett, Belinda. *How Long? How Long? African-American Women in the Struggle for Civil Rights.* New York: Oxford University Press, 1997.

Ross, Rosetta E. *Witnessing and Testifying: Black Women, Religion, and Civil Rights.* Minneapolis: Augsburg Fortress, 2003.

Rowan, Carl T. *Dream Makers, Dream Breakers: The World of Justice Thurgood Marshall.* Boston: Little, Brown, 1993.

Russell, Letty M., and J. Shannon Clarkson, eds. *The Dictionary of Feminist Theologies.* Louisville: Westminster John Knox, 1996.

Sadler, Rodney S., Jr. *Can A Cushite Change His Skin? An Examination of Race, Ethnicity, and Othering in the Hebrew Bible.* New York: T & T Clark, 2005.

Sanders, Cheryl J. *Empowerment Ethics for a Liberated People.* Minneapolis: Augsburg Fortress, 1995.

———. *Saints in Exile: The Holiness-Pentecostal Experience in African-American Religion and Culture.* New York: Oxford University Press, 1996.

Sernett, Milton C. *Black Religion and American Evangelicalism: White Protestants, Plantation Missions, and the Flowering of Negro Christianity, 1787–1865.* Metuchen, N.J.: Scarecrow Press, 1975.

———. *Bound for the Promised Land: African-American Religion and the Great Migration.* Durham: Duke University Press, 1997.

Shannon, David T. "'An Ante-bellum Sermon': A Resource for an African American Hermeneutic." In Felder, *Stony the Road We Trod,* 98–123.

Shockley, Grant H. "Black Pastoral Leadership in Religious Education." In *The Pastor as Religious Educator.* Edited by Robert L. Browning. Birmingham, Ala.: Religious Education Press, 1989.

———. "Black Theology and Religious Education." In *Theologies of Religious Education*. Edited by Randolph Crump Miller. Birmingham, Ala.: Religious Education Press, 1995.

Simms, James M. *The First Colored Baptist Church in North America*. New York: Negro Universities Press, 1969.

Sitkoff, Harvard. *The Struggle for Black Equality, 1954–1992*. 1981. Reprint, New York: Hill and Wang, 1993.

Smith, R. Drew, ed. *New Day Begun: African-American Churches and Civic Culture in Post-Civil Rights America*. Durham: Duke University Press, 2003.

Smith, Timothy. "John Wesley and the Second Blessing." http://wesley.nnu.edu/wesleyan_theology/theojrnl/21-25/21-09.htm.

Smith, Yolanda Y. "Christian Educators of the 21st Century Project." Biographical information on Olivia Pearl Stokes. www.talbot.edu/ce20 (accessed July 8, 2006).

———. *Reclaiming the Spirituals: New Possibilities for African-American Christian Education*. Cleveland: Pilgrim, 2004.

Snowden, Frank, Jr. *Blacks in Antiquity: Ethiopians in the Greco-Roman Experience*. Cambridge: Harvard University Press, 1970.

Sobel, Mechal. *The World They Made Together: Black and White Values in Eighteenth-century Virginia*. Princeton: Princeton University Press, 1987.

Spencer, Jon Michael. *Protest and Praise: Sacred Music of Black Religion*. Minneapolis: Augsburg Fortress, 1990.

———. *Sacred Symphony: The Chanted Sermon of the Black Preacher*. New York: Greenwood Press, 1987.

Stampp, Kenneth M. *The Peculiar Institution: Slavery in the Ante-bellum South*. New York: Knopf, 1956.

Stanford University. www.stanford.edu/group/King/about_king/encyclopedia/nash_diane.htm.

Staples, Robert, and Leanor Boulin Johnson. *Black Families at the Crossroads: Challenges and Prospects*. San Francisco: Jossey-Bass, 1993.

Staudenraus, P. J. *The African Colonization Movement, 1816–1865*. New York: Columbia University Press, 1961.

Synan, Vinson. *The Holiness-Pentecostal Tradition: Charismatic Movements in the Twentieth Century*. 1971. Grand Rapids: Wm. B. Eerdmans, 1997.

Taylor, Clarence. "African American Religious Leadership and the Civil Rights Movement." *History Now: American History Online*, no. 8 (The Gilder Lehrman Institute of American History, 2006). http://www.historynow.org/06_2006/historian4.html.

———. *The Black Churches of Brooklyn*. New York: Columbia University Press, 1994.

Terrell, Joanne Marie. *Power in the Blood? The Cross in the African-American Experience*. Maryknoll, N.Y.: Orbis Books, 1998.

Thomas, Frank A. *They Like to Never Quit Praisin' God: The Role of Celebration in Preaching*. Cleveland: United Church Press, 1997.

Thomas, Frank A., and Martha Simmons. *The African American Pulpit*. Hope for Life International, Inc. www.theafricanamericanpulpit.com.

Thomas, Latta. *Biblical Faith and the Black American*. Valley Forge: Judson, 1976.

Thurman, Howard. *Jesus and the Disinherited*. Boston: Beacon Press, 1976.

———. *The Luminous Darkness*. New York: McGraw-Hill, 1964.

————. *With Head and Heart: Autobiography.* New York: Harcourt Brace Jovanovich, 1979.

Tillich, Paul. *Dynamics of Faith.* New York: Harper, 1957.

Townes, Emilie. *In a Blaze of Glory: Womanist Spirituality as Social Witness.* Nashville: Abingdon, 1995.

————. *Troubling in My Soul: Woman Perspectives on Evil and Suffering.* Maryknoll, N.Y.: Orbis Books, 1993.

————. "Womanist Ethics." In Russell and Clarkson, *The Dictionary of Feminist Theologies,* 91.

Trimiew, Darryl. "Ethics—Moral Evolution: From Customary Societies to Atomistic Individuals." In *Handbook of U.S. Liberation Theologies of Liberation,* edited by Miguel De La Torre. St. Louis: Chalice, 2004.

Trinity United Church of Christ. www.tucc.org/ministries.htm (accessed July 7, 2006).

Tushnet, Mark V. *Making Civil Rights Law: Thurgood Marshall and the Supreme Court, 1936–1961.* New York: Oxford University Press, 1994.

Unity Fellowship of Christ Church. http://www.ufc-usa.org/history.htm.

University of New Hampshire. "Definition of Interdisciplinary Work." http://extension.unh.edu/AboutUs/Workdef.pdf#search=%22definition%20interdiscipli-nary%22.

Van Deburg, William L. *New Day in Babylon: The Black Power Movement and American Culture, 1965–1975.* Chicago: University of Chicago Press, 1992.

Veling, Terry A. *Practical Theology: "On Earth as It Is in Heaven."* Maryknoll, N.Y.: Orbis Books, 2005.

Walker, Alice. *In Search of Our Mother's Gardens: Womanist Prose.* San Diego: Harcourt Brace Jovanovich, 1983.

Walker, David. *David Walker's Appeal; Together with a Preamble, to the Coloured Citizens of the World, but in Particular, and very Expressly, to Those of the United States of America.* Black Classics Press, 1993.

Walker, Wyatt Tee. *The Soul of Black Worship: A Trilogy—Preaching, Praying, Singing.* New York: Martin Luther King Fellows, 1984.

Washington, Booker T. *A New Negro for a New Century.* New York: Arno Press, 1969.

————. Speech at the Atlanta Cotton States and International Exposition. September 18, 1895. http://teachingamericanhistory.org/library/index.asp?document=69.

Washington, James M. *Frustrated Fellowship: The Black Baptist Quest for Social Power.* Macon, Ga.: Mercer University Press, 1986.

————. *A Testament of Hope: The Essential Writings of Martin Luther King, Jr.* San Francisco: Harper San Francisco, 1991.

Waters, Kenneth L., Jr. *Afrocentric Sermons: The Beauty of Blackness in the Bible.* Valley Forge: Judson, 1993.

Watley, William D., and Raquel Annette St. Clair, *The African Presence in the Bible: Gospel Sermons Rooted in History.* Valley Forge: Judson, 2000.

Weems, Renita. *Just A Sister Away: A Womanist Vision of Women's Relationships in the Bible.* Philadelphia: Innisfree Press, 1988.

————. "Reading *Her* Way through the Struggle: African American Women and the Bible." In Felder, *Stony the Road We Trod,* 57–80.

West, Cornel. *Prophesy Deliverance! An Afro-American Revolutionary Christianity.* Philadelphia: Westminster John Knox, 1982.

————. *Race Matters*. Boston: Beacon Press, 1993.

West, Thomas R., and James W. Mooney, eds. To Redeem a Nation: A History and Anthology of the American Civil Rights Movement. St. James, N.Y.: Brandywine Press, 1993.

Westfield, Nancy Lynne. *Dear Sisters: A Womanist Practice of Hospitality*. Cleveland: Pilgrim, 2001.

White, Deborah Gray. *Too Heavy a Load: Black Women in Defense of Themselves, 1894–1994*. New York: Norton, 1999.

Wiggins, Daphne C. *Righteous Content: Black Women's Perspectives of Church and Faith*. New York: New York University Press, 2005.

Williams, Delores. "What Does It Mean to Reconcile the Bible with Black Christian Identity?" Keynote address presented at the Seventh Annual Black Religious Scholars Group Consultation, San Antonio, Texas, November 19, 2004.

Williams, Juan. *Thurgood Marshall: American Revolutionary*. New York: Times Books, 1998.

Williams, Juan, and Quinton Dixie. *This Far by Faith: Stories from the African-American Religious Experience*. New York: W. Morrow, 2003.

Williams, Preston. "Afro-American Religious Ethics." In Childress and Macqurrie, *The Westminster Dictionary of Christian Ethics*, 1986, 12.

Wilmore, Gayraud S. *Black Religion and Black Radicalism: An Interpretation of the Religious History of African Americans*. Garden City, N.Y.: Anchor Press/Doubleday, 1973.

Wimberly, Anne E. Streaty. *Nurturing Faith & Hope: Black Worship as a Model for Christian Education*. Cleveland: Pilgrim, 2004.

————. *Soul Stories: African American Christian Education*. Revised edition. Nashville: Abingdon Press, 2005.

Wimberly, Anne E. Streaty, and Evelyn Parker. *In Search of Wisdom: Faith Formation in the Black Church*. Nashville: Abingdon, 2002.

Wimberly, Edward P. *African American Pastoral Care*. Nashville: Abingdon, 1991.

————. *Pastoral Care in the Black Church*. Nashville: Abingdon, 1979.

————. *Relational Refugees: Alienation and Reincorporation in African-American Churches and Communities*. Nashville: Abingdon, 2000.

Wimbush, Vincent L. *African Americans and the Bible: Sacred Texts and Social Textures*. With Rosamond C. Rodman. New York: Continuum, 2000.

————. "The Bible and African Americans: An Outline of an Interpretive History." In Felder, *Stony the Road We Trod*, 81–97.

Wolf, Eric C. *Europe and the People without History*. With a new preface and cartographic illustrations by Noel L. Diaz. Berkeley: University of California Press, 1997.

Wood, James W. *One Hundred Years of the African Methodist Episcopal Zion Church*. New York: AME Zion Book Concern, 1895.

Wood, Peter H. *Black Majority: Negroes in Colonial South Carolina from 1670 through the Stono Rebellion*. 1974. Reprint, New York: Norton, 1996.

Woodson, Carter G. *The History of the Negro Church*. 1921. Washington, D.C.: Associated Publishers, 1992.

————. *The Mis-Education of the Negro*. 1933. Washington, D.C.: Associated Publishers, 1992.

Woodward, C. Vann. *The Strange Career of Jim Crow*. New York: Oxford University Press, 1955.

Bibliography

Wormser, Richard. *The Rise and Fall of Jim Crow*. New York: St. Martin's Press, 2003.

Wright, Richard. *Uncle Tom's Children*. 1940. Reprint, New York: Harper & Row, Perennial edition, 1965.

Zane, Wallace W. *Journeys to the Spiritual Lands: The Natural History of a West Indian Religion*. New York and Oxford: Oxford University Press, 1999.

AUTHOR BIOGRAPHIES

STACEY M. FLOYD-THOMAS is Associate Professor of Ethics and Director of Black Church Studies at Brite Divinity School, Texas Christian University in Fort Worth, Texas and an ordained pastoral counselor within the American Baptist Churches USA and Progressive National Baptist Convention. Dr. Floyd-Thomas is a graduate of Vassar College (BA), Emory University's Candler School of Theology (MTS), and Temple University (MA and PhD). As executive director and cofounder of the Black Religious Scholars Group, her scholarly research examines the effects that church, education, family, and government have on defining people of color and the subversive tasks that marginalized people take in order to define their own identities, virtues, and destinies. She is the recipient of the 2007 American Academy of Religion of the Teaching Excellence Award, author of *Mining the Motherlode: Methods in Womanist Ethics*, and editor of *Deeper Shades of Purple: Womanism in Religion and Society*.

JUAN M. FLOYD-THOMAS is Associate Professor of History at Texas Christian University in Fort Worth, Texas. Dr. Floyd-Thomas is a graduate of Rutgers University (BA), Temple University (MA), and the University of Pennsylvania (PhD). His research fields are African American Intellectual History; American Religious History; Twentieth Century American Social Movements; Pan-Africanism and the African Diaspora. He teaches various courses including "The Black Religious Experience in America," "The Black Church and the Civil Rights Struggle," and "Religion in American Life." Dr. Floyd-Thomas has had the unique opportunity to teach undergraduates, graduate students, and seminarians. He is the author of *The Origins of Black Humanism in America: Reverend Brown and the Unitarian Church*. In addition to being a cofounder and associate director of the Black Religious Scholars Group, he is also a member of several scholarly and church organizations.

STEPHEN G. RAY JR. is Associate Professor of African American Studies and Director of the Urban Theological Institute at the Lutheran Theological Seminary at Philadelphia. Prior to joining the faculty at Louisville Seminary he taught at Louisville Presbyterian Theological Seminary and lectured at Yale Divinity School and the Hartford Seminary. Dr. Ray received his PhD in Theology and African American Studies from Yale University and his MDiv (*summa cum laude*) from the Yale Divinity School. He has written numerous articles and lectured on African American religion, human rights, and the

275

intersection of religion and politics. Dr. Ray is the author of several published works including: *A Struggle from the Start: The Black Community of Hartford, 1639–1960* and *Do No Harm: Social Sin and Christian Responsibility*. In addition to his own monographs he has been a contributor to the recently published books: *Constructive Theology: A Contemporary Approach to Classical Themes*, *Who Do You Say That I Am: Christology and Identity in the United Church of Christ*, and *Human Rights: Christian Influences and Issues*. In 2002 he was the recipient of the Kentuckiana Metroversity Distinguished Teacher of Adult Learners Award. He is an ordained minister of the United Church of Christ and has served as the pastor of churches in Hartford and New Haven, Connecticut, and in Louisville, Kentucky.

CAROL B. DUNCAN is Associate Professor in the Department of Religion and Culture at Wilfrid Laurier University in Waterloo, Canada. A sociologist of religion, she earned a BA in sociology at the University of Toronto and MA and PhD degrees in sociology from York University (Toronto). Her areas of interest include Caribbean religions in diasporic and transnational contexts, especially the Spiritual Baptist faith; religion and post-colonialism; critical pedagogy in religious studies; and religion and popular culture. In addition to numerous articles on the Spiritual Baptist faith in Canada, Duncan has published on Black Caribbean women's religious lives; Black women and motherhood; and gender, race, and cultural representation in film and video. She consulted on, and appears in, the award-winning documentary, *Seeking Salvation: A History of the Black Church in Canada*, and is author of the forthcoming book, *This Spot of Ground: Spiritual Baptists in Toronto*.

NANCY LYNNE WESTFIELD is an ordained deacon with The United Methodist Church and Associate Professor of Religious Education at Drew University, Madison, New Jersey. She attended Murray State University taking a BS in Agriculture, earned her MA from Scarritt Gradutate School, then PhD from Union Institute. She has served several churches in Philadelphia and was on staff at The Riverside Church, New York City, as Minister of Christian Education. As a Religious Education scholar, her areas of interest include: engaged pedagogy, Womanist pedagogy, Black Church studies, cultural studies, spirituality, imagination, and popular culture. Her research has explored such topics as practices of African American women for resilience; the embodiment of Blackness in theological classrooms; and prayer as a cultural and psychological element of African American people. Rev. Dr. Westfield is author of *Dear Sisters: A Womanist Practice of Hospitality* as well as numerous articles on Christian education, Womanist pedagogy, and culture.

INDEX

Index